1983

SPORTS
in Modern America

SPORTS
in Modern America

William J. Baker
John M. Carroll

Introduction: Bob Broeg

RiverCity
Publishers
LIMITED

Saint Louis, Missouri

To Jeanne Belaire
and
Willie Clinton Baker
(1901-1972)

Second Printing January 1983

Copyright © 1981 by River City Publishers, Limited. All rights reserved. No part of this publication may be reproduced or transmitted in any form or by any means electronic or mechanical, including photocopy, recording or any information storage system now known or to be invented, without permission of the publisher, River City Publishers, Limited, Box 28665, St. Louis, Missouri 63141, except by a reviewer who wishes to quote brief passages in connection with a review written for inclusion in a magazine, newspaper or broadcast.

Published by River City Publishers, Limited

Printed in the United States of America

Published simultaneously in Canada

Library of Congress Catalog Number: 81-51300

ISBN: 0-933150-30-X

Cover and text designed by Jerry Moore and Janet Moody

Contents

Contents

Preface

This book contains fourteen original essays on themes that reflect the growth of sports in modern America, 1865 to the present. The essays relate the events and trends in the world of sports to the larger social, economic, and political problems in modern American society. Although they are concerned with sophisticated, scholarly material, the authors have made a real effort to write clearly and understandably for the undergraduate student and general sports fan so that their reading in sports history will be both meaningful and enjoyable. Designed to complement a standard textbook in a recent American survey course, a more specialized course in modern sports history, or courses in physical education and the sociology of sports, the book presents interpretive material, new viewpoints as well as traditional ones, and can, therefore, assist in stimulating class discussion. The authors are representative of the various academic disciplines concerned with the study of sports. They have not hesitated to express opinions or to pass judgments, and thus they present modern sports history as an exciting, thought-provoking study rather than a mere collection of facts. They hope that the general sports enthusiast will find the book as stimulating as the college undergraduate does.

Sports in Modern America is divided into three interrelated parts with a general introduction. The general introduction by Bob Broeg focuses on the meaning of sports in America's recent past to both the fan and the society as a whole. Broeg, Sports Editor for the *St. Louis Post-Dispatch*, a columnist for *The Sporting News* for ten years, and the author of nine books, is eminently qualified to analyze the impact of sports in modern America. He was recently given the prestigious J.G. Taylor Spink Award at the National Baseball Hall of Fame in Cooperstown, N.Y. Broeg's thesis is that sports have had a democratizing and stabilizing effect on American society.

Part I, "The Growth of Industrial Society and Sports, 1865-1920," deals with the rise of sports from an informal casual pastime to a highly organized and standardized activity. It covers such diverse topics as the origin and development of organized sports, the impact of social elites on athletics, sports and political reform, and the particular problems which American sports faced at the time of World War I. Part II, "American Sports Come of Age, 1920-1950," analyzes the growth and maturation of American sports in the important eras of the "Golden '20s," the Depression, and World War II and its aftermath. It focuses on baseball and intercollegiate athletics and highlights the manner in which the sports hero has been depicted in both film and literature. An essay on the black athlete details how sports reflect social problems in the larger society. In Part III, "Recent Changes and Challenges, 1950 to the Present," essays on women, violence, the Olympic movement, and the expansion of American sports abroad demonstrate the central role which sports have played in American life and the problems which they pose for our society.

We would like to acknowledge the numerous people who contributed to the completion of this book. Many friends offered suggestions; many colleagues read parts of the book in manuscript. To all our friends and colleagues, we thank you. A special thanks goes to William J. Miller and Patrick T. Conley, who offered suggestions concerning the topics to be selected, and to Ms. Frances Shelton and her staff for preparing the essays for publication. We are grateful to the various museums, picture agencies, archives, and especially the *St. Louis Post-Dispatch*, that helped us to locate and obtain illustrations. We also wish to express our gratitude to Erby Young and the staff of River City Publishers, especially to Irene Miller for editorial assistance, to Carole Young, who directed the project during production, and to Janet Moody and Jerry Moore for their many efforts on our behalf. We wish, finally, to express our appreciation to the scholars who contributed essays to this book. They were helpful, met deadlines, and accepted our editorial revisions with remarkable courtesy.

William J. Baker
John M. Carroll

Introduction

The Impact of Sports on Americans

Bob Broeg

What do sports mean in America? That's easy. The games we play and watch, especially those in which we spectate rather than participate, often keep us from the psychiatrist's couch.

As one who has made a living for more than forty years primarily by putting one word after another, most of them about sports, I do not delude myself into over-emphasizing sports. As a newspaperman, I rarely care to see sports on Page One even though—for a fact—sports do help sell newspapers and preferred-advertising space just as they attract radio listeners and television viewers and commercial time.

But even though I like to believe I know sports' relative significance compared with the crime, time, wherewithal, and weather of the day, I do feel that America's games have a value far in excess of dollars and sense.

Sports keep a lot of guys and gals, too, from going nuts. It's in rooting or raving, grandstand managing or officiating, praising or arguing on behalf of this team or that player, that a person lets off the steam built up with the pressure cooker of life.

Whether saddled with an unpleasant or monotonous job, confined by a barely tolerable marriage or the pangs of four-wall loneliness, or weighted down by ill health, financial worries, or family problems, too many people need relief.

That's relief as in the antacids of a heroic home-team relief pitcher coming up with an inspiring side-retiring performance when the chips went down for the other team. It's the ecstasy of a game-winning home run, touchdown, or field goal. The joy of victory, the sorrow of defeat. It's the chance to blow the mental cork over a stupid mistake by the manager or coach of the team of your choice or to scream fair words or foul at a blue-jerseyed umpire or striped-shirted referee whose vision and judgment you question.

It helps to brush back the perspiration on a hot night at the old ballpark, easing the pain and strain of the brushoff the boss gave you when you asked

II for a raise. On a foggy, rainy night's ride to an athletic arena to watch towering guys run around in their basketball BVDs, it's possible to forget the missus' or the mister's slave-galley treatment back home, where the mortgage is due and the roof leaks. And it helps on even a snowy, skidding drive to the stadium, wondering whether that high-salaried so-and-so at quarterback will be able to hit the inside of a barn this week, to forget briefly that junior is hurting from whooping cough or cocaine or unable to make a scholastic first down.

Yes, that's what sports do. (I always want to say "does" because I think of sports as all-inclusive, singular.) Sports serve as men and women's safety valve and an escape hatch from mischief for kids who have too much time on their hands.

Sports are the greatest common denominator this side of the last inhale and exhale. Although merely reading, listening, or watching at home while the boss sits out there in fifty-yard or box-seat comfort, a bank janitor doesn't mind telling the head man—nicely, of course—that he's all wet if he thinks Rocky Marciano could lick Muhammad Ali. The boss, who'd tell the custodian to mind his manner or cuspidor in other areas of disagreement, doesn't seem to take umbrage often at a difference of opinion over athletics.

Rich man or poor, whether butcher or baker or electric-bulb maker, each man has his own athletic castle, the team he thinks he owns or wishes he did. In his world he'd tell that inflated-salaried talent to get lost in the horse latitudes instead of losing so many blasted ball games.

When a man in Chicago arranged in 1980 to be buried in a Cubs' baseball uniform, at a time the Toddlin' Town's National League team hadn't won a pennant in thirty-five years, he was just doing a bit more than a lot of chaps elsewhere would if they had the gumption. Even if the poor fella was a little nutty, just think what he MIGHT have proposed if he hadn't had a life-long love affair with rinky-dinks of the diamond?

Again, sports do indeed keep most individuals from making bigger fools of themselves where it counts most—on the job or at home. So it's with a sense of curiosity about life's fun-and-games, the sports John Q. Public and dear Jane take seriously enough to avoid going nuts and a trip to a padded cell, that the authors in this volume have probed sport from the middle of the nineteenth century to within a chip shot of the twenty-first.

Actually, of course, Egyptian hieroglyphics show representation of sports, and laurel-crowned bodies beautiful in Greece and ancient Romans took part in sport. Some of it was grisly, of course, and paganistic, the lions versus the Christians. I don't think I'd have had the heart to cover the gladiatorial one-on-one of early trained professionals in which death claimed the loser. And it certainly couldn't have helped the appetite to watch Aztecs, Incas, and others kick around the cranium of a bloke who had lost his head in battle or to play a rudimentary form of basketball with an unhinged sloped dome.

I believe, though, that the psychological side of me that pulls so often for the underdog would have reached lyrically for the nearest scroll or scrimshaw when little David wound up his pitching arm and plunked giant Goliath between his evil eyes. What a story that would have been to write, even if the circulation was small. I'd have reveled, too, if that legendary archer in green, Robin Hood, had come out of Nottingham's Forest to beat the sheriff's long-bow best with more bull's-eyes. I KNOW I would have liked to be there the day that a tall Virginia horseman named George Washington slung or skipped a silver dollar across the Rappahannock, smug that I knew it wasn't the Potomac.

Presidents have taken time out from their toil to pursue sports, either with clubhead or racquet or rod or trigger in hand or, if not, an ample seat in the stands. William Howard Taft, the old Yale pitcher, had become so over-stuffed that when the Washington Senators' crafty clubowner, Clark Griffith, persuaded Mr. Taft to begin the long-time tradition of throwing out the first ball in 1913, the President was too cramped in a box seat. He stood in relief, and that's how baseball's so-called "seventh-inning stretch" began.

Andrew Jackson, that hot-blooded, hearty and haughty Tennessean, was a good man with a blade in his hand or his long legs in the stirrups. Even longer-limbed with bonier knees, Abraham Lincoln could burst a sack of flour or grain when practicing a wrestler's scissors hold. Theodore Roosevelt, beneath that weak squint, loved to box off a fella's ears for the bully exercise of it, and the old Rough Rider liked to charge up a beauteous western hill in pursuit of fair game just as he did facing the Spanish at San Juan Hill.

Why, even stone-faced Calvin Coolidge, who fished with a proper high collar, found relaxation in a cold stream if not a smile. Silent Cal didn't know a foul tip from a fowl, but, apparently, he wasn't without amusement. When the President was told in the middle of the Roaring Twenties that owner George Halas would be happy to drop around with professional foot-ball's biggest new name, Red Grange, and the Chicago Bears, Mr. Coolidge thought that would be fine indeed.

Said the President, "I always did like animal acts."

Fact or fancy, that's good sport enough about one who was no sport, yet at least, was good enough to report that one opening day, when pre-pared to suffer through an opener with wife Grace at his side, the Yankees' Babe Ruth shook hands with him at the ballpark and said:

"Geez, Prez, it's hot, ain't it?"

However, Mrs. Coolidge kept score as if she ought to have a card in the Baseball Writers' Association of America. Herbert Hoover, though he might have looked a bit like a stuffed shirt, was a former football waterboy and a keen baseball fan.

Franklin D. Roosevelt tried 'em all, particularly steering a yacht with seaman's skill before polio forced him to stick to swimming. Harry Truman's faulty vision limited his athletic ability, but he loved to twit the press and others opening day by throwing out the ceremonial ball with dexterity, one time left-handed, the next right-handed. And as a judge in western Missouri, hurrying back to Kansas City from a 1930 World Series game at St. Louis,

IV   he reported a Philadelphia Athletics' victory to a curious gas-station operator this way:

"Jimmy Foxx 2, Cardinals 0."

The old soldier who'd banged up a knee on the gridiron at West Point, Dwight D. Eisenhower, never lost his interest in football, but it paled before his love of golf. Why, you'd have thought Ike was coming out against motherhood, if not baseball, when he skipped opening day at Griffith Stadium one year to sharpen his golfing touch down at Augusta, Georgia, the magnificent home of the storied Masters Tournament.

If you want to capsule why golf became such a blazing participant sport and, especially, a television drawing card that enabled winners' fees to climb astronomically, you've got to credit the golfing nut in the White House. Yes, General Eisenhower, the charismatic, pants-hiking player from Pennsylvania, Arnold Palmer, and the sophistication of TV's red-eyed camera.

Golf might have been something even before Mary Queen of Scots swung a knobby-nosed club back home where the game began. Golf lost its upper-crust exclusivity when an engaging American named Walter Hagen ignored the servants' entrance requirements in England of the '20s and waltzed boldly through clubhouse front doors. But it wasn't until Ike's era in the late '50s that the humbling game became a favorite of many who didn't know a birdie putt from a parakeet.

Golf and television's impact on it symbolize the changes over the years from when I was a kid, standing on a street corner awaiting the late-afternoon editions with the skeletonized play-by-play of the day's games. (Night ball didn't turn every day into Sunday in the majors until 1935.) Golf then was drastically underplayed both in the counting house and in the press.

College football had a pretty sizeable following, but pro football was rinky-dink, even after Red Grange came right off the campus at the University of Illinois to the Chicago Bears for the game's first uplift on Thanksgiving Day in 1925.

College basketball still was breaking out of the low-score, low-ceilinged image that had been in vogue in that era of narrow basement-gyms where fly-by-night pro basketball players who traveled days cooped up in cars for coffee and cakes tried to pot-shot two-handed set shots. Pro basketball was then played by pygmies, relatively speaking, and had about the same dwarfish impact on the restricted national sports scene. Boxing was everywhere or somewhere, at least, on any given night until killed off or, more accurately, nearly suffocated by the same feature that made pro football and golf in particular and aided most other sports: television.

The boob tube, it's called, customarily by a jealous press, but the money and interest created primarily by commercials ranging from big automobiles to small cameras, from beer-bucolic sunrise scenes to sunset, from toothpaste to hygienic unmentionables, have turned sports into boxcar-salaried big business. The ma-and-pa kind of confectionery owner, athletically speaking, has had to get out of the large corporation's or well-heeled syndicate's way.

Sophisticated, faster travel has run a definite second in making sports big-league as well as big-money. When teams traveled by trains, limited time restricted scheduling and, therefore, the boundaries of the majors. As the so-called national pastime, though now it probably merits only a photo finish for first with football, baseball on a big-league basis didn't even get beyond the west banks of the Mississippi or south of the Ohio until 1958.

History DOES play a part in sports, if only inferentially. Baseball obviously was played before Abner Doubleday was a plebe at West Point, much less a Civil War general. Chances are, like Topsy, it just grew out of an old British game called rounders, diagrammed into baseline boundaries, nine innings and nine men on a side by a New Jersey gent named Alexander Cartwright. Baseball's Johnny Appleseed took the game all the way to Hawaii and himself into baseball's Hall of Fame at Cooperstown.

As early as the War Between the States, blue-bellied Yankees and the road-uniformed lads in gray were playing a form of baseball. A reformed British cricketeer named Henry Chadwick became the father of baseball writers. Father Chadwick, as he was called, not only invented the baseball box score, which probably rivals the *Wall Street Journal* for daily tabular newspaper perusal, but he also established a baseball rulebook as early as 1858.

Baseball had come so far that on a hot, windy June day in 1876 when George Armstrong Custer and his valiant Seventh Cavalry regiment met s-o-o many Sioux out there on the Little Big Horn, massacred to a man, big-league baseball was played in its infant season (1876) on the west banks of the Mississippi at St. Louis. Think of that one for a moment: Civilization in the country's heartland, as reflected by a sport, simultaneous with raw, savage killing out on the frontier beyond the Central Plains.

From where I sit and stand, a writer who'll always be a fan, I regard that incongruity, geographically and actually, as ranking with the magic of sports for its impact on aiding immigration's melting pot and the flight from the ghetto of the last century.

I don't like to see sports used politically because—to repeat—I don't believe they have that much significance, despite Communism's national over-emphasis on games for international standing. Nor did I feel comfortable even when an American President, Richard M. Nixon, the one-time reserve football end at Whittier College, diagrammed football plays for the coach (George Allen) of a team in which he had a rooting interest, the Washington Redskins.

Mostly, I thought it was beneath the dignity of that impressive presidential seal for the man in the White House to telephone a victorious athlete, coach, or team in its dressing room or clubhouse of triumph. Maybe, yes, there could be some virtue in Jimmy Carter's honoring the United States Olympic hockey team for its astonishing gold-medal upset over the rugged Russkies in the 1980 winter games at Lake Placid, New York. But I felt, putting aside politics, if you will, that sports became as uncontrolled as a hydrogen-filled football. The U.S.'s action to express disapproval of the Soviet invasion of Afghanistan, when the softball player from Georgia played hardball by keeping American athletes away from the Olympics in Moscow, seemed superficial.

Even if the President was right, I thought the recourse was wrong. I

Bob Broeg of the *St. Louis Post-Dispatch* and Jack Buck, sportscaster for **KMOX**-Radio in St. Louis, discuss escalating salaries in professional sports. *(St. Louis Post-Dispatch)*

respect sports for the early-mentioned assist to mental health and—before the largely unbelievable salary situation of the late 1970s and early 1980s— for the fact that the games we play did so much for the immigrants and the down-and-out.

Over the years, I've been astounded that in baseball alone, largely a home-grown game except for growth in Japan, where it took over with even greater mania than in America in the early 1930s, so many men still speaking with an accent of a foreign tongue became rabid fans.

When they came from the Old World in the late 1800s and stepped into a saloon for a nickel beer and a bite of free lunch, they longed for camarad-erie. It came when timid immigrants overheard controversy over the ferocity of Michael "King" Kelly's slides in Boston, Adrian "Cap" Anson's base hits in Chicago and, ultimately, the red-necked fury of that lithe Detroit demon from the Deep South, Ty Cobb. Later, the foreigner would be out there at the ballpark himself, whether in the two-bits or half-buck boards of the bleachers or the high-rent dollar seats of the grandstand, to watch pot-bellied Babe Ruth create as much excitement striking out magnificently as when he homered with high, majestic flight.

And still later, the wiry little Hungarian who cut my hair from age four to forty or the stocky Greek produce-work prodigy who struck it comfortably with his own restaurant glowed with apple-pie Americanism over what baseball had meant to them. And woe to the native-born sportswriter who didn't get his records right. These old-timers knew.

They knew other things, too. Essentially, they knew boxing second best. They might have kicked soccer, as the old-timers put it with quaint redundancy, and they would glow if their old homeland's team did well in the World Cup, the Holy Grail of international sports' number-one game.

But even though Pele, the Black Pearl of Brazil, might be better known around the globe than his proper name, Edson Arantes do Nascimento, the bootblack who became a national treasure was not the world's most famous athlete into the 1980s. It was a loud-mouthed yet often charming fighter from the United States. Of course, that would be Muhammad Ali, born Cassius Clay, vaccinated with a phonograph-record needle and gifted with the nimble feet of a 200-pound-plus ballet dancer.

Best known for flitting like a butterfly and stinging like a bee, as he described himself with characteristic self-esteem, Ali capped for boxing an acceptance that began late in the last century.

At the end of the Gay Nineties, a handsome, former San Francisco bank clerk named James J. Corbett, "Gentleman Jim," spurned the bare-knuckle brawling of often-outlawed, riverboat-barge brawls to outbox John L. Sullivan. The Great John L., as he was advertised, could lick any man in the house—your favorite neighborhood watering trough or his—but he couldn't beat the dandy Irishman who brought science and class and definition to the manly art of self-defense.

By then, the Irish were battling as the Germans had previously to get out of the ghettos. One Irish immigrant's son, James J. "Gene" Tunney, born above a grocery store in New York City, furthered Corbett's efforts to take the mucker and the mugger out of the squared circle, as prize-ring press poets called the area of combat.

Tunney, a World War I Marine in France, was a good-looking, green-eyed guy whose close-cropped upright hair made him look as if he'd just seen Lon Chaney, Sr., in the "Phantom of the Opera," the silent horror movie of the era (1926) when Gene outjabbed Jack Dempsey for the heavyweight championship.

Tunney, who read Shakespeare and developed a pen-pal and personal acquaintanceship with George Bernard Shaw, showed how a poor boy could strike it rich in the ring and get the hell out of there. In 1927, repeating his victory over Dempsey even though knocked down in an infamous "long-count" bout, Tunney listened again to the promoter's reckoning of the champion's cut of a fight seen by more than 100,000 at Chicago's Soldier Field.

Tunney nodded pleasantly. "Okay, Tex," he said, "now I'm going to write you a check for $10,000 so that you can give me an even $1,000,000. And, if you don't mind, when the check clears, I'd like to have it so I can frame it."

A million bucks then, with a dollar king-sized even before the Depression

VIII

and income tax a token, made Tunney a millionaire overnight. He fought once more, using a New Zealand trial horse named Tom Heeney as a punching bag in 1928. He retired, married a wealthy Connecticut socialite, sired a senatorial son (John Tunney), and lived happily until a ripe-age death.

Boxing was the magic carpet not only for the Germans and the Irish. The Jews, the Italians, the blacks, and the Caribbean-country refugees came out of the ghetto, willing to make the physical sacrifice necessary to qualify for the chance at the blue chips.

Television, in its live-action infancy a time of the small set and limited-camera mobility of the late 1940s and much of the 1950s, found boxing such a ready-made product that TV killed it. There wasn't enough talent around for the insatiable thirst of either the television industry or the beer-peddling sponsors. They could do everything with the suds except stop the nick of a rival razor-blade commercial.

Based on years of study, Jimmy Jacobs, former United States handball champion and the country's foremost collector of fight films throughout the century, concluded that more of the best fights were between the two World Wars, roughly 1919 to 1942. Certainly, fighters boxed more often in that twenty-year stretch.

It's the controversy over which era is the best in any sport, whether Joe Louis could beat Jack Dempsey, O. J. Simpson outrun Jim Brown or Jim Thorpe, or whether Babe Ruth still outperformed single-season and career-record conquerors, Roger Maris and Henry Aaron, that lent charm to the games. It also provided an outlet for the up-tight feeling of the closed-in-candidate for the cuckoo couch.

It's hard to argue against the time clock in track events or swimming or wherever the yardstick and tape measure are involved. Back in 1935 the University of California's long-time track coach, Brutus Hamilton, also a former Olympic athlete and mentor, sought to project mankind's physical potential thirty-five years down the road. Hamilton was a prophet in his belief that man—and woman—had far to go, but still had the mental and physical capacity to break records until. . .

He was so right, but not right enough. In the mile, for instance, Hamilton didn't think anyone ever could break a tape under four minutes, but England's Roger Bannister, a medical student, did it first in 1954, after which the accomplishment became almost commonplace. By 1980, Britain's Steve Ovett had lowered the mark to 3:48.8.

Obviously, in some events, such as the pole vault, in which the pole went from bamboo to steel to glass and to an entirely more modern spring-board that turned the performer into part weight lifter and part gymnast flinging himself over the barrier, the rapid increase to the neighborhood of nineteen feet was almost jet-propelled. I can remember, amusedly now, having covered the annual Boston Gardens' games for *The Associated Press* in early 1942 and wiring an excited bulletin when Cornelius "Dutch" Warmerdam, far ahead of his athletic day, soared over the fifteen-foot height.

Right on, the difference in rules and regulations as well as conditions has had some effect on records. For one, Johnny Weissmueller, best known as the most enduring of the movie Tarzans, could describe in detail the pool-and-rule changes that enabled skinny-dipping or bikini-clad swimmers to break records he or Eleanor Holm had set. If you're old enough to remember when Edward gave up the throne of England for Wallis Warfield Simpson's hand, thereafter making "The Student Prince" as obsolete as an out-dated track record or an Edsel, you're old enough to remember when Miss Holm was kicked off the 1936 Olympic team. Dear Eleanor had had the indecency to sip a champagne on the ship enroute to Berlin.

Maybe I overstate the case or underestimate the amount of bubbly grape; still it's a nostalgic reminder of an era that was as golden as the Roaring Twenties.

Everything was bigger and better almost overnight. In baseball, a rash of new ballparks had been built just before and after 1910. Club-owners had prospered by paying coolie wages. A $2400 salary limit in the National League ultimately led to the American League and even, briefly, to the Federal League. But the pinch-penny operation of Charley Comiskey, the Chicago White Sox owner who should have been called the Old Skin Flint instead of the Old Roman, set the mood for the 1919 Black Sox World Series.

The Chisox were so underpaid that even the grand illiterate, "Shoeless Joe" Jackson, a career .350 hitter, was drawing only $6000 after nine major-league seasons. Consequently, too many of the angry Sox sold out.

This is not intended, please, to condone dishonesty but merely to explain that there are two sides to a nickel even if the proprietor owns it and squeezes it until, as they used to say, the buffalo screams.

At any rate, a scraggly-haired, sharp-featured and scowling Federal judge and baseball fan, Kenesaw Mountain Landis, came in as commissioner to take the heat off baseball. With foreign substances barred except for seventeen certified spitball pitchers, more baseballs were used (white ones, too), and then there was Ruth.

The Babe, a converted pitcher, was traded by the myopic Boston Red Sox clubowner, Harry Frazee, later producer of the theatrical musical "No No Nanette," to the New York Yankees. Overnight, the Babe thundered from twenty-nine homers, a staggering record, to an unbelievable fifty-four followed by fifty-nine.

The 1920s were off to a start as roaring as the machine guns of rival bootleggers involved in the big business of Prohibition days. And from the length and breadth of the land, colleges began to erect stadia to match the famed Yale Bowl. Wartime memorial-fund drives gave universities an excuse to build the kinds of athletic operations that would permit big-time football.

The National Collegiate Athletic Association, born in 1906 when Teddy Roosevelt threatened to bar football if the colleges didn't take the mayhem off the gridiron, had not yet refined its operation. A famed Carnegie report in 1929 would expose excesses, but not until the full-fledged athletic scholarship was authorized early in the 1950s were athletes hired for anything except winding seven-day clocks.

The sham was a shame, almost as bad as more recent developments. Athletes not only were surreptitiously subsidized, above and beyond a healthy le-

X gal limit that included high-salaried summer jobs, but many also were not even official university students. If guys weren't going to have to study EVEN Early-Morning Bird Calls or Basket Weaving, you could win with Gregory Gorilla running behind Rhinegold Rhinoceros and Harry Hippopotamus.

This was, truly, a far cry for those of us brought up to read about our athletic heroes performing with luck and pluck, honesty and humiliation in Burt L. Standish's pulp-magazine stories of the Merriwell brothers at Yale. Personally, I was smitten by "Baseball Joe," a series of books off the pen of Lester Chadwick, who took a kid named Joe Matson from high school through the majors. A great pitcher, dead-armed through sinister science-fiction rays, blossomed into a home-run hitter who would make the Babe look like a bunt.

The corn on the celluloid cob was even worse than the literature, in reflection, but I guess I was just a gullible kid or not sufficiently sophisticated. I didn't realize in those twelve-to-fifteen-week movie serials, some fifteen minutes of action with a gasping, improbable ending each week, just what lousy actors athletic favorites such as Babe Ruth, Jack Dempsey, Gene Tunney, and Red Grange were.

I'd been spoon-fed, too, with the purple prose of the period, inspired writing of many who flung around the word "courage" much too frequently for sheer athletic derring-do. Others larded their paeans with italicized faces of poetry better than mine, I guess, because—honest, Mr. Publisher—I can't rhyme "June" with "moon."

But I don't intend to demean. Writers of my youth helped mould me as a person and as a performer, hopefully with some success. To this day, though I like to think I can temper criticism with more compassion than some more youthful colleagues, I still have confidence enough in my ability to observe so that I'll watch and write as a play critic or a movie reviewer, without running down to have someone tell me that the other guy hit a "hanging curve" off him. I could see that!

To this day, you'll see reference to an athlete's accomplishing a "Merriwell," meaning he's hit an unbelievable game-winning home run or scored an unlikely basket or goal, and you will hear or read about a "Garrison finish."

At times I really wonder whether a young reader knows or cares who Merriwell was or is even aware that, yes, Virginia, there was a real-life James "Snapper" Garrison? (Snapper was a jockey who came from behind so often to win that a rallying runner or athletic team often was given Garrison's name for its final get-up-and-go.)

I'm not trying to debunk what obviously is my hobby as well as my habit, but, merely, to show that I'm not completely blind to the growth of sports, the obviously big-business, boxcar-salaried development of a major phase of Americana.

I have seen golfers grow and golf courses, too, even though it's tough to yield lush, yawning, green acreage for subdivided homes when the building interest rates aren't too high. I've seen tennis go from the sissy to the spectacular, a sport played with the cardiovascular fervor of jogging, and the immediate post-World War II boom of bowling.

Ultimately, some bowling alleys went the way of trampoline sets and hula hoops, but, still, though walking less and riding more, Americans play more games for the fun and health of it. Presumably, this offsets our sitting around watching more basketball and football.

Professional football has had a remarkable impact on the country's way of life. Anyone who gives an afternoon party on Sundays is seeking no-shows or, if he or she has no television set, a grumpy crowd. And Monday night, because of TV's pro football impact, would be a good one to give the Great Depression come-on, free dishes, at the movies.

I don't like to see violence in athletics, especially football, but there's a bit of unlikely touchiness in baseball, where the availability of plastic helmets with earpiece protection and the old reliable jock-strap cup should protect an athlete. In the first 104 years of professional baseball, only one player (Ray Chapman, Cleveland, 1920) ever was killed playing ball. And who really worries about getting hurt? Such players as Bucky Harris, Solly Hemus, Frank Robinson, Minnie Minoso, and the champion human pin-cushion, Ron Hunt, accepted a pitch in the rump, ribs, or wrist as part of the game—and first base.

Gambling, minor and major, is interwoven more with football especially and basketball secondarily than any other sport. In football, some of the more successful coaches didn't always please the most zealous rooter with a bit of green on the line. They won games but didn't always beat the infernal point spread.

Although hockey has made dramatic inroads among small fry in areas new to the Canadian game's newest major-league entries, basketball has kept burgeoning to the point where, as I recall Atlanta sports editor Jesse Outlar putting it in verse:

"Up from the valleys of Haversham, down from the hills of Hall, everybody and his sister is bouncing the bleeping ball."

Sports' Taj Mahals for indoor sports, particularly basketball and a new sleeping giant of a booming, relatively recent American game, soccer, have brought the larger and smaller inflated round balls into constantly greater focus. Television has found college basketball more acceptable nationally than pro basketball. "True bounce," as Oklahoma State's venerable Iron Duke, Hank Iba, nicknamed basketball in humorous rivalry with "bad bounce" (football), has come a long way from when a Canadian-born man invented it in 1891 at Springfield, Massachusetts, YMCA College.

James Naismith, first a divinity student, then a physical education instructor, and later a medical doctor, spent most of his years at Kansas University, where years ago a young student asked him for recommendation as basketball coach at Baker University.

Dr. Naismith was highly amused as he said to Forrest C. "Phog" Allen, who would win more than a little reputation and many games at KU, "Why, Phog, my dear boy, you don't coach the game. You just play it."

As one getting mighty old, I guess—old enough to have met Naismith at our fraternity house when I was visiting Kansas in 1937, a couple of years before he died—I've seen women go from passive to active in sports. Sports also provided "open sesame" for blacks before the courts did.

XII Athletes black and white, male and female, have hit the financial jackpot. Many haven't handled the wealth or the media or even the freight-paying public with consideration, but, then, it's as heady as Cyclops' vino to reach such smashing overnight financial heights, guided by a sports agent often as sharp as an athlete's ability to throw or hit a baseball, pop a shoulder pad or pass in football, or score a birdie in golf, an ace in tennis, or dunk a basket rather than a doughnut.

In the incongruity of the moment when sports are big-time with a Superman's capital "S," when athletic interest is probably greater than it really ought to be, it's important and timely that the authors have seen fit to describe, diagnose, and analyze the rise of the games we play or watch in the twentieth century.

Part I

The Growth
of Industrial Society and Sports

1865-1920

During the half century separating the fall of Johnny Reb from the day that Johnny came marching home at the close of World War I, American society underwent massive change. As the frontier closed, cities grew by leaps and bounds, in no small measure because of a vast influx of immigrants from afar. Rural, small-town patterns of life gave way to city culture. Industry boomed, monopolies prospered, and the gap widened between affluent and socially marginal Americans. Despite dramatic technological innovations in transportation, communications, and creature comforts on a scale never before imagined, Americans in the late nineteenth century became polarized into urban, suburban, and rural communities; rich, comfortable, and indigent levels of life; native white, immigrant, and segregated black ethnic groups. Reformers could do little to reverse these trends. In the Progressive movement, city, state, and national government attempted to bring efficiency and some degree of justice to a chaotic social order in the early years of the twentieth century.

Like the society which gave it birth, organized sport grew rapidly in size and complexity from 1865 to 1920. In the first essay of this section, John M. Carroll, a political and diplomatic historian, explains the urban, technological, ideological, and commercial factors that gave rise to organized sports. He suggests that by the turn of the century Americans had successfully adapted their own loosely organized frontier pastimes and new European (mostly English) sports and games into a structured, highly competitive enterprise that was uniquely American. First in the industrial Northeast, then in the fast-developing upper Midwest, professional baseball and college football especially flourished.

In the second essay, Benjamin G. Rader revises a portion of his forthcoming *American Sports: From the Age of Folk Games to the Age of Spectators* (Prentice-Hall) for an assessment of the role of upper-class "social elites" in forming athletic clubs, building fine facilities, creating rules and

2   tournaments, and generally promoting amateur competition in yachting, cricket, track and field, polo, golf, and tennis. Rader, a cultural and social historian, suggests that the amateur code was more a badge of affluence and social distinction than a philosophical principle. Only wealthy Americans could afford the luxury of expensive amateur sports. The cost and rules of membership in private sports clubs barred most immigrants, poor native whites, and blacks alike. Yet by 1920 even elite amateurs such as golfers and tennis players were set on a course destined to turn their exclusive pastimes into spectacles on the order of professional sports.

On the seamier underside of sports at the turn of the century, an essay by Randy Roberts depicts boxing as a relic of barbarism in the age of reform and progress. A lecturer in history, Roberts draws from his research on *Jack Dempsey: The Manassa Mauler* (Louisiana State University Press, 1979) to show how the introduction of padded gloves and orderly rules in the late nineteenth century made pugilism momentarily attractive to a more respectable clientele until the emergence of "Bad Nigger" Jack Johnson frightened white Americans into turning their backs on prize fighting. When the Progressive Era ended at the outset of World War I, scarcely could anyone foresee that boxing would have a prominent place in the postwar world.

Not even professional baseball and college football would have emerged as popular spectacles in the 1920s had they not successfully negotiated their way through several crises during the first two decades of the twentieth century. In the final essay of this first section, a social-intellectual historian of Modern Britain, William J. Baker, expands a section of his forthcoming *Sports in the Western World* (Rowman and Littlefield) for an analysis of organized baseball's administrative reform in 1903, college football's stylistic changes of 1906-12, and the Black Sox scandal of 1919. Perilous moments all, these crises forced patrons and players to set their houses in order for future respectability and prosperity.

The Rise of Organized Sports

John M. Carroll

The swift growth of organized sports in America is closely linked to the rapid urbanization and industrialization in the late nineteenth century. Between 1860 and 1900 the percentage of people living in urban areas increased dramatically from about seventeen to over forty. The urban society was conducive to the rise of organized sports because it was more complex and interdependent than that of rural America. Urbanites became dependent on more formalized and structured activities for their amusement, including sports for both the participant and the spectator. It is not surprising, therefore, that organized sports first took root in the urban Northeast and spread to the South and the West as the nation grew.

Although the rise of organized sports is usually associated with the post-Civil War era, the origins of this movement can be seen in the ante-bellum period. The growth of American cities was well under way by the early decades of the nineteenth century, and by the eve of the Civil War nearly one out of five Americans lived in urban areas. In prewar cities, several forces existed which tended to legitimize organized sports as a respectable leisure-time activity. It was in this urban atmosphere that one could see most clearly the erosion of the "Puritan Ethic," which held that sports, games, and other idle amusements were a frivolous waste of time and potentially evil. Dating back to colonial New England, the "Puritan Ethic" was never universally observed or enforced, but it did have a great impact on the general perception of sports in early America and for centuries thereafter. The slow but steady decline of the Puritan influence throughout the nineteenth century led to the wider acceptance of sports as a valid pursuit during free hours.

The regimentation of factory work and the restrictive nature of city life, moreover, caused a concern about the physical deterioration of city dwellers in the two decades prior to the Civil War. Numerous magazine articles pointed out that long hours in cramped factories and very limited opportunities for physical exercise were responsible for undermining the health of many

4   Americans. Various efforts were made to introduce physical education into school curricula and to encourage the public to engage in some form of exercise. Of particular importance in this regard was the establishment of the *Turnverein* movement in the United States. Introduced to America by German immigrants in the 1820s, the *Turnverein* movement stressed the need to combine physical and mental development to attain the ideal of a well-rounded individual. The turners emphasized gymnastic training and had established more than 150 societies throughout the country by 1860. They were particularly successful in encouraging the development of physical education programs in the nation's schools. The *Turnverein* movement helped to popularize gymnastics and physical training in general. But more importantly, it offered a rationale for the acceptance of sports as a worthwhile endeavor.

Despite the growing awareness of the importance of physical exercise and sports for overall well-being and as a release from the pressures of city life, most ante-bellum urbanites did not engage in organized sports as either spectators or participants. For the most part, they did not have the free time or the money to pursue organized sporting activities. Working-class city dwellers were more likely to spend their limited leisure time at saloons, poolrooms, or sporting halls where they might view and wager on cockfights or billiard games. The organized sports that did exist in ante-bellum America were mainly established and controlled by the social elites for their own benefit and amusement. From colonial times, the elites had the leisure, wealth, and inclination to support various kinds of organized sports. In the pre-Civil War era, horse races and boating regattas were popular spectator events for the social elites. It was not unusual during this period for ten to fifteen thousand spectators to turn out for an important horse race. Although people from all segments of urban society did attend these events as well as boxing matches, footraces, and baseball games, it would be incorrect to conclude that organized sports had a wide following in the pre-Civil War period.

The Civil War (1861-65) was a watershed in the rise and development of organized sports. It had both a direct and indirect effect in promoting and popularizing sports. The war brought together millions of men who in their leisure time participated in or viewed organized sporting events for the first time. After the conflict, they took back with them to their towns and cities the knowledge of and enthusiasm for various sports. The spectacular rise of baseball to a dominant position among postwar sporting events, for example, can be partially attributed to its wartime popularity in military camps in both the North and South. The war had a similar although less dramatic impact on other sports such as horse racing, wrestling, and boxing. Beyond these direct effects, the war influenced public attitudes and mores. The wartime emphasis on strength, stamina, and physical conditioning tended to undermine the widely held view that sports were a waste of time and energy. As in the case of most wars, the Civil War clouded many established religious and moral beliefs and to some extent further eroded the traditional opposition to sports. The unusual destructiveness of the war in both a physical and psychological sense also created tensions and anxieties among the people

Sports during the Civil War: A drawing of a horse race held by the Army of the Potomac, 1863. *(Library of Congress)*

on both sides, who sought some form of emotional outlet or release. In the postwar years, organized sports provided one such avenue of escape from the emotional strain of four years of civil strife. But what is of greater importance is that the war triggered an industrial "take-off" which transformed the United States from a rural, agricultural nation into an urban, manufacturing country in the course of the next fifty years. It is in this sense that the Civil War can be considered a watershed in the development of American sports, because it was in this urban-industrial environment that organized sports developed and prospered.

Several notable historians and sociologists have wrestled with the intriguing question of the connection or relationship between the growth of urban-industrial society and the development of organized sports. The historian Frederic Paxson, elaborating on Frederick Jackson Turner's "Frontier Thesis," maintained in a 1917 article that sports acted as a kind of "safety valve" to release pent-up urban tensions and frustrations. Once the natural "safety valve" of the frontier and free land was gone, he maintained, urbanites asserted their pioneer heritage by seeking some new form of escape from city pressures and anxieties—organized sports. Thus, organized sports were one of the releases that the urban masses used to cope with the stresses of urban-industrial life. Implicit in Paxson's interpretation and especially in the work of Foster Rhea Dulles, *A History of Recreation* (1965), is the assumption that the masses have contributed significantly to the direc-

6   tion and development of organized sports and that organized sports and other recreational activities have been a democratizing agent in American society.

Other observers have not been as optimistic concerning the role of organized sports in moderating the rigors of urban society or improving the quality of life in the industrial environment. They have argued that organized sports in modern society have become more an appendage to the industrial structure than a creative activity designed to cope with the tensions, pressures, and anxieties of urban life. The regimentation and standardization associated with organized sports, Johan Huizinga and others have observed, reflect the influence of the urban-industrial system in which these sports developed. A few radical critics of capitalism, including Paul Hoch, *Rip Off The Big Game* (1972), have suggested that organized sports are controlled by a capitalist elite with the main objective of immunizing or desensitizing the urban workers to the exploitive and alienating currents of capitalist society. While it is not the purpose here to resolve the question of whether organized sports were/are an agent of democracy or authoritarianism, it can be stated that the development of sports in post-1865 America was, as John R. Betts has pointed out, "as much a product of industrialization as it was an antidote to it."

Betts, a pioneer American sports historian, has placed particular emphasis on technological innovations associated with the industrial "take-off" in accounting for the rapid development of organized sports. Although the Civil War initially retarded the growth of sports, most observers agree that it stimulated expansion and innovation in the fields of transportation and communication which contributed to the urban-industrial surge after 1865. These developments were of particular importance in paving the way for organized sporting activity on a national basis. The dramatic increase in railroad building in the postwar era linked towns, cities, and regions of the country which previously had been relatively isolated. By 1890, almost 100,000 miles of track served the needs of the nation as compared with 30,000 in 1860. The new railroads made possible inter-city and inter-regional competition, which in turn heightened interest in organized sports. In 1869, for example, the Cincinnati Red Stocking Club, the first all-salaried professional baseball team, utilized the newly completed Union Pacific Railroad to stage a coast-to-coast tour in which it went undefeated. The success of the Cincinnati nine and other professional teams focused attention on highly competitive athletic contests, helped to standardize rules and procedures, and led to the establishment of regional and national leagues and associations. The formation of the National Baseball League was partly due to the cheapness and availability of railway transportation. Organized in 1876, the National League established teams in various cities in the northeastern quadrant of the country extending from Boston to St. Louis on the Mississippi River. After surviving a shaky start, the National League soon became the most successful and prestigious professional sporting association in America. Similarly, the development of intercollegiate athletics depended on the railroad. Many of the first interscholastic contests in rowing, baseball, and football were in part subsidized by railway companies eager to increase their business. The practice of providing special trains, ferries, or trolley cars to service sporting contests at both the professional and amateur levels was an important stimulant to the rise of organized sports.

In addition to transportation, improved communications were an important factor in popularizing sports. The telegraph, which was invented before the Civil War, was improved, and service was expanded after 1865. Telegraph lines, which crisscrossed the nation by the 1880s, aided newspapermen in covering sporting contests. The John L. Sullivan-James J. Corbett championship boxing match of 1892, for example, was one of the best-reported sporting contests in the nineteenth century, owing to the telegraph and other postwar technical innovations. Newspaper coverage of major sporting activities was also enhanced by the improvement in printing methods and the development of the Eastman Kodak camera (1888). The more rapid reportage of national and international athletic contests and the more vivid portrayal of these events through the use of still pictures intensified interest in sports. By the end of the century, the sporting page became a feature in many urban newspapers. Advancements in printing, moreover, contributed to the development of the dime novel, which brought the exploits of fictional athletic heroes such as Frank Merriwell and Dink Stover within the reach of millions of Americans, young and old.

The invention of the incandescent light bulb by Thomas Edison in 1879 and the wider application of electrical innovations thereafter contributed to the refinement of organized sporting activity. Electric lighting, which was installed in New York's Madison Square Garden by 1882, increased interest in indoor sporting events and allowed promoters to stage new and more spectacular evening attractions. By the last decade of the nineteenth century, as Betts has noted, the electric light acted as a lure for players and spectators alike to Young Men's Christian Associations, athletic clubs, and high school and college gymnasiums. In addition, the development of electrical technology helped to revolutionize the urban transportation systems. Electric streetcars replaced horse-drawn vehicles and made travel in the city more rapid and convenient. Urban sports fans could now more easily attend events such as horse races and baseball games in suburban areas. Those living outside the city also found it more convenient to travel to downtown athletic clubs or sporting arenas. As has already been noted, transit companies often subsidized athletic teams in order to increase passenger traffic. By the 1890s, it was quite common for streetcar companies to set up trolley parks in suburban areas. These parks offered various kinds of recreational activities and often included a baseball diamond with the home team, of course, sponsored by the transit company. Clearly, the electric streetcar was a stimulant to both sporting activity in general and organized sports in particular. As Betts has stated, "a decade of electrification, paralleling improvements in transportation, had elevated and purified the atmosphere of sport." Other inventions or technical innovations which contributed in a minor way to the development of organized sports were the stop watch, ball bearings, artificial ice, moving pictures, and the percussion cap.

Dramatic social changes which took place in the late nineteenth century

8   were also important factors contributing to the growth of organized sports. The new social elites of the post-Civil War era, whose wealth and leisure were largely a product of the industrial "take-off" period, were influential in legitimizing and popularizing sporting activities. Although social elites had been engaged in sporting and recreational pursuits since colonial times, the *nouveaux riches* of the urban-industrial era embraced sports in an ostentatious manner and with a peculiar zest which set them apart. Although some of their sporting activities, such as yachting and polo, were beyond the means of even the middle classes and never became important popular sports, other athletic interests of the elites, such as tennis, golf, and football, later became major organized sports for all classes. In addition, as Benjamin Rader points out in a later essay in this volume, the social elites were instrumental in the formation of athletic clubs which promoted sports such as track and field and tennis and helped to standardize rules and procedures in amateur athletics. In late-nineteenth-century America, where society was much less stratified than in Europe, the lower and middle classes tended to respect the social elites and emulate their enthusiasm for sports. Many laborers and shopkeepers dreamed of the day when they too might enjoy the fruits of wealth and leisure, which included athletic activities. The acceptance of organized sports by the social elites also helped to further erode the traditional moral and cultural opposition to athletics.

The influence of European ideas concerning sports and the influx of large numbers of immigrants from Europe were other factors which contributed to the growth of organized sports. The views of upper-class Englishmen regarding the role of sports in society had an important impact on America's elite classes, who set social trends. England was the first country to experience the process of industrialization, and as a result organized sports developed there first. By the mid-nineteenth century, Britishers participated in or watched a variety of organized athletic events. For social and cultural reasons, America's social elites emulated their British cousins and organized many of the same sporting activities. Such sports as tennis, track and field, and football first became popular organized activities in England. It is important to note that many upper-class Englishmen considered vigorous sporting activity an essential ingredient in the proper education of youth. At private schools and universities in England, it was widely held that rugby, cricket, and other athletic contests helped build moral character in students and complemented their scholastic achievements. This connection between organized sports and character building was popularized in America through such books as *Tom Brown's School Days* (1857) by the Englishman Thomas Hughes, who extolled organized sports as providing needed moral training for youth. This concept, which became known as "muscular Christianity," was advocated at first by only elite groups in America, but as the twentieth century approached it became accepted more widely by less-privileged Americans. To this extent, the English influence helped to undermine some of the religious opposition to sports.

The great tide of immigrants who poured into the United States between 1850 and 1900 contributed to both the growth and diversity of organized

Swedish immigrants enjoy a skating party in Montana. *(National Archives)*

sports. Each national group which migrated to America seemed to specialize in some particular athletic activity and helped to popularize and organize that sport. As we have seen, many German immigrants supported the *Turnverein* movement and were instrumental in promoting gymnastics and physical education in the schools. The Irish, who came to the United States in large numbers both before and after the Civil War, contributed to the rise of boxing as a major sport. Partially as a result of their low economic and social status, many Irish-Americans focused their attention on prize fighting, a sport which most middle- and upper-class Americans viewed as brutal and dishonest. For young Irishmen, however, boxing was an avenue toward financial and social success in a society in which many opportunities were closed to them. Boxing became so popular and Irish-American boxers so successful that many other Americans began to view the Irish immigrants with greater respect. Two Irish-American champions, John L. Sullivan and James J. Corbett, in fact, were among the most widely heralded sports heroes in the nineteenth century.

Other immigrant groups had similar success in promoting and popularizing specific athletic activities. Scottish-Americans were particularly important in developing track and field into a major American sport. Scandinavian immigrants were equally successful in popularizing Nordic sporting events associated with skiing and ice-skating and in advocating physical education. In general, the great wave of immigration of the nineteenth century added to the richness and diversity of American sports and contributed to the urban-industrial growth which sparked the development of organized sports.

In the period immediately after the Civil War, few urban immigrants and other working-class city dwellers were either participants or spectators at organized sporting events. As a rule, only the social elites and some middle-class Americans enjoyed the leisure and wealth to engage in organized sports. The typical factory worker earned between one and two dollars a day and thus could not afford the fifty-cent to one-dollar admission price at many athletic contests. In addition, he worked long hours Monday through Saturday, which were the only days on which sporting events were permitted in

10   most cities. As in the ante-bellum era, the urban laborer was more likely to spend his free time and seek his entertainment in saloons or sporting halls where a variety of crude contests such as cockfights, "rat worries," and dog-fights were staged. Gambling and rowdyism were a constant problem in these quasi-sports centers. As the industrial surge continued, however, more urban workers and their families were able to participate in organized sports. America's phenomenal industrial growth generated immense wealth, which slowly but surely trickled down to the laboring classes in the form of higher wages and free time. This was particularly true by the beginning of the twentieth century after frequent and bloody strikes in the 1890s frightened businessmen, touched the public conscience, and helped to spark an urban reform movement, the Progressive Era. By the end of the nineteenth cen-tury the working day was generally reduced from twelve hours to ten and, in a very few instances, to an eight-hour day. This gradual increase in both wages and free time allowed more working-class people to participate or spectate at sporting events. Beyond this, the ban on athletic activities on Sundays, which was linked to moral and religious opposition to sports, was altered or abol-ished in many cities. This allowed even greater numbers from the working class to become part of organized sporting activity. By 1900, organized sports were no longer the exclusive domain of America's upper classes.

Another influence which stimulated the rapid development of organized sports in the late nineteenth century was the increasing interest which businessmen took in athletics. For the most part, businessmen became active in sports for the profit that it might bring them. This was nothing new, since even before the Civil War transportation companies had recognized that promoting sporting events was one way of increasing passenger traffic and profits. As sports grew in popularity among a larger sector of the population, businessmen began to realize that sports teams or athletic events could be run like a business and return a profit. Even the athletic clubs of the social elites, which nominally adhered to the code of amateurism, often compen-sated top athletes to ensure victory and increase the prestige of the club. For businessmen who owned teams or promoted sporting events, it was equally important, if not more so, to provide the very best sports entertainment for the paying customer. As sports began to be covered more widely in news-papers and magazines and fans became more sophisticated, it was essential to provide top-flight performances and standardized procedures at sporting events. These developments contributed to the rapid organization of sports in the late nineteenth century.

In many ways, the development of organized sports between 1865 and 1900 reflected the social, political, and economic changes that were taking place in the larger industrial society. American sports in 1865 were, for the most part, loosely controlled by the participants who set up the games or events. Although professionalism did exist in some sports, most athletes were amateurs who participated for the joy of competing and the comradeship that it provided. Rules and practices in many sports varied from one area of the country to another and were often haphazardly enforced. There were few national or regional associations which attempted to regulate sporting activities, and there was almost no interference from government bodies at any level. This era in sport coincided with a period in American industrial development which many historians describe as the era of modified *laissez-faire* practices, that is, when business was relatively unrestrained from outside control or regulation. In such a climate, the free market reigns, and competition—sometimes fierce or cutthroat competition—prevails. In the case of baseball, which was the most popular game of the day, this competitive atmosphere in combination with the increased interest in the game led to greater professionalism. Some baseball teams, seeking to win and attract larger crowds, became semi-professional and then all-professional organizations. The Cincinnati Red Stocking Club of 1869 demonstrated the profitability of a highly competitive professional baseball team. In other sports such as football and track and field, which remained amateur, practices such as offering lucrative jobs or payments to athletes indicate that the same competitive forces were at work which resulted in the partial professionalization of baseball.

In the larger society, businessmen, particularly big businessmen, were the first group to respond to the problems caused by unrestrained competition. Specifically, cutthroat competition decreased profits, caused inefficiency and duplication, and created instability in the marketplace. The main thrust of big business's response was the movement toward combination and monopoly. Industrialists such as John D. Rockefeller attempted to bring order to the economic system and, at the same time, increase their own wealth by absorbing small companies, combining with them in trust agreements or forming pools and associations to share markets. In sports, businessmen or other executive interests often were able to bring about the same kind of consolidation and control of loosely organized teams and athletic events. It should be noted, however, that some organizations or associations were formed to prevent the commercialization and professionalization of sports. Such groups as the National Association of Base Ball Players (1858), the National Association of Amateur Oarsmen (1872), and the League of American Wheelmen (1880) attempted to eliminate the creeping commercialism that was invading sports. These organizations met with varying degrees of success.

In the case of baseball, the NABBP failed to stem the tide of professionalism. Highly talented pro or semi-pro teams under player control became common in the decade after the Civil War. The players, however, found it difficult to cope with the complex problems of management along with the high incidence of gambling and rowdyism which plagued the game. As a result, more teams came under business control. The culmination of this movement toward business control came in 1876 with the formation of the National League. Although it would be incorrect to assume that the National League reformed baseball by eliminating operating losses, gambling, and rowdyism, it did put professional baseball on a business basis and in the long run helped to standardize rules and procedures of operation.

In college football, another major team sport of the period, one can also see the process of centralization taking place. Although football retained its amateur status, control of college teams passed from the students to the

12   faculty and administration. Football, like pro baseball, became more commercialized, and standard practices with regard to rules, coaching, equipment, and eligibility were adopted. Clearly baseball, football, and other
major sports of the late nineteenth century reflected to a large degree the
highly competitive, commercial, and increasingly centralized society of
which they were a part.

In professional and amateur athletics, the passing of control over organized sports from the athletes to businessmen or administrators created
much friction. Many athletes resented the rules and restrictions placed on
them by owners, college officials, or national associations. At the college and
athletic club level, regulations to preserve amateurism were often violated or
side-stepped. In pro baseball, the conflict of interest between players and
owners resulted in major labor problems. This was not surprising, since the
American society of the late nineteenth century was plagued by bitter and
sometimes violent labor-managment disputes. A major cause of the problem
was the cavalier attitude with which management regarded labor. Like most
nineteenth century capitalists, baseball owners looked upon their players as
replaceable cogs in a machine. Players, they believed, should have no say in
the operation of a team or recourse to any protest against league policies or
rules. In keeping with the trend of the era, National League owners attempted
to monopolize pro baseball by driving rival leagues out of business or forcing
them to adhere to National League regulations. By the early 1880s, the
National League was in a strong enough position with regard to its rivals to
begin a campaign to maximize profits by restricting players' rights and
salaries. The "reserve clause" (1882) was one method used to undermine the
bargaining position of the players. It stipulated that a player was the sole
property of a club and could not move to another unless he was sold, traded,
or released. Prior to the "reserve clause," players could "jump" from one
team to another if higher wages were offered. At first, the "reserve clause"
applied to only a certain number of players on a team but was later expanded to include all players. It took away a fundamental right of the ballplayer—the right to sell his services to the highest bidder. In addition, the
National League in 1885 imposed a player salary ceiling of $2,000 per year,
which was well below the wage of star players of the day.

The players, led by John M. Ward of the New York Giants, organized a
protest against the "reserve clause," the salary ceiling, and other National
League practices. In 1885 Ward set up the Brotherhood of Professional Base
Ball Players, an association which had some of the earmarks of a labor union.
Failing to achieve results through the Brotherhood, Ward led an open revolt
against the National League in 1890 when he organized a rival Players'
League. During that season, the two leagues battled each other to determine
whether the players or the owners would control pro baseball. In one of the
most bitter labor disputes in professional sports, the National League was the
victor when the Players' League folded after the 1890 season. Financially
shaken, but with the "reserve clause" and salary ceiling intact, the National
League owners resumed their authoritarian and tight-fisted control over pro
baseball. As in the larger society, labor, even specialized laborers like pro

Early football games were informal and violent, such as this one between Cornell and Rochester, 1889. *(Library of Congress)*

baseball players, stood little chance of successfully challenging the power of nineteenth-century capitalists. By the end of the century, organized sports had been transformed by the industrial surge which radically changed life in America. Standardization of operating procedures, which was an important innovation in stimulating the industrial "take-off," became an integral part of organized sports. Baseball, which was a gentleman's sport played in a casual manner before the Civil War, became highly organized. Systems of teams, associations, and leagues were established throughout the country at both the amateur and professional levels. Schedules were set up in advance, and as a result of the transportation revolution, intercity and regional rivalries were established. Rules were also standardized to provide maximum excitement and fan interest. The "liveliness" of the ball was adjusted on several occasions, for example, to create a better balance between offense and defense and, perhaps more importantly, to ensure an exciting contest within the two or three hours which fans could afford to spend at the ballpark. The same was true with regard to football, which evolved from a rudimentary form of English rugby into a highly technical game. Rule changes which emphasized the running game and the institution of the first down and set scrimmage added excitement, precision, and order to the game. As in the case of baseball, more diverse scheduling of games and the organization of leagues made intercollegiate football a national sport by the 1890s. The same

Chicago White Stockings, 1885-86, "Champions of the United States." "Cap" Anson, front row left; Mike Kelly, second row extreme right. *(Library of Congress)*

kind of standardization took place in other sports, including golf, boxing, and horse racing.

Another outgrowth of the industrial process which made its mark on organized sports was the increase in specialization. The complex and interrelated industrial society needed specialists, and sports reflected this trend. In baseball, field positions such as catcher, pitcher, and first baseman became highly skilled assignments requiring specific equipment and talents. Players who were adept at bunting, throwing a curve ball, or stealing bases were important assets to any team. The same was true in football, where positions such as center, punter, and tailback required special skills. In football and baseball, the advent of the paid referee or umpire and the professional coach added to the degree of standardization and specialization. The increasing specialization in sports, combined with its growing popularity and the commercialism that engulfed it, led to the rise of sports heroes. Adrian "Cap" Anson of the Chicago White Stockings baseball team of the 1880s was a multi-talented athlete who specialized in hitting, playing first base, and managing. During the '80s, Anson led the Chicago team to five pennants and became one of the most celebrated players in the game. A Chicago teammate in that decade, Mike "King" Kelly, earned nearly equal acclaim for his aggressive play and particularly for his ferocious slides into the bases. Kelly became so popular that his feats were celebrated in a song of the day, which some sports fans still remember today—"Slide, Kelly, Slide." As has already been mentioned, John L. Sullivan, the Boston Strong Boy, became the most popular athletic hero of his era for his knockout blows and endurance in bare-knuckle boxing. The increasing popularity and commercialization of sports made many athletes, especially those who lent their names to advertising promotions, household words by the end of the century.

Between 1865 and 1900 organized sports had changed dramatically from a mainly amateur, gentlemanly pastime into a commerical, standardized, and highly competitive enterprise. The forces that transformed organized sports in this era can be best understood by focusing on the shift of the United States from a rural, agricultural society to an urban, industrial nation by 1900. Rapid changes in moral values, methods of transportation and communication, economic organization, and social status all contributed to the rapid rise and development of organized sports. In 1901 organized sports entered the new century with the popularity and potential for further development which would make it a central preoccupation for many Americans during the next eighty years.

Sources and Suggested Readings

Barth, Gunther. *City People: The Rise of Modern City Culture in Nineteenth Century America* (New York, 1980).

Betts, John R. *America's Sporting Heritage, 1850-1950* (Reading, Mass., 1974).

——————— . "The Technological Revolution and the Rise of Sport, 1850-1900," *Mississippi Valley Historical Review*, 40 (Sept. 1953), 231-56.

Dulles, Foster R. *A History of Recreation: America Learns to Play* (New York, 1965), Chaps. 8, 11, 12, 13.

Huizinga, Johan. *Homo Ludens: A Study of the Play-Element in Culture* (Boston, 1955).

Lucas, John A. and Ronald A. Smith. *Saga of American Sports* (Philadelphia, 1978).

Nevins, Allan. *The Emergence of Modern America, 1865-1878* (New York, 1927).

Paxson, Frederic Logan. "The Rise of Sport," *Mississippi Valley Historical Review*, 4 (Sept. 1917), 143-68.

Somers, Dale A. *The Rise of Sports in New Orleans, 1850-1900* (Baton Rouge, La., 1972).

2

The Impact of the Social Elites on Sports

Benjamin G. Rader

Those who stood at the apex of the American social structure, the social elites, played a central role in the growth of amateur sports in the United States. In the middle decades of the nineteenth century upper-class Americans, imitating their counterparts in England, began to engage in sports with unbounded enthusiasm. They formed dozens of clubs in the larger cities for the playing of sports, especially for amateur track and field, cricket, polo, golf, and tennis. They built lavish athletic facilities, formulated rules of play, formed national associations, and sponsored competition from the local to the national levels. Apart from engaging in sport for the sheer joy of play, the elites used sport as a vehicle for enhancing or maintaining their social status and for nurturing certain values among their children. To serve these social functions, the elites employed the principle of amateurism to exclude the "outsiders," that is, ethnics, blacks, and workingmen, from "their" sports.

Sports and sport clubs served as one means of building socially-exclusive subcommunities within the larger society. As the society became more impersonal in the nineteenth century, as burgeoning cities became more important than small geographic communities, and as the nation became more culturally heterogeneous, more and more Americans formed subcommunities based upon ethnicity, status, or other considerations. Central to the development of much nineteenth-century sport was the emergence of subcommunities based upon status. Apart from clubs, elite groups used residence in a particular neighborhood, adherence to a certain religious denomination, attendance at a specific college, and the like, to exclude social "inferiors" from their subcommunities.

That the American social elites often turned to sport clubs as a means of forming status communities should occasion no surprise. Only those with wealth could play games that required expensive equipment, immense acreage, a staff of assistants, and an abundance of leisure time. Participation in expensive and time-consuming sports necessarily excluded lower-income groups unless the sport became professionalized. Furthermore, participation in sport per se did not threaten any deeply held personal beliefs that might otherwise divide members of the elite. Sport, which by definition was subordinated to rules, encouraged a temporary equality among the players; it strengthened the bonds among athletes and facilitated direct communications.

The sudden rage for sport in England in the middle of the nineteenth century decisively influenced the American elites. Since colonial times would-be American aristocrats had always been inclined to imitate the latest fashions of the English upper classes. Prior to the 1850s the English gentleman's leisure activities had consisted largely of country weekend excursions, balls, riding to the hounds, a bit of cricket, horse racing, and much time devoted to gambling and hard drinking. Then, beginning in the 1850s, many upper-class Englishmen joined the organized sports movement, forming literally hundreds of clubs for cricket, "athletics" (track and field), football, rowing, yachting, lawn tennis, and eventually golf. While the early English clubs served as models for the Americans, they, unlike the American clubs, subordinated status considerations to interest in sport itself.

Like their English counterparts, the American elites came to see sport as an important mechanism for socializing youth. As early as the 1850s a minority of the New England literati launched a minor crusade for a "muscular Christianity" which urged the compatibility of "physical and spiritual sanctity." In the latter half of the century and the first half of the twentieth century, a barrage of boys' sport fiction, in the mold of the classic *Tom Brown's School Days* (1857) by the Englishman, Thomas Hughes, asserted that participation in sport by youth would result in personal moral improvement and even enhance one's probability of gaining material success. Sports, many believed, would counteract the tendencies of the nation's youth toward softness and effeminacy. Theodore Roosevelt, the elite Easterner turned cowboy, the "Rough Rider" of the Spanish-American War, and the supercharged President of the United States between 1901 and 1909, believed that only aggressive sports could create the "brawn, the spirit, the self-confidence, and quickness of men" that was essential for the existence of a strong nation. By the 1890s even middle-income groups, who once looked upon sport with suspicion, began to accept certain sports under the supervision of adults as tools for shaping the character of youth. The result was a mammoth program of adult-managed sports for youth (especially boys) sponsored by the Young Men's Christian Association, Public Schools Athletic Leagues, city playgrounds, and the nation's high schools.

At an early date New York City assumed and maintained the leadership of elite sports. In the nineteenth century the social elites of New York developed in a quite different fashion from the elites in Philadelphia or Boston. While early in the century the Boston-Philadelphia "mercantile-Federalist" elites founded virtual dynasties that perpetuated their status and power, the tremendous surge of commerce, railroad building, and the growth of the factory system in the latter half of the nineteenth century fractured the old

18   New York elite. The absence of a clear-cut dynasty or social arbitrator in New York encouraged the presence of the "beautiful people," a "smart set," or "Upper Four Hundred," that derived its status primarily from reputation, that is, highly publicized activities available only to the super-wealthy. Sport furnished them with one convenient means of self-advertisement.

However, the New York Yacht Club, the first major voluntary sport organization of the city, originated among the families of the older elite. John Cox Stevens, a major-domo on the New York sporting scene, organized the yacht club on board his schooner, *Gimcrack*, on July 30, 1844. The following year the club erected a handsome Gothic clubhouse at the Elysian Fields, Hoboken, New Jersey, the site of Stevens' estate. For twenty years thereafter the club held an annual regatta off the clubhouse promontory. Membership in the club came to be the equivalent to acceptance at the very top rung of New York "Society."

International competition in 1851 increased interest in yacht racing. In that year Stevens, the long-time commodore of the New York Yacht Club, entered a race in a regatta sponsored by the Royal Yacht Squadron of Great Britain. Stevens commissioned a special boat, christened the *America*, for the occasion. Against eighteen British yachts in a race around the Isle of Wight, *America* won easily. The victory by the representatives of the small yacht club in New York over the yachtsmen of the oldest yacht club in the world encouraged the formation of exclusive clubs in all the major cities along the Eastern seaboard. In 1857 Stevens presented the cup won in England to the New York Yacht Club as a perpetual challenge cup open to competition by yachts of all nations. Through 1980 twenty-four international challenge matches had been held for the *America's* Cup, all won by American yachts. To participate in the race for the cup required large outlays of money either from syndicates or wealthy individuals. Thus yacht racing remained perhaps the most exclusive of American sports.

From the late 1850s to the late 1870s James Gordon Bennett, Jr., the colorful and eccentric owner of the *New York Herald*, replaced John Cox Stevens as the premier of the New York sporting scene. Bennett had a direct influence on several sports. In 1866, as a member of the New York Yacht Club, he won the world's first yacht race across the Atlantic. Beginning in 1873 he awarded cups and medals to college track and field champions. After witnessing a polo match played by English army officers while visiting England in 1875, Bennett returned to the United States with polo mallets and balls. The next year he and his rich friends formed the Westchester Polo Club in New York and took the sport to Newport, Rhode Island, where the fashionable of the nation's super-rich spent their summers. In 1886 Newport hosted the first of several international matches with the Hurlingham Club. Finally, in 1909, to the utter amazement of the English, the Americans established their superiority in polo, a position they retained until 1939. In the post-World War II years Argentina dominated international competition.

Bennett's assistance to the sport of lawn tennis had more bizarre origins. According to legend, in 1878 he obtained for a British army officer a guest card to Newport's most exclusive club, the Reading Room. He then dared his friend to ride a horse up the steps of the club's front hall, a challenge that the Englishman accepted. The Reading Room revoked Bennett's membership for instigating such a provocative act. Miffed, Bennett retaliated by building an even more lavish sports complex, the Casino, a few blocks away. The Casino subsequently became the site for the first thirty-four national lawn tennis championships. Later in the century Bennett also contributed to the Olympic movement and promoted horse, auto, and air races.

Beginning in the 1860s the elites initiated the formation of a large number of athletic clubs. At first, the members of New York Athletic Club (NYAC), incorporated by well-to-do young athletes in 1868, appeared to be more concerned with promoting young men in "amateur" track and field than in using sport as a status-enhancing mechanism. They simply wanted to offer an alternative arena of competition to the existing world of track and field which was dominated by professional athletes, gamblers, and "rowdies."

In the 1870s the club built the first cinder track in the country at Mott Haven, introduced the use of spiked shoes, and sponsored the first national amateur championships in track and field (1876), swimming (1877), boxing (1878), and wrestling (1878). In 1879 the newly organized National Association of Amateur Athletes of America (popularly known as the N4A) took over sponsorship of the national track and field championships. By then six large clubs modelled after NYAC had been formed in New York; large clubs also had been organized in Baltimore, Buffalo, Chicago, Detroit, and St. Louis. The 1880s witnessed further growth of the clubs. In 1887 an observer reported that "Athletic Clubs are now springing into existence in the United States in such profusion as to baffle the effort to enumerate them. Scarce a city can be found having a population of more than 30,000 inhabitants, in which there is not at least one club of this class." Only a severe economic depression in the 1890s reversed the growth of athletic clubs. Many of them went bankrupt.

Ironically as the clubs prospered, they tended to become more socially oriented. Athletics often took second place to the social functions of the clubs. In the 1880s NYAC, by inviting some of the leading social arbiters of the city to become members, became part of a socially exclusive network of the most prestigious clubs in the city. In 1885 the club built an elegant five-story, Venetian-style clubhouse at a cost of $150,000 which contained a gymnasium, swimming pool, dining rooms, bowling alley, rifle range, billiards room, wine cellar, and sleeping rooms. In 1888 NYAC acquired a country home at Travers Island where it built a clubhouse, boathouse, track, and clay tennis courts. Each club began to sponsor an elaborate social calendar. "Wine, women, and song," according to the historians of NYAC, "became more than a catch phrase—they were woven into the texture of NYAC activities."

The trend away from an athlete-centered orientation alarmed the NYAC Old Guard, that is, the founding members. They protested the decision of the club to "go social." "The social element in the clubs is like 'dry rot'. . ." exclaimed one critic; "it soon causes them to fail in the purpose for which they are organized . . . palatial clubhouses are expected and money is spent adorning them that, if used to beautify the athletic grounds and improve

20 tracks, would cause a widespread interest in athletic sports and further the development of the wind and muscles of American youths." But the protests were futile. To the "social element," sport was primarily a means of enhancing the prestige of the club, not something to be pursued for its own sake. The social activities of the club were essential for it to serve effectively as an agency of status ascription.

Championing amateur principles was also an essential ingredient in promoting status. In due time the clubs insisted upon the adoption of an amateur code of athletics. Supporting amateurism permitted the clubs both to imitate their upper-class English counterparts and to exclude social "undesirables" such as blacks, ethnics, and working men from "their" sporting activities. Yet the amateur code was less restrictive in practice than in principle. The amateur code in the United States, unlike that in England, stemmed from neither a body of established customs nor the sponsorship of an inherited aristocracy. In England centuries of tradition and the perquisites of social standing had prescribed appropriate behavior for a gentleman and a sportsman. To win at all costs was bad form; work and play were distinct spheres of gentlemanly activity; no gentleman could claim such a status if he made his living from sport. In contrast to the English upper strata, the American social elites often consisted of men of new wealth who brought with them the acquisitive values of the marketplace. While nominally accepting the concepts of "fair play" and amateurism, defeating rivals by any means within the rules was consistent with their experiences in the world of commerce and industry. Thus, the major metropolitan athletic clubs placed high priority on winning, even if it meant extending thinly disguised subsidies to the most-talented athletes and violating the ethos of amateurism.

The major clubs engaged in intense rivalries for athletic supremacy, which led to the demise of the N4A and the formation of the Amateur Athletic Union in 1888. The AAU, however, did not eliminate conflicts between the clubs or settle eligibility controversies. Smaller clubs complained that the larger clubs "stole" their best athletes by promising higher subsidies. Colleges and high schools also resented the authority of the AAU and the restrictions that it attempted to impose upon them. Beginning in the early twentieth century and continuing into the 1980s, the governance of amateur sport was the center of an incredibly complex running controversy. Several competing organizations tried to establish their control over nonprofessional athletes. The athletes appeared to be the chief victims of the struggle among different groups for hegemony over amateur sports.

Despite a history rent with controversy, social discrimination, and blatant hypocrisy, the elite athletic clubs and the AAU played significant roles in the promotion of amateur sport, especially track and field. Prior to 1900 the clubs produced most of the country's outstanding runners, jumpers, pole vaulters, and shot putters. At a celebrated international meet between the London Athletic Club and NYAC at New York in 1895, the Americans swept to victory in every event. The following year, American athletes, mostly from the Boston Athletic Association, participated in the revived Olympic Games in Athens, Greece. Though America's best athletes did not make the trip, the Americans won nine of the twelve track events. For both the 1908 and 1912 Olympic Games, the AAU made a concerted effort to field the strongest American team possible. In the twentieth century the AAU and the clubs continued to sponsor many of the major amateur meets, but a steadily increasing share of the athletes of championship calibre came from the colleges and the high schools.

The elites used sports other than track and field to build status subcommunities. In Philadelphia, old-stock Americans became cricket enthusiasts. By the 1890s, within a ten-mile radius of Philadelphia, there were four beautifully kept, spacious cricket grounds with lavish clubhouses; London, by comparison, had only two grounds of equal stature. Membership in the fine "first-class" clubs ranged from 500 to 1,300 persons, who were representatives of Philadelphia "Main Line" families (established families of old wealth). Before 1900 Philadelphia teams played over a dozen international matches, and each year the clubs engaged in intense competition for the Halifax Cup, awarded to the most powerful eleven in the city. In the twentieth century, cricket in Philadelphia declined rapidly. Other diversions such as lawn tennis, which could be played more quickly, tended to replace cricket as a sport favored by the Philadelphia elites. William "Big Bill" Tilden, the world's greatest tennis player in the 1920s, learned to play the sport on the courts of the Germantown Cricket Club. By the 1920s the cricket clubs could hardly be distinguished from any other metropolitan athletic or country club.

The metropolitan athletic and cricket clubs were forerunners of the great country club movement that flourished first in the 1920s. The first "Country Club," founded in 1882, was far more exclusive than later imitators. The Brookline Club was one of the primary agencies for preserving the exclusiveness of Boston "Society." In the twentieth century, the country club became a haven for those seeking to establish status communities in the smaller cities and the metropolitan suburbs. Membership in a country club became a salient badge of distinction, almost obligatory for anyone striving for status in communities both large and small.

While golf did not furnish the initial impetus for the formation of the first country clubs, it, more than any other sport, induced the rapid spread of the clubs throughout the country. In 1887 John Reid, a transplanted Scotsman and an executive of an iron works at Yonkers, New York, organized the St. Andrews Club, named after the historic club in Scotland. In the 1890s business tycoons in New York, Boston, Philadelphia, and Chicago took up the sport. In 1891 William K. Vanderbilt brought over Willie Dunn, famed Scottish golfer, to build the first eighteen-hole links, the Shinnecock Hills course, located in Southampton, Long Island, where many wealthy New Yorkers had summer homes. By 1900 rich golfers could follow the seasons. When cold winter winds began to blow, they could play on courses in Florida, Georgia, and North Carolina. Golfers formed the United States Golf Association in 1894, which each year scheduled a national tournament. Initially, Scottish immigrants dominated championship play. With but few exceptions, a reporter wrote in 1898, golf "is a sport restricted to the richer classes of the country."

A game of polo, a favorite pastime of the rich, ca. 1882.

Yet in the twentieth century golf began to appeal to active business and professional men who stood a notch or two below the apex of the American status structure. In the earliest days of golf, commented one wag, it had been the exclusive sport of the upper "Four Hundred," but in the 1920s it became the sport of the "Upper Four Million." In 1913 there were 742 links in the entire nation; by 1930 the number had leaped to 5,586, an eight-fold increase. Apart from being a conspicuous status mechanism, golf furnished business and professional men with an escape from the close confinement and annoying details of their downtown offices. They could presumably retreat to the open, verdant, serene, pastoral countryside. However, men reassured their anxious wives and their bosses that they got as much business done in the locker room and on the course as they did in their offices. Sometimes playing golf seemed to be only a pretext for convivial gatherings at the "nineteenth hole," the club-house bar.

As early as 1913 golf exhibited its potential as a public spectacle. That year a crowd of more than 3,000 watched Francis Ouimet, a twenty-year-old amateur golfer, upset Britain's two leading professional golfers—Harry Vardon and Edward "Ted" Ray—in the United States Open Tournament. Overnight Ouimet was a national hero. In 1916 millionaire Rodman Wanamaker furnished the funds for the formation of the Professional Golfers' Association. While a professional tour of sorts developed in the 1920s, ama-

A singles game of tennis at the Staten Island Club grounds, ca. 1881.

teur play, especially that of Robert "Bobby" Jones, held the spotlight. However, in the 1930s the professional players began their total domination of play at the championship level. Only one amateur (in 1933) ever again won the United States Open.

Lawn tennis flourished first on the estates and in the summer resorts of the super-rich. At Newport, where the nation's wealthiest families built large Gothic palaces for summer homes and entertained one another royally, tennis became the "in" sport. Dixon Wector captured the flavor of Newport in the late nineteenth century when he wrote, "Other than social consciousness, the only bond which drew this summer colony together was sport—which might consist of sailing around Block Island, or having cocktails upon one's steam yacht reached by motorboat from the landing of the New York Yacht Club, or bathing at Bailey's Beach or the Gooseberry Island Club, or tennis on the Casino courts." Tennis buffs founded the United States Lawn Tennis Association in 1881 and scheduled the first national tournament the same year at Newport. In 1913 the tournament moved to the West Side Tennis Club at Forest Hills, New York. Lawn tennis long remained a sport dominated by clubs of impeccably high status aspirations.

In the first two decades of the twentieth century, tennis began to lose some of its image of being a delicate, effeminate sport. In 1900 a wealthy Harvard player, Dwight F. Davis, encouraged national rivalries by establish-

Lawn tennis at the Seventh Regiment Armory, New York City. Tennis was a popular sport among the social elites, ca. 1881.

ing the International Lawn Tennis Challenge Cup (Davis Cup), one of the most coveted prizes in tennis until the 1960s. In 1909 Maurice McLaughlin brought a new brand of tennis to Newport. His power and speed, learned on the fast, hard-surfaced courts of California, excited an interest never before felt on the hallowed grounds of the East. In the 1920s the appearance of Big Bill Tilden, Suzanne Lenglen, and Helen Wills marked an end to the conservative, casual, and social age of tennis and the beginning of the age when tennis players became public celebrities. Yet tennis clung to the principles of pristine amateurism while practicing "shamateurism," that is, secretly subsidizing players, until the late 1960s, when the major tournaments became affairs open to professional and amateur players alike.

The sponsorship of tennis and golf by the elite clubs expanded the opportunities for women to participate in sport. While the aggressive physical activity essential to success in most sports violated the prevailing Victorian image of femininity, upper-class women seemed to be less inhibited than their middle-class counterparts. Women from rich families pioneered in breaking down the sex barrier in amateur sports. The elite clubs built some of the first tennis courts specifically for the wives and daughters of club members. In the early years, the women preferred doubles to singles, possibly because they were encumbered by bustles and full-length skirts. In 1887 the women scheduled the first national women's tennis tournament. Like the men's sport, women's tennis at the championship levels, from the 1920s through the 1960s, was characterized by "shamateurism."

The task of breaching the sex barrier in golf was more difficult. In the closing years of the nineteenth century, the golf clubs began reluctantly to set aside the links on certain afternoons for female players. Only thirteen women participated in the first national tournament held on the Meadow-brook course on Long Island in 1895. In 1898, H. L. Fitz Patrick an-nounced—prematurely—that "the American golf girl has arrived!" Women golfers helped initiate a more liberal style of dress. By 1898 a few brave ladies played without hats and with sleeves extending only to the elbows. The great women golfers, such as Alexa Stirling and Glenna Collett of the 1920s, never received the public attention given to their female counterparts in tennis. Women's golf at the highest performance levels remained an ama-teur affair until the 1940s, when the great Mildred "Babe" Didrikson Zaharias took up the sport as a professional.

By mid twentieth century the role of social elites in sports was remark-ably different than it had been in earlier times. Legacies of the earlier era sur-vived, but in sharply attenuated forms. For instance, the principle of ama-teurism continued, wreaking havoc in college sports and the Olympic Games. Everyone recognized that athletes could not achieve top-level performances without devoting full time to the task. To do this, they had either to be inde-pendently wealthy or to obtain subsidies of some sort. Yet Americans were reluctant to abandon totally a principle that was rooted in the elite-domi-nated sports of the nineteenth century.

Vestiges of the earlier era of elite sports remained in yachting, tennis, and golf. Yet even such an expensive and socially exclusive sport as yacht-racing took on many of the characteristics of a professional sport. In 1980 Bob Banier, president of the *Yachting* magazine, declared, "I just a little bit deplore that you've got to work for two years—every working day—to pre-pare for a sailboat race." While few blacks played tennis or golf at the cham-pionship level—or nonprofessionally, for that matter—the principal reason did not appear to be racial or status discrimination. Rather, blacks simply did not have the financial resources to launch professional careers in sports requiring the use of expensive facilities and individual coaches.

To sum up, those who aspired to achieve a position at the top of the American status structure in the latter half of the nineteenth century had found in the playing and promotion of certain sports a means of building subcommunities based upon status ascription. In so doing these elites, or would-be elites, encouraged a tremendous growth of amateur yachting, crick-et, track and field, polo, golf, and tennis. Yet, the elites permitted, some-times encouraged, or were unable to halt the transformation of these sports from a player to a spectator-centered orientation. Once the sports were fash-ioned to satisfy the needs of spectators, the power of the elites to dictate the future of American sports sharply declined. By the latter half of the twenti-eth century, the spectators through such intermediaries as educational insti-tutions, sporting entrepreneurs, and television were far more important than the elites in shaping the contours of American sport history.

Sources and Suggested Readings

Considine, Bob and Fred B. Jarvis. *The First Hundred Years: A Portrait of NYAC* (London, 1969).

Janssen, Frederick W. *History of American Amateur Athletics* (New York, 1885).

Lester, John A., ed. *A Century of Philadelphia Cricket* (Philadelphia, 1951).

Outing magazine (1882-1923). A valuable journal devoted almost exclusively to elite sports.

Rader, Benjamin G. "The Quest for Subcommunities and the Rise of American Sport," *American Quarterly*, 29 (Fall 1977), 355-369.

——————————. *American Sports: From the Age of Folk Games to the Age of Spectators* (Englewood Cliffs, N.J., in press), Chaps. 3, 11, 15.

Wector, Dixon. *The Saga of American Society: A Record of Social Aspiration, 1607-1937* (New York, 1937).

Willis, Joe D. and Richard G. Wettan. "Social Stratification in New York City Athletic Clubs, 1865-1915," *Journal of Sport History*, 3 (Spring 1976), 45-63.

3

Boxing and Reform

Randy Roberts

Thomas Pye, a pioneering New Orleans photographer, froze the scene forever. It was clearly another age. Men wearing black bowlers and white shirts with turned-down, starched collars stand next to large-wheeled buggies; other men wearing straw hats, vests, and even tails look on. These men, who seem today to be pathetically over-dressed, had gathered in complete secrecy in a remote corner of Mississippi to watch two Irish-Americans break the law. And how they shattered it! The illegal activity—bare-knuckled prize fighting—commenced at 10:30 in the morning of July 8, 1889, and continued for the next two hours and sixteen minutes. Although by noon the temperature exceeded one hundred degrees, both men fought and drank as if they were locked in a Homeric epic. In the forty-fourth round John L. Sullivan, who had been drinking a mixture of tea and whiskey between rounds since the start of the fight, began to vomit. One ringside wag said that the Great John L. was getting rid of the tea but retaining the whiskey. Recovering from this condition, Sullivan proceeded to butcher Jake Kilrain. After round seventy-five, Kilrain's ringside representative "threw up the sponge." There was real fear that Sullivan might add murder to the crime of prize fighting. So the fight ended. Sullivan retained his World's Heavyweight crown. It was the last time that two men would fight for that title using just their bare fists. Years later when the poet Vachel Lindsay tried to recapture the mood of the 1880s, he wrote:

> Nigh New Orleans
> Upon an emerald plain
> John L. Sullivan
> The strong boy
> Of Boston
> Fought seventy-five rounds with Jake Kilrain.

How could such an activity exist in an age which was consciously devoted to progress and reform? On the surface, prize fighting seemed to be a

28   sport struggling against the current of an age. The dominant theme of the period between the end of Reconstruction and the start of World War I was reform. Year by year the consensus on this issue swelled; it started as a lonely voice of reform-minded politicians and intellectuals who coalesced in the Liberal Republican movement, grew louder with the passage of the Pendleton Act (1883) and the Sherman Anti-Trust Act (1890), and positively shouted after the assassination of William McKinley placed "that damn cowboy" Theodore Roosevelt in the Oval Office. So powerful had the issue become that the years between 1901 and 1917 have been labeled the Progressive Era. Through reforms politicians hoped to curb the abuses of industrialism and bring order to a rapidly changing society. In reform they saw improvement, in improvement progress, and in progress perfection.

As it was practiced in the 1870s and 1880s, prize fighting was a *non sequitur* and an embarrassment. It conjured images men would have preferred to forget—scenes of mortal combat in the blood-soaked sand of the Roman Colosseum or of brutish Regency nobles wagering on whether a fallen fighter would survive or die. In an age that viewed itself as reasonable and progressive, bare-knuckle prize fighting was illogical and retrogressive. As Don Atyeo has suggested, bare-knuckle fighting was quite simply "beyond the pale of sporting sanity. . . . Only a madman would ever contemplate entering a contest in which *inevitably* one side retired with at best a swollen head or a battered face and the other with bruised or broken hands." It was a contest with few rules and no time limit or institutionalized sympathy. A round ended only with a knockdown, and a fight concluded only when the felled fighter could not be revived within thirty seconds.

Everything about the sport was brutal and primitive. Because the sport was illegal throughout most of the nation, rings were hurriedly constructed and any sort of salutary supervision was absent. Given these conditions, a fighter's career was usually violent and short. Often it would take six months to a year to recover from a fight, and it was unusual for a prize fighter to engage in more than a dozen bare-knuckle matches. Retired fighters commonly complained of arthritis in their hands, and signs of traumatic encephalopathy (a neurological syndrome also known as dementia pugilistica or the punch-drunk syndrome) were alarmingly frequent. Those who chose prize fighting as a career normally died young and broken—physically, psychologically, and financially.

That such a career opportunity existed at all is a sad commentary on the age. Reform was a dominant theme in the Gilded Age precisely because so much reform was needed. Labor abuses, especially among women and children, low wages, an appalling lack of health and safety measures, and squalid working conditions were the gloomy facts of life for most working Americans. Among men blessed with hard hands or hard heads, prize fighting was an alternative, an escape from the sweat shops, coal mines, steel mills, and railroad camps that scarred the map of industrial America. In either world—pugilistic or industrial—violence was the norm; however, the ring held out the promise of fame and fortune. If the cheers and dollars were achieved only

in dreams, then at least there *were* dreams. For the laborer in industrial
America, even the dreams were absent.

Not surprisingly, prize fighting became the territory of the most despised and depressed ethnic groups in America. As S. Kirson Weinberg and Henry Arond's study illustrates, until the 1920s Irish-Americans comprised the largest single ethnic group in prize fighting. Such noted American bare-knuckle fighters as Yankee Sullivan, John Morrissey, John C. Heehan, Ned O'Baldwin, Joe Coburn, Mike McCool, Paddy Ryan, and John L. Sullivan spoke with the brogue of the old country and wore their names like badges. The first four heavyweight champions were Irish-Americans, and they also dominated the lighter divisions. Although most of the champions between 1877 and 1917 were Irish, there were also several black champions. Such blacks as Jack Johnson, Sam Langford, George "Kid Chocolate" Dixon, and Joe Gans are still considered among the very best of American boxers.

The lure of this brutal trade was simple: for the lowest rungs of society it offered one of the few avenues for advancement. In his essay, "The Road To Business Success, An Address To Young Men," Andrew Carnegie, a leading spokesman for and example of success in America, told eager readers to aim high, work hard, live cleanly, and concentrate all energy toward a single goal. The result, Carnegie assured, would be success and the fruits of success—money, prestige, and power. For an uneducated, unconnected, and uncouth Irish-American or black, Carnegie's message translated into the pursuit of a championship belt. If Scottish immigrants could look longingly toward Carnegie as an apotheosis, then every brawny Irish-American male could so view the Great John L. Without catching a leprechaun, Sullivan found his pot of gold.

This is not to say that prize fighting was generally accepted as a legitimate form of social elevation and success. It was not. For most Americans, who chose to speak of themselves as "respectable," prize fighting remained beyond the pale. It was viewed as a ghastly trade, practiced by brutal and brutalized men and watched only by the sadistic and debased. In 1893 the "respected" magazine, the *Nation*, remarked that the clientele of prize fighting "consists almost always of the offscourings of human society—gamblers, thieves, drunkards, and bullies. . . . The pugilists themselves . . . are generally persons whose manners and morals are a disgrace to our civilization." To watch a fight, the article continues, is to "make human nature seem a cheaper, viler thing." The editor concludes by asserting that no "respectable" newspaper would even cover such a demoralizing event.

Yet, although the sport was brutal and thus the object of much criticism, nevertheless boxing imbibed liberally of the elixir of reform that affected the rest of America. Between 1889 and 1900 the promoters of prize fighting made an attempt to transform their sport into a more ordered and respectable profession. Actually, the most significant step toward bringing order to the prize fighting world took place almost a generation before the 1889 fight between Sullivan and Kilrain. In England in 1867, John Graham Chambers wrote and John Sholto Douglas, eighth Marquis of Queensberry, popularized

30   a new boxing code. The Queensberry Rules changed boxing from a bare-fisted sport to a gloved sport, and the code abolished wrestling throws and hugging holds. In addition, the new rules called for three-minute rounds with a one-minute rest period between rounds, installed the concept of a knock-out, and allowed contests to be decided by a referee's decision. The goal was to transform boxing from a contest for thugs into a match for gentlemen. As a result, the rules were considered effeminate and were slow in gaining acceptance. But by 1889 even the most hardened devoté of the bare-fisted sport reluctantly had come to realize that the future belonged to fighters wearing gloves.

By adopting the use of gloves and allowing a bout to be resolved by a decision, the sport appealed to a larger audience. The move introduced the idea of scientific fighting into boxing. No longer did one have to knock out an opponent to win; now a fighter could be victorious by landing light blows and avoiding his foe's punches. Defense gained parity with offense. The manly art of self-defense, as taught by gentlemen instructors such as Ned Donnelly, thus was transformed into a noble art, a "precise science in which a legitimate parry existed for every possible offensive move." In Donnelly's book *Self-Defense or the Art of Boxing* (1879), the sport became an intellectual exercise. Any gentleman could master the sport simply by study-ing—in a book, not in the ring—the correct body movements for each different situation. One of Donnelly's best pupils, George Bernard Shaw, became so enamored of the sport that he wrote a novel about a champion prize fighter. In *Cashel Byron's Profession* (1886), the boxer hero is unique, being both a gentleman and a scientific pugilist. Cashel is the sort of chap that any gentleman would be proud to take home for dinner and to introduce to his mother and sister.

This new sort of prize fighter was not confined simply to gentlemen's gyms and the pages of fiction. Just such a man defeated John L. Sullivan on September 7, 1892. "Gentleman Jim" Corbett could have been Cashel's brother. A former bank clerk, Corbett was scrupulous in both dress and speech, with a penchant for stiff collars, canes, gloves, and the passive voice. His true ambition was to be an actor, and the ring was his stage. The Sullivan-Corbett bout was a study in contrasts, pitting the old against the new. Corbett's victory, noted a writer for the Chicago *Tribune*, "was a triumph of youth, agility, intelligence, and good generalship over age, lack of science, and brute force." Sullivan was the bruiser, whose friends were strictly hoi polloi. But Corbett, if not an aristocrat by birth, was a different breed entirely.

Increasingly then, boxing became a sport that transcended class lines. If the wealthy and aristocratic Americans seldom became boxers, they were attracted to the ring as patrons and spectators. If the champions learned their trade in south Boston, Pennsylvania mines, or San Francisco's Barbary Coast, their patrons gained an appreciation of the sport in places like the Olympia Club, the Young Men's Gymnastic Club, and the Southern Athletic Club. At a major fight rowdy fans and pickpockets could be found shoulder-to-shoulder, hand-in-pocket with Shaw, Arthur Conan Doyle, and members of the leading New York and Southern families. Indeed, Professor William

Lyon Phelps of Yale remembered reading the newspaper to his Baptist min-
ister father the day after the Sullivan-Corbett fight: "When I came to the
headline CORBETT DEFEATS SULLIVAN, I read that aloud and turned
the page. My father leaned forward and said earnestly, 'Read it by rounds!'"
Boxing certainly had moved up in the world.

With its rules reformed and its clientele expanded, boxing enjoyed a new
status in the 1890s. However, several less attractive aspects of the decade
also were reflected in the sport. Social Darwinism and jingoism, for example,
became part of prize fighting. As Dale A. Somers has observed in his fine
book, *The Rise of Sports in New Orleans, 1850-1900* (1972), "When the
prize ring produced men capable of beating all rivals in such rigorous, prime-
val struggles, it seemed to justify America's competitive system and to prove
the value of the system's scientific underpinning." When Sullivan was champion, the New York *Sun* asserted that he was " the most phenomenal production of the prize ring that has been evoluted during the nineteenth century." With ideas such as the "survival of the fittest" and the "hierarchy of
races" drifting about the intellectual atmosphere, such an opinion seemed
logical. In America a thrilling syllogism was cast: Sullivan is the greatest
fighter in the world; Sullivan is an American; *ergo* America is the world's
greatest country. Indeed, in few areas of life did the Darwinistic principles
seem so evident. In the ring the "march onward and upward" and the "progress of the species" were visible. And that the best fighters were produced
in America seemed a clear indication of America's special fitness.

Changes in racial attitudes also affected late-nineteenth-century boxing.
Throughout the South Jim Crow was flexing his muscles; that is, institutionalized segregation was spreading. Between the end of Reconstruction and the
1890s, blacks and whites had lived without any formal code of segregation.
They had not lived on terms of equality, and they had not enjoyed a particularly friendly or peaceful existence together; but gains were made, problems were solved, at least temporarily, and violence was kept to a minimum.
Then in the 1890s, the races were officially and legally separated. In 1896,
the Supreme Court in the *Plessy* vs. *Ferguson* decision laid down the "separate but equal" doctrine, thereby justifying a separate and distinctly unequal
society. The races were kept apart in all forms of public transportation,
from steamboats to trains; in hospitals, penal institutions, state parks, soda
fountains, waiting rooms, and circuses; in education, from kindergarten to
graduate school. Jim Crow was extended to extremes that would be amusing
were they not so serious. For example, in North Carolina and Florida, state
law required that textbooks used by public school children of one race be
kept separate from those used by the other race. Even when the textbooks
were put into storage during the summer months, they had to be separated
into different closets. Thus even "separate but equal" textbooks had to be
kept apart.

Similarly, in the 1890s Jim Crow entered the ring. Before then, contests
between blacks and whites had been frequent. In the early 1890s such bouts
became less common. First, John L. Sullivan barred black boxers from fighting for the highest prize, the Heavyweight Championship. Expressing his will-

ingness to fight all contenders, Sullivan said in 1892, "In this challenge I include all fighters—first come, first served—who are white. I will not fight a Negro. I never have and I never shall." True to his word, he never did. Next, blacks were excluded from fighting for many of the lighter titles. On September 6, 1892, George "Little Chocolate" Dixon, a black, soundly defeated Jack Skelly, a white. After the fight, the New Orleans *Times-Democrat* announced that it was "a mistake to match a Negro and a white man, a mistake to bring the races together on any terms of equality, even in the prize ring." After the Dixon-Skelly bout, promoters simply refused to arrange interracial contests. If promoters failed to uphold Jim Crow, a high-minded citizen could be counted on to correct the oversight. For instance, in 1897 the Mississippi Pleasure Company sponsored an interracial match. As soon as the bout began, Henry Long, described as "a loyal Southerner," stopped the fight, commenting: "The idea of niggers fighting white men. Why, if that darned scoundrel would beat that white boy the niggers would never stop gloating over it, and, as it is, we have enough trouble with them."

By 1900 then boxing had become something of a national institution. To be sure, it was still illegal throughout most of America, and fights were stealthily planned and staged on moored barges and backwater sections of Mississippi. Yet if the fights themselves were largely clandestine affairs, the results were always widely publicized, and millions of Americans waited impatiently for the results. The reason was simple: boxing transcended matters of legality. As a popular national institution, it reflected something higher than the base, brutal activity within the ring. It mirrored America and the most sacred of American institutions—democracy, capitalism, and racism. Boxing was open to all men, and its champions formed a true "natural aristocracy" in the Jeffersonian sense. Economically it was unregulated; literally only the fittest did survive. Money was there to be made by the most intelligent or most ruthless, whether fighter or entrepreneur. Unlike football or baseball, boxing was the closest sport to American capitalism, because it was the most individualistic. In both capitalism of the Gilded Age variety and boxing the goal was domination, whether over the manufacturing of a specific product or a roped-in patch of turf. The differences between Rockefeller or Swift and Sullivan or Corbett were more a matter of species than genus. Finally, within the ring racism gained ascendancy. As much as possible, within society and the ring, the object was to render the black man invisible, and *Plessy* vs. *Ferguson* and Sullivan's drawing of the "color line" were giant steps in that direction.

In part, the glorification of boxing in the 1890s was illustrative of a larger ethos, for during that decade there was a discernible quickening in the national temper. The prophet of the era, Theodore Roosevelt, best summarized the new feeling in his 1899 essay, "The Strenuous Life." One must, Teddy intoned, "boldly face the life of strife . . . for it is only through strife, through hard and dangerous endeavor, that we shall ultimately win the goal of true national greatness." Perhaps even more graphically, a year later in an address to "The American Boy," he said that "in life, as in a football game, the principle to follow is: Hit the line hard; don't foul and don't shirk, but hit the line hard." Roosevelt expressed this attitude every day of his life. He hunted animals in most parts of the world, played football on the White House lawn, and was firmly convinced that every male should be conversant with the "manly art of self-defense." His large-toothed grin sent off electric currents, which seemed to light up a nation. If Roosevelt was the bugleman of the martial spirit, there was no shortage of troops to follow. The millions of Americans who enjoyed the music of John Philip Sousa or were thrilled by the adventure novels of H. Rider Haggard or found pleasure in the masculine poetry of Rudyard Kipling understood the mood that Roosevelt represented.

The ultimate expression of this ethos was, of course, war. And it came in 1898 against Spain. In many ways a needless conflict—and certainly one that could have been prevented—the Spanish-American War allowed men to test their grace under fire. It provided Roosevelt with a chance to prove himself, and as a war correspondent, naturalist-writer Stephen Crane even stood during a crossfire to experience firsthand the sensation of being fired upon. This attitude, along with the internal reforms in the sport, permitted boxing to become a national passion in the 1890s.

Nevertheless, by the end of the Spanish-American War, boxing's popularity had begun to diminish. In part, this was due to the increasing difficulty promoters confronted in arranging bouts. Throughout the 1880s and early 1890s, New Orleans had been the national center of boxing. With a long record of moral laxity and a tradition of being the city that promoted forbidden pleasures, New Orleans allowed boxers to ply their trade openly. In the middle 1890s this situation changed. First, the major boxing club, the Olympic Club, ran into financial troubles; then Louisiana's governor turned against the sport; and finally, public opinion vis-á-vis boxing underwent a sharp reversal. In 1894, a local favorite, Andy Bowen, died as a result of a beating administered by George "Kid" Lavigne. After this match, boxing became an endangered species in New Orleans; and if the climate was inhospitable in Louisiana, it was far worse in other areas. By 1900 the other two areas that had once allowed prize fighting, California and New York, had also abolished boxing.

The reasons legislators called for the abolition of boxing are surprising, but they serve as a flash of lightning in the night, illuminating for a brief moment the social landscape. Generally, politicians were not concerned about the brutality of the sport. That fighters were beaten senseless, often retired without a penny, or sometimes were blinded or killed as a result of boxing does not seem to have weighed heavily on politicians' minds. Instead, they attacked boxing as being demoralizing financially. Politicians decried the amount of money a superior fighter could earn; that a boxer might make $15,000 or $20,000 in a year was seen as somehow unhealthy and demoralizing to the average man. In addition, they criticized the amount of money bet on prize fights. Always concerned about how the lower classes lived, politicians believed it was their duty to guarantee that hard-earned dollars were not frittered away on drinking and gambling. Nowhere is this patrician attitude more apparent than in Theodore Roosevelt. Although he was eager to note that he enjoyed boxing—indeed "encouraged" it "among boys and

James J. Jeffries, rated No. 1 among heavyweight boxers by many experts, was undefeated from 1899 to 1904. After retirement
he returned in 1910 as "The Great White
Hope" to fight Jack Johnson.
(St. Louis Post-Dispatch)

young men generally"—and that he counted a prize fighter or two "among
his friends," nevertheless, as governor of New York he oversaw the abolition
of professional boxing. "The money prizes fought for are enormous," he
wrote, "and are a potent source of demoralization in themselves, while they
are often so arranged as either to be a premium on crookedness or else to
reward nearly as amply the man who fails as the man who succeeds." In
short, the idea that a defeated pugilist should be rewarded offended Roosevelt's sense of justice. His boxer friends, after all, were not losers.

Perhaps another reason for the decline in public interest in boxing can
be discovered in the times. After Roosevelt became President in 1901, the
pace of American life seemed to pick up. The old source of boxing's popularity, newspapers, found a new way to sell advertising space. Instead of
printing lurid tales of pugilistic struggles, they published lurid tales of industrial abuses. In the crusades against child labor, corrupt government, dangerous working conditions, and tubercular meat, journalists found material
to titillate even the most jaded reader. Boxing seemed out of place in this
brave new world, as anachronistic as a pike. Boxing belonged to the world of
street corner saloons, cheap liquor, rank cigars, loud laughter, and fat bosses
who lorded over their slum fiefdoms. This world stood opposed to the major
tenets of the Progressive Era. Therefore, newspapers lumped booze, bosses,
and boxing together and told their readers, "Let us be done with all this."

In this atmosphere, boxing was forced into the more lawless corners of
the nation, areas still untouched by the cleansing impulse. Between 1900 and
1915 not a single Heavyweight Championship fight was staged east of the

Jess Willard, who was known as the Pottawatomie Giant, defeated the great black fighter, Jack Johnson, for the heavyweight title in 1915. Willard lost the title to Jack Dempsey in a 1919 bout.
(*St. Louis Post-Dispatch*)

Mississippi River. Gone were the great title fights staged in Coney Island. Instead matches were held in places like Reno, Los Angeles, Colma, Las Vegas, and San Francisco. Boxing became a western sport, a miner, rancher and cowboy sport. In the dusty western towns, western fighters battled one another for the amusement of other westerners. Often important fights were not covered by the influential eastern press. What is more, after James J. Jeffries retired in 1904, even westerners lost interest in boxing. Jeffries' successor, the one-eyed Marvin Hart, was an insipid fighter who generated no public interest. When he lost the title to Canadian Tommy Burns, it drew little more than a yawn. To make any money from the championship, Burns had to pack suitcase and title into an ocean steamer and go abroad. He defended his title in London, Dublin, and Paris. When the Europeans lost interest, he went to Australia, defending his title successfully in Sydney and Melbourne. Back in America nobody cared. For the vast majority of Americans boxing had become a dead issue, not worthy of either a crusade against it or a rally of support for it.

On the day after Christmas, 1908, the complexion of the heavyweight division and, by extension, the fortunes of boxing changed in a sudden, dramatic, and ominous manner when Tommy Burns defied tradition. The tradition Burns flouted was the "color line," for he became the first modern heavyweight champion to defend his crown against a black fighter. At the time, the championship was not worth much to him; consequently, when Hugh D. "Huge Deal" McIntosh offered Burns a big payday to defend his title against Jack Johnson, the champion agreed. The two fought in an arena

36   at Ruschcutters Bay in Australia at a time when the American goodwill fleet was harbored at Sydney. Johnson easily won the one-sided match and became the new champion. Suddenly, America again became interested in boxing. The very idea of a black heavyweight champion was a discomforting thought to most white Americans. It forced a new syllogism: Johnson is the greatest fighter in the world; Johnson is black; *ergo* black is best. Pondering the development, a New York reporter wrote, "Never before in the history of the prize ring has such a crisis arisen as that which [now] faces the followers of the game." Other writers concluded that boxing was bad enough when the champion was white; now it was unbearable.

Johnson's actions as champion were hardly calculated to mollify public opinion. He was the sort of black known to Southern folklore as a "bad nigger," one who lived on the border between sanity and insanity, with no fear of death and, therefore, no fear of life. Johnson boasted, flashed a gold-toothed grin, swaggered, and displayed an annoying habit of doing exactly what he claimed he could do. For this he was hated by white Americans in direct proportion to how much he was admired by black Americans. Perhaps the novelist Jack London best expressed white opinion. Sitting at ringside and watching Johnson humiliate Burns, he was moved to write, "One thing remains. Jeffries must emerge from his alfalfa farm and remove that smile from Johnson's face. Jeff, it's up to you!"

Jeffries became the focal point in the search for a white fighter who could defeat Johnson. Urged to come out of retirement for patriotic, psychological, and even genetic reasons, Jeffries soon responded to the public mandate. He would fight Johnson and return the heavyweight title, the very symbol of physical superiority, to the Caucasian race—or so he and his supporters believed. Johnson and Jeffries battled on July 4, 1910, on the one hundred and thirty-fourth anniversary of America's birth. There was an apocalyptic air about the contest, almost as if it were a racial Armageddon. Bands blurted forth the national anthem, flags hung limp in the Nevada summer sun, and an overwhelmingly white audience shouted racial slurs at Johnson. But once the fight began, the mood turned serious and the spectators quiet. It was not the scenario that Jeffries' supporters had hoped for. Crouching, swinging wildly, Jeffries tried, and as Johnson cut him with cold, cruel, precise jabs and right-hand leads, the former champion continued to try. Johnson taunted, "Whatsa matta, Misah Jeff? I's can go on like dis all affanoon!" and carried on a lively repartee with Jeffries' handlers and ringside spectators. It ended in the fifteenth round when the referee counted "ten" over Jeffries.

No sooner were Johnson's gloves cut off than a wave of interracial rioting and violence washed the country. Scores of blacks were killed, and even more were injured. White gangs, such as New York's Hounds of Hell and Pearl Button Gang, swept through black sections assaulting residents with no provocation save skin color. Never before had a single event caused such widespread rioting. No section of the country was immune; north, south, east, and west were unified in their response to Johnson's victory. Reviewing the ugly mood of the country, Theodore Roosevelt commented, "I sincerely trust that public sentiment will be so aroused and will make itself felt so effectively, as to guarantee that this is the last prize fight to take place in the United States." In this wish, Roosevelt was joined by millions of other red-blooded, white-skinned Americans.

It was not the last fight staged in the United States, but after 1910 boxing was most certainly a vilified sport. Many of the same organizations that were found in the forefront of the progressive moral reforms now turned their attention to boxing. William Shaw, general secretary of the United Society of Christian Endeavor, declared that "Independence Day has been dishonored and disgraced by a brutal prize fight; the moral sense of the nation has been outraged." He pledged his support in the battle against such an outrage of public decency. He was joined by members of the influential Anti-Saloon League of America, who viewed Johnson in particular and boxers in general as friends of publicans, frequenters of saloons, and the epitome of every type of sleazy and licentious sinner. As a first step in the elimination of boxing, such organizations in 1912 pushed a bill through Congress to prevent the interstate transportation of fight films.

Johnson proved to be a guest who did not know when to leave. His every action, whether public or private, upset white Americans. He drove fast cars, wore flashy clothes, and showed an utter disdain for traditional morals. He transformed a series of Great White Hopes into Great White Jokes. But especially, he exposed a sensitive American nerve—miscegenation. He married one white woman, and when she shot herself in the temple, he married another. For this Johnson was scorned in every public forum. For preachers Johnson served as an example of moral decay; for politicians he was an indication of a lawless society. In a speech before Congress, Representative Seaborn A. Roddenberry of Georgia denounced Johnson in particular, blacks in general, white women who would have anything to do with blacks, and the American Constitution because it did not prohibit blacks from marrying whites. When Johnson was forced to flee the country to avoid prosecution under the Mann Act (on charges that had been trumped up to put him behind bars), white America exhaled a sigh of relief. Finally the unwanted visitor was out of the house, even if he did take the jewelry with him.

However, by 1914 when Johnson went into exile, the jewelry—the heavyweight crown—was as unwanted as the guest. Americans were tired of Johnson and boxing. The world was changing, and boxing belonged to the past. Progressive reformers such as Woodrow Wilson spoke in visionary language about the future, and in that close-at-hand land boxing would have no place. Pugilism was a reflection of a violent world, reformers argued, and in the future there would be no violence to mirror. This was the accepted attitude toward boxing when Europe went to war in June of 1914, a conflict that America entered in 1917. The war ended the Progressive Era and gave a startling glimpse of the future. The glimpse was of a world where boxing would still have a place.

Sources and Suggested Readings

Atyeo, Dan. *Blood and Guts: Violence in Sports* (London, 1970).

Farr, Finis. *Blacks Champion: The Life and Times of Jack Johnson* (London, 1964).

Gilmore, Al-Tony. *Bad Nigger! The National Impact of Jack Johnson* (Port Washington, 1975).

Green, Benny. *Shaw's Champions: G.B.S. and Prizefighting from Cashel Bryan to Gene Tunney* (London, 1978).

Higham, John. *Writing American History: Essays on Modern Scholarship* (Bloomington, 1970).

Roberts, Randy. *Jack Dempsey: The Manassa Mauler* (Baton Rouge, 1979).

Sullivan, John L. *Life and Reminiscences of a 19th Century Gladiator* (Boston, 1892).

Wiebe, Robert H. *The Search For Order, 1877-1920* (New York, 1967).

Woodward, C. Vann. *The Strange Career of Jim Crow* (New York, 1966).

4

Sports at the Crossroads

William J. Baker

At the outset of the twentieth century American's two most popular spectator sports, professional baseball and intercollegiate football, tottered on the brink of destruction. Without drastic change, both would have been irreparably damaged, possibly to be relegated to the rubbish heap of exciting but short-lived games. Like the regulating, standardizing, modernizing tendencies of American government in the Progressive Era, administrative alterations insured the survival of sport. Reformed, baseball and football not only survived but thrived. The crisis through which they successfully passed between 1900 and 1920 made possible the "Golden Age" of sports in the 1920s.

At the end of the nineteenth century, major-league baseball especially seemed bent on self-destruction. For two decades clubs had engaged in ruthless competition for players and spectator support. Owners quarreled bitterly until they had to close ranks against outsiders. Rival leagues rose and fell with debilitating regularity. Clubs consistently lost money, especially after a players' strike in 1890 soured public attitudes toward the game. Accounting for baseball's difficulties, the *New York Times* in 1900 blamed "the brotherhood trouble in 1890 . . . from which the game has not yet recovered" and the rapid recent "growth in popularity of other sports" but also cited "rowdyism by the players on the field, syndicalism among the club owners, poor umpiring, and talk of rival organizations."

Since the collapse of the American Association in 1891, the National League had been the whole of major-league baseball. Now the threat of yet another rival organization was more than mere talk. A new league emerged in 1900 when Byron Bancroft "Ban" Johnson, president of a minor Western League, boldly claimed "major league" status for his group, renamed it the American League, and immediately began raiding National League rosters. A salary ceiling ($2,400) imposed by National League owners made their players eager to consider better offers. Beginning with strong clubs in several of the cities previously monopolized by the National League, Ban Johnson's

40 upstart American League played havoc with the salary structure, attendance figures, and media attention of the older league. Once again major-league baseball seemed on the verge of tearing itself apart.

Finally, in 1903, National League owners agreed to recognize the American League as a junior partner in "Organized Baseball," a kind of owners' monopoly regulating player trades, territorial rights, minor-league affiliations, and team schedules. Most importantly, under the National Agreement of 1903 owners united to crush any further teams or leagues threatening their investments. At the head of their cartel, they established a National Commission composed of the two league presidents and a third person mutually agreed upon. For all its inadequacies as an administrative body, the National Commission brought stability to the game sufficient to withstand a business recession in 1904-5, an economic "panic" in 1907-8, a new players' union in 1912, and yet three more rival leagues in 1911-15.

In order to sustain spectator interest to the end of each season (when crowds usually diminished once the league title was decided), the National Commission pulled an old rabbit out of the hat. They renewed a so-called World Series between the champions of the two major leagues. In 1903, the newly formed Boston Americans beat the representatives of the senior circuit, the Pittsburgh Pirates, five games to three. From the outset, the interleague rivalry was fierce. In 1904 the tough manager of the National League pennant-winning New York Giants, John McGraw, refused to allow his team to play in the Series against the American League champions, whom he dismissed as "a minor-league aggregation." In the following year, however, the World Series commenced again, destined to flourish as America's oldest team championship competition. The path to today's green pastures began in the early years of this century.

Intercollegiate football at the turn of the century similarly stood in need of drastic change. The most popular spectator sport at the college level, its reputation was nevertheless notoriously bad. Long since had American footballers replaced the old English code of amateur sportsmanship with an emphasis on winning at all costs. Once a simple, student-organized game, football had become an enterprise run by "professional" (full-time and salaried) coaches who recruited vigorously, secretly offered "subsidies" (scholarships), and worked players mercilessly long and hard to prepare them for victory. Rules of eligibility were vague. Players jumped from one team to another, often extending their playing careers past the normal four years required for graduation. All the while, college coaches, faculty, and presidents gave out uncertain signals. Often they preached the virtues of sportsmanship and the need for clearer, better-enforced rules but in the next instance succumbed to alumni pressures to do whatever was necessary to win. The pressure cooker atmosphere of "big-time college football" is no recent invention.

In the early years of the century, however, the worst and most obvious problem was the brutality of the game. In their zeal to win, players recklessly bent rules and broke opponents' arms, legs, and necks. Illegal slugging, kicking, and piling on were infractions common to the game. Football was scarcely an isolated feature of American life. "The spirit of the American

Harvard's tandem formation in a game versus Yale in 1905. Yale won the game at Cambridge, 6-0, before 43,000 spectators. The stacked defense shown was used before the introduction of the forward pass. Note the grid pattern of the field.

youth, as of the American man, is to win, to 'get there,' by fair means or foul," observed the editor of the *Nation*, "and the lack of moral scruple which pervades the struggles of the business world meets with temptations equally irresistible in the miniature contests of the football field." At home and abroad, brute force "by fair means or foul" dominated. College football was no worse, if no better, than politics and business in that age when the tenets of Social Darwinism took on the aura of gospel truth in the corridors of power.

Even the rules of the game left a wide expanse for savagery. In variations on old mass formations such as the "flying wedge" and the "turtleback," brawny linemen continued to surround offensive backs in pulverizing attacks on the opposition. A conservative rules committee headed by Walter Camp refused to open up the game, leaving it in the hands of a juggernaut mentality. In 1903-4 a new rule specified the number of men required on the offensive line of scrimmage, but still the casualties mounted. By the autumn of 1905, injuries and deaths on the field created something of a national scandal, prompting President Theodore Roosevelt to summon representatives of Harvard, Yale, and Princeton to the White House. Himself a keen advocate of "manly" sports, Roosevelt had no intention of banishing the game. He detested "sentimental humanitarians" but in good Progressive fashion insisted that "brutality and foul play" be removed from football in order to preserve

Bill Sprackling of Brown University was one of the first players to popularize the forward pass in the early 1900s. *(Brown University)*

the game. Like American capitalism, football needed to be regulated, not radically changed and certainly not abolished.

Promises to clean up the game had little effect. Within two months of Roosevelt's mini-conference, no less than eighteen young men died from injuries received on the football field. Administrators at Columbia, the Massachusetts Institute of Technology, Northwestern, California, Stanford, and several lesser institutions momentarily disbanded their programs. "The game of football," declared the President of the University of California, "must be entirely made over or go." They made it over. In late December, 1905, officials from sixty-two colleges and universities convened to create an organization called the Intercollegiate Athletic Association of the United States. Five years later the name was changed to the National Collegiate Athletic Association (NCAA), which survives to the present as the supreme governing body of intercollegiate sports. Originally this new organization attended solely to football. Moreover, at first it merely sought to revise and enforce the rules of play. It tinkered with larger issues, such as scholarships and eligibility requirements, but mainly left those problems in the hands of local institutions and regional conferences. Overhauling the tactics of the game proved to be sufficiently difficult.

For years Walter Camp's older, conservative rules committee had resisted any radical changes in the rough mass-formation style of football. Finally in January, 1906, Camp's group was incorporated and outflanked by a new rules committee intent on reform, sponsored by the Intercollegiate Athletic Association. In order to break up mass mauls, they established a neutral zone ("the line of scrimmage") between the offensive and defensive teams and restricted linemen from dropping back on offense. In place of the customary three attempts to gain five yards for a first down, they sought to encourage more wide-open end runs by doubling the first-down requirement to ten yards. Most importantly, they legalized the forward pass, but with severe restrictions. A ball had to be thrown across the line of scrimmage downfield into a ten-yard-wide alley, five yards on either side from the point at which it had been snapped. Chalk lines running up and down as well as across the field assisted officials in detecting infractions, making popular a new term for the field of play: the gridiron. According to the rules of 1906, a pass touched but not caught by an offensive player could be recovered by the defense. Passing was risky business.

Infrequently used, the forward pass nevertheless initially increased the brutality suffered by defensive tackles. Earlier, defensive backs all bunched up as linebackers behind the tackles. With the new threat of the forward pass, tackles were left alone to confront assaults of blockers whose interlocked arms made for a most formidable charge. In 1909 six tackles died of injuries, provoking the rules committee in 1910 to forbid blockers from interlocking their arms and from pushing or shoving the ball carrier. Still determined to open up the game, the committee also decided that a pass could be thrown from any angle but not more than a distance of twenty yards. Subsequent changes in 1912 virtually completed the transformation of football into the game that is played today. The twenty-yard limit on forward passes was

44   removed, a fourth down was added to make ten yards for a first down, an
end zone ten yards deep was created, and (after several previous changes in
the scoring system) the value of a touchdown was set at six points and a
field goal at three.

Amidst all these struggles for orderly rules and new styles of play, the
Rose Bowl was born. It was a difficult birth. In 1902 a "Tournament of
Roses Association Game" was held on New Year's Day in Pasadena, Califor-.
nia, but apparently more people smelled the roses than watched the game.
Only 8,000 turned out to see the University of Michigan romp over Stanford, 49-0. For fourteen years no further Pasadena game was held. In 1916,
however, Washington State beat Brown 14-0 before 25,000 spectators, setting the Rose Bowl on its way as the premier post-season game. Not until
the 1930s were the other major bowls created.

The major teams of the prewar era were the University of Chicago under
the tutelage of Amos Alonzo Stagg, the University of Michigan under F.H.
"Hurry Up" Yost, and Harvard under Percy Haughton. All three of these
coaches were stern disciplinarians and master tacticians, representing the
new "professional" era of paid coaches who worked full-time to produce
winning teams. The hiring and supporting of Haughton especially exempli-
fies the tenor of the times. Before he signed on at Harvard in 1908, the Crimson had regularly suffered through abysmal seasons. Always the leading
apologists for strictly amateur sports on the English pattern, Harvard presidents and faculty had effectively blocked undergraduates from taking football too seriously. Graduates and team captains "coached" but with little
consistency and negligible success in terms of winning. Most embarrassing of
all, Harvard annually served as a doormat on which Yale footballers wiped
their feet. Percy Haughton changed all that. He brought a rigid discipline to
the game, and with discipline came victory, the staple of alumni enthusiasm.
From 1908 to 1916 the Crimson enjoyed winning seasons, losing only one
of nine games to Yale. Once they went thirty-three games without a loss;
three times they emerged as the mythical national champions.

Ironically, it was the last hurrah of the old elite Eastern schools on the
national scene. Cornell went undefeated and untied in 1915, and Brown performed honorably in the 1916 Rose Bowl, but by World War I football was
much stronger elsewhere than in the Northeast. Larger state universities with
lower entrance requirements produced powerful squads at Purdue, Wisconsin, and Michigan in the Big Ten, at Georgia Tech (under John Heisman, after
whom the Heisman Trophy was later named) in the South, at Oklahoma and
Nebraska in the Corn Belt, and in California, Oregon, and Washington in the
far West, where the Pacific Coast Conference was formed in 1915. Two
perennially strong independents, Army and Notre Dame, also first came into
public view on the eve of the First World War.

A dramatic game between Notre Dame and Army in 1913 not only
brought both teams into the limelight; it also put a glamorous seal of approval on the recent tactical changes introduced by the rules makers. Definite underdogs going into the game, Notre Dame had a "secret" weapon at
its disposal: the forward pass. All summer long the Notre Dame quarterback,

Gus Dorais, and a light but quick end, Knute Rockne, had worked together at a resort on Lake Erie. Already displaying the savvy that was to make him a coach of renown, Rockne ran set patterns and practiced catching the ball with the hands rather than in the customary bread-basket fashion. Early in the season, he and Dorais accidentally discovered the effective "button-hook" play. Just as Dorais released the ball, Rockne fell down but bounced back to his feet to catch the ball free of defenders. With buttonhooks and slant patterns, the Dorais-Rockne combination demolished Army, 35-13. The sports public was astonished to read of the aerial circus of thirteen completions in seventeen attempts for 243 yards and five touchdowns.

For several decades, of course, the forward pass was to remain a minor, though integral, part of the college game. Though it was the cornerstone of the many tactical changes that opened up football, thereby making it less dangerous and consequently more acceptable to Americans in the early years of the twentieth century, it still was not often employed. Jim Thorpe, a fast, strong runner for Glenn "Pop" Warner's Carlisle Indians, was the star of the prewar era, just as running backs Harold "Red" Grange and Ernie Nevers headed the list of Saturday's heroes in the golden '20s. Thorpe added to his athletic fame by winning two gold medals in the Stockholm Olympics of 1912. The King of Sweden rightfully called him "the most wonderful athlete in the world," but shortly thereafter Thorpe was stripped of his medals because he had played professionally for a minor-league baseball team. The tragedy was twofold. Not only had Thorpe received a pittance for his efforts, but when he later signed to play baseball for the New York Giants, he proved to be mediocre on the diamond. While college football weathered its storm of criticism and self-doubt to become firmly entrenched as the leading autumn spectacle throughout the United States, baseballers far more gifted than Jim Thorpe lent lustre to the summer game that had recently passed through its own critical phase of administrative disarray.

Colorful players and managers were the magnets that caused major-league attendance to soar from less than five million in 1903 to more than seven million in 1910. John McGraw, fiery manager of the New York Giants, was color personified. Blessed with abundant doses of both Irish temper and charm, he sometimes fought with his own players but more often with opponents, fans, and league officials. He was coarse of tongue and demeanor; he loved the race track and gambling casino as much as the diamond. Authoritarian by nature, he drilled his players endlessly in the fundamentals of place-hitting, bunting, base running, and defensive play. In 1902 he began his thirty-year reign at the head of the Giants, leading them to ten National League pennants and four World Series crowns.

In that "dead ball" era, pitchers such as Cy Young, Joe McGinnity, Rube Waddell, Christy Mathewson, Grover Cleveland Alexander, Rube Marquand, and "Smoky Joe" Wood dominated the game. Young incredibly won 511 games in a twenty-two year career that began in 1890. Of Johnson's 414 victories (all with the weak Washington Senators), 113 were shutouts. Mathewson shares with Alexander the record of 373 victories in the National League. Briefest but most spectacular was the performance of Joe Wood. He joined the Red Sox in 1908, struggled for two years, then in 1911 won twenty-three games (including a no-hitter). In 1912 he won sixteen consecutive games on his way to a 34-5 season, with three more victories in the World Series. Years later a Chicago White Sox fan recalled how "Wood threw smoke": "With the shadows pushing over the ball park he would stand out there on the pitching mound with his red-trimmed gray road uniform, hitch up his pants, and throw. To this day, I have a recollection of a strange sensation as if my head emptied, when he fired the ball in the shadowy park. The White Sox couldn't touch him." Only twenty-two years of age, Wood was the youthful god of Beantown. But his prowess was short-lived. During spring training the following year, he slipped on wet grass and broke his thumb. Returning to the mound too soon, he strained his shoulder, injured his arm irreparably, and saw his powers diminish to the point of painful retirement in 1916. After a year's layoff, he returned to play in the outfield for five years in Cleveland beside his old Red Sox roommate, Tris Speaker.

Expert punch-hitting and base running distinguished the outstanding offensive players. While Honus Wagner, shortstop of the Pittsburgh Pirates, won eight of twelve National League batting titles from 1900 to 1911, he also led the league five times in base stealing. The master of the art, however, was Detroit's "Georgia Peach," Tyrus Raymond "Ty" Cobb. Between 1907 and 1919 he claimed twelve of thirteen American League batting titles, set a bevy of base-stealing records, and earned the reputation for being perhaps the most aggressive, respected, and disliked player in the history of the game. With spikes flying, fists ready, and tongue always spewing out venom, Cobb asked for no mercy and gave none. Unfashionable southern roots and his father's tragic gunshot death at the hands of Cobb's own mother bred in him an uncontrollable rage. He was a loner, with few friends. Faced with opposition, he became a man possessed. On the base paths, especially, he intimidated by his very presence. Fans everywhere detested him but turned out in huge numbers to taunt the man they loved to hate.

Yet Cobb was merely a flagrant exaggeration of the general run of hard-drinking, heavy-gambling, loose-tongued individualists who played the game around World War I. Minus Cobb's abrasiveness, the young George Herman "Babe" Ruth was little different. A castoff son of a Baltimore bartender, Ruth was retrieved from the gutter by men who recognized his baseball talent. He carried gutter language and behavior with him to Boston in 1915, where he immediately starred as a brash but strong left-handed pitcher. His greatest fame, of course, lay in the future as a power-hitting outfielder for the New York Yankees. But for all his later mythological gloss, the Babe's character, talents, and style were rooted in the rocky soil of social deprivation.

For the numerous major-league players who were similarly from the wrong side of the tracks (or worse still, from simple rural backgrounds), exploitation was inevitable. Despite the good salaries of Ty Cobb and his exceptional kind, most baseballers were poorly paid. Yet they worked hard, for hard work was all they knew. Largely uneducated, they were fun-loving in the simplest terms, especially on road trips. Always in need of an extra

Ty Cobb, "The Georgia Peach," in the classic batting stance which produced 4,191 base hits, a record that may never be broken. *(St. Louis Post-Dispatch)*

buck, they were easy prey for the numerous gamblers who hovered like vultures in the third-base box seats.

Rumors of "fixed" games frequently surfaced. In 1908 John McGraw was accused of offering bribes to some Philadelphia pitchers to let up against the Giants, but the matter was never investigated. At the end of that season, two National League umpires filed an official complaint that the Giants had offered them $3000 to allow the Giants to beat the Chicago Cubs in a play-off for the pennant. At the head of the committee appointed to investigate the charge was none other than John T. Brush, the owner of the Giants. The entire affair was swept under the carpet by scapegoating the team doctor and barring him from baseball. Yet again in the World Series of 1917, McGraw was rumored to have thrown two games. In the fifth game of the series, the Giants built up a 5-2 lead against the White Sox only to have McGraw—famously shrewd in his handling of pitchers—leave his pitcher in the game long enough for the Sox to even the score. When the White Sox finally won, McGraw blamed his second baseman for not cutting off a couple of ground balls. At the end of the series, McGraw deflected criticism by immediately trading his second baseman to another team.

Even more bizarre was the case of Hal Chase, a first baseman for the New

48   York Highlanders (Yankees), who was censured by his manager for throwing games during the season of 1910. Chase was not merely cleared of the charges, but his manager was fired, and Chase himself was given the position. In 1913, however, he was implicated in another "fix" and was finally traded. With the Cincinnati Reds in 1918, he was yet again charged with bribery. Four players and two managers testified that Chase had offered them money to throw games, but the president of the National League dismissed the case, hushed up the scandal, and put a good face forward for baseball.

If custodians of the game did too little to preserve its integrity, defenders of baseball's image did too much. "Baseball is a national game, our national game," droned the New York *Evening Telegram* in 1909, "for all good Americans are proud of it, and its great prosperity is the most conclusive testimony to its purity, its honesty, its attractiveness and the hold which it has on the national heart." Prosperity, in other words, meant purity. President William Howard Taft, who attended the opening game of the Washington Americans in 1909 and thereby established a tradition which lasted for well over half a century, extolled baseball as "a clean, straight game" attractive to "everybody who enjoys clean, straight athletics." Shortly before the scandal of 1919, no less a public figure than the moralistic fire-and-brimstone evangelist, Billy Sunday, declared baseball "the cleanest sport in America": "Gamblers have never been able to creep in and spoil the game. Men in control, both magnates and players, have always been united in the effort to keep the game clean. All this talk about baseball being crooked, the game being decided before it is played, is all bosh. Such a charge is an unmitigated lie." Dramatically simplistic as ever, Billy Sunday was apparently as ignorant of the facts as were most Americans who needed untainted athletic heroes to go along with God, motherhood, and the flag during the era of the Great War.

The war itself provided the backdrop for the infamous Black Sox affair. During the last year of the war, 1918, baseball attendance dropped some forty per cent, prompting owners to shorten the season under the guise of supporting the war effort. They summarily released all players to avoid paying them their full salaries called for in contracts but entered into one of their notorious "gentlemen's agreements" not to tamper with each other's property. The few players who took their contractual disputes to court were branded "Bolsheviki" by owners and sportswriters.

So the 1919 season began in an uproar, with disgruntled players on all teams. Dissension was especially rife in the clubhouse of the Chicago White Sox. Although the White Sox had won the pennant and World Series in 1917, their salaries were among the lowest in the major leagues. Owner Charles Comiskey was a skinflint of the first order. Still, the White Sox won the American League pennant again in 1919 and entered the World Series as heavy favorites to swamp the Cincinnati Reds. Professional gamblers seized the opportunity to make a killing. They bribed first baseman Chick Gandil and pitcher Eddie Cicotte, who in turn let several other White Sox in on the deal. In Boston on the final road trip of the season, Gandil approached outfielder Joe Jackson with an offer "to frame something up" for the lordly sum of $10,000. A simple man from a Southern mill town, Jackson had

made only $6,000 for the entire 1919 season in which he had batted .351
and ranked among the American League leaders in virtually every hitting category. He informed Comiskey of the talk of "fix," only to have his owner ignore the warning. The gamblers had their way, as the White Sox lost to the Reds, five games to three.

Rumors of the "fix" swirled throughout the winter and into the next season. At the end of the 1920 season, a grand jury investigating further accusations of gamblers' involvement in a Phillies-Cubs game suddenly switched its attention to the World Series of 1919. Under oath, eight members of the White Sox admitted their guilt to the grand jury. Curiously, their testimonies were not to be found when their case came to trial a year later. A jury found the players not guilty, but the incident shook the baseball world so severely that all eight were banned from the game for life.

Of all the players involved in the scandal, the case of "Shoeless" Joe Jackson was surely the most poignant. He had received his nickname early in his semi-professional career at Brandon Mills in Greenville, South Carolina, when he once played barefooted in order to avoid blisters while breaking in a new pair of shoes. Baseball writers popularized the yarn that he never wore shoes until his adulthood; his nickname conveyed a country-bumpkin image of the illiterate southern boy who could not cope with the complexities of northern big-city life and temptations. Yet Jackson was one of the finest players of his day. His lifetime major-league average of .356 is the third highest in the history of the game. Babe Ruth copied his swing at the plate. In the World Series of 1919, in fact, Jackson collected twelve base hits for an average of .375, a most impressive performance for a man who supposedly helped "throw" the Series. During his trial, a journalist created colorful copy with an account of Jackson coming out of the courtroom to be met by a small boy pleading, "Say it ain't so, Joe." A fictitious concoction, the incident nevertheless represented the sentiment of baseball fans everywhere, whose faith in the integrity of the game was severely shaken.

The Black Sox crisis prompted baseball owners to dismantle the three-commissioner system which had resulted from the earlier crisis of 1903. In its place they decided on a single commissioner whose respectability and unquestioned authority would restore the image of purity to the game. A thin, white-haired federal judge from Chicago, Kenesaw Mountain Landis, was the ideal man. He was an avid baseball fan but had no prior formal connection to baseball. Most importantly, he was a stern defender of law and order. From the bench he had protected management's interests against labor unions and agitators and during the war had served as a super-patriot in cracking down on draft dodgers. He was rectitude incarnate, an individual uniquely equipped both in temperament and reputation to put baseball back on the pedestal from which it had fallen.

He succeeded brilliantly. Even rich, powerful baseball owners bowed to his command. Players especially felt his wrath. He adamantly refused ever to reconsider the ban on the eight Black Sox despite legal evidence and personal pleas to the contrary. Within his first year at the helm of organized baseball, he banned three other players for life; by 1924 a total of fifty-four players

50   were listed as ineligible to play in the big leagues, fifteen permanently. Though the Commissioner became more lenient as he ruled major-league baseball until his death at seventy-eight years of age in 1944, his first few years earned him the nickname "Czar" Landis.

At the crossroads of 1900-1920, both baseball and college football chose the road of reform, consolidation, and respectability. Both entered the decade of the '20s fortified for a popular and prosperous pilgrimage. Like John Bunyan's Christian, athletes and sports officials in 1920 turned their backs on the Valley of Despond, setting their eyes on the Celestial City, whose streets were paved with gold.

Sources and Suggested Readings

Asinof, Eliot. *Eight Men Out: The Black Sox and the 1919 World Series* (New York, 1963).

Danzig, Allison. *The History of American Football: Its Great Teams, Players, and Coaches* (Englewood Cliffs, N.J., 1956).

Gropman, Donald. *Say It Ain't So, Joe! The Story of Shoeless Joe Jackson* (Boston, 1979).

Riess, Steven A. *Touching Base: Professional Baseball and American Culture in the Progressive Era* (Westport, Conn., 1980).

Ritter, Lawrence S. *The Glory of Their Times: The Story of the Early Days of Baseball Told by the Men Who Played It* (New York, 1966).

Spink, John George Taylor. *Judge Landis and Twenty-Five Years of Baseball* (New York, 1947).

Voigt, David Quentin. *American Baseball: Volume II: From the Commissioners to Continental Expansion* (Norman, 1970).

Weyand, Alexander M. *The Saga of American Football* (New York, 1955).

Part II

American Sports Comes of Age

1920-1950

An American boy born in 1920 entered school with the sound of jazz ringing in his ears. In his living room sat a newfangled piece of furniture, the radio. His parents talked about prohibition, government corruption, mediocre presidents, Hollywood stars, and the aviation exploits of Charles Lindbergh. More and more people owned new homes, automobiles, and various luxuries of life. Then the world came crashing down into economic depression touched off by the collapse of Wall Street. High school civics classes discussed dreadful poverty in the land and examined President Roosevelt's New Deal as a means of recovery. Still, the spectre of unemployment stalked the minds of high-school seniors on the eve of graduation. Worse still was the threat of impending war, until news from Pearl Harbor on December 7, 1941, fired patriotic resolve to resist the Japanese in the Pacific and the fascists in Europe. At the war's end, a mushroom cloud hung over the whole of civilization. By mid-century a thirty-year-old American had a heap of living tucked under his belt.

Tucked away in his mind were images and references to various sports heroes. Like radio and the cinema, sports in the 1920s added a spice of excitement to urban and rural Americans alike; during the Depression, sports provided momentary diversion from the harsh realities of economic disaster. For Americans living outside the Northeast and the industrial Midwest, top-level athletes were distant figures about whom one read newspaper accounts or whose feats were dramatized over the radio. Their nicknames made them seem bigger than life: the Sultan of Swat, the Galloping Ghost, the Four Horsemen, the Manassa Mauler, the Brown Bomber, the Yankee Clipper, the Splendid Splinter. Before television reduced them in size, they inhabited a pantheon formerly reserved for the untouchable ancient gods of Mount Olympus, mythologically shrouded in mystique.

America's oldest organized game, baseball, was the first to be glamorously packaged and sold to the American public. James Harper, a diplomatic historian, suggests in the first essay of this section that baseball flourished after World War I not only because it had been intrinsically linked to the growth of urban America but also because it conjured up nostalgic images of a simple, rural past for millions of Americans who had moved into cities. Moreover, the game and its stars adapted well to the changing tenor of the times. George Herman "Babe" Ruth and the new "live ball" era uncannily reflected the restless, action-packed character of the "Roaring Twenties." For the difficult years of the Depression, the unpredictable Jerome "Dizzy" Dean and his "Gas House Gang" mirrored the unsteady period of which they were a part, just as the efficiently respectable Stan Musial embodied the grey-flannel-suit conformity of mid-century America. By 1950 baseball reached its pinnacle as the National Pastime.

College football was its only serious rival for public attention in the interwar years. The second essay in this section, by Jack W. Berryman and Stephen H. Hardy, professors of kinesiology and sports studies, examines the conflict between the educational and economic functions of college football, setting it in a campus context of physical education and intramural sports in which women as well as men participated. Grouped around the throne of King Football were college track and baseball programs; in the 1930s a potential usurper, basketball, came to the fore. In telling this story, and telling it well, the authors admirably illustrate the solid scholarship that is being generated within the North American Society for Sport History and its publication, the *Journal of Sport History*, of which Berryman is editor.

Long before historians became interested in sports, literature and films attended to sports themes. Homer was first off the mark, of course, but in American literature a persistent concern for sport runs all the way from James Fenimore Cooper's frontier outdoorsmen through Mark Harris's recent baseball trilogy. Some novelists sentimentally idealize athletics; others write satirically in a fashion recently made popular by former athletes such as Jim Bouton and Dave Meggysey. In terms of quality, sports literature ranges from the artistic to the awful. So do films on sports themes. In the third essay in this section, Charles T. Summerlin, a professor of English, appropriately casts his net wide to catch pictures of the American athlete in fiction and film.

Another theme requiring expansive treatment is the place of blacks in sports. William MacDonald, a twentieth-century historian, concludes this section with an essay proposing reasons for the present dominant position of black athletes and offering an historical perspective on their rise to prominence. Jim Crow had his way in sports as in every other aspect of American life at the turn of this century, consigning black athletes to separate and decidedly unequal opportunity to participate in organized sports. In the 1920s collegiate and professional football practiced token integration, but major-league baseball remained lily-white for the entire interwar period. All the while, Negro baseball leagues ran a brilliant but unstable course. Just after the Second World War, Jackie Robinson emerged from that pool of black talent, and things have never been the same since. The entrance of black Americans into the mainstream of sports completed the process whereby sports came of age between 1920 and 1950.

5

Baseball: America's First National Pastime

James Harper

By 1920 professional baseball had firmly established itself as the national pastime. Historians David Voigt and Harold Seymour have given us masterful chronicles of the rise of the sport, and Richard Crepeau has recently provided a thoughtful focus on the years 1920 to 1940. All agree that the main reason for baseball's retention of the designation "national pastime," is the game's uncanny ability to reflect the changing currents of American life. Baseball's changing pace of play epitomized the raucous era of bathtub gin, jazz, flappers, and the flivver. Its most notorious scandal anticipated an era of public immorality, and its heroes personified what Americans wanted to idolize. Economically, baseball's structure represented the dominant trend in American business—the search for order and monopoly in an unregulated marketplace. Baseball boomed with the surface prosperity of the 1920s, suffered with the Depression, experienced disruption with World War II, and prospered in the post-1945 era. In many areas of life such as race relations, business trends, and literature, baseball mirrored the larger society.

The national pastime enjoyed spectacular success during the 1920s, led by the hitting exploits of its most enduring hero, George Herman Ruth. "The Babe" emerged as a giant just when the sport needed a super-hero to counteract the harmful publicity of the Black Sox scandal of 1919. In September, 1920, Ruth grabbed sports headlines by hitting ten home runs in his last fourteen games. His total for the 1920 season was a shattering fifty-four, twenty-five more than the record of the previous season, forty more than his nearest rival, and more than any team in the major leagues save one. Ruth surrounded his homers with nine triples, thirty-six doubles, one hundred and thirty-seven runs batted in, and a .376 batting average. His slugging percentage of .847 remains sixty years later as one of baseball's apparently untouchable feats. For an encore, in 1921 Ruth hit fifty-nine home runs. In both seasons, if one includes his enormous number of walks, Ruth was a better-than-even bet to reach base every time he came to the plate.

Babe Ruth, "the greatest player ever," taking his home-run swing as a New York Yankee. *(New York Yankees Baseball Club)*

Ruth quickly became the sports colossus of the 1920s, perhaps of all time, and his heroic posture eclipsed memories of the scandal. Born in 1895 the son of a bartender, the rambunctious Ruth had been sent to Baltimore's St. Mary's School for Boys to curb his delinquency. Baseball proved to be the constructive outlet for his energies, and by 1914 his skills, especially as a pitcher, had earned Ruth a professional contract. From 1914 to 1920 Ruth established himself as the star left-handed pitcher of the Boston Red Sox with a skill that showed Hall of Fame potential and a surprising ability to hit the baseball a long way. By 1919 Ruth preferred hitting and playing the outfield to the demands of the mound. As the baseball grew livelier, hitting seemed more fun, and in 1919 Ruth established a new record for home runs with twenty-nine.

On January 3, 1920, Harry "Bud" Frazee, better at producing Broadway hits such as "No No Nanette" than judging baseball talent, sold Ruth to the New York Yankees for $100,000 in what became the greatest steal in baseball history (despite the belief of some sports writers that the deal would benefit the Red Sox). Ruth's presence in the media center of New York mixed all the necessary ingredients for super-hero status. He quickly seized the pinnacle of attention in an age of celebrities such as Red Grange, Charles Lindbergh, and Bobby Jones. The public found and wanted its politicians dull after the charisma of Theodore Roosevelt and Woodrow Wilson. Public idols were to be discovered elsewhere. Motion pictures, radio, and tabloids found "The Babe" excellent copy to transfix the public in a period of political apathy. Ruth's exploits were action in a time of action, and the hooplah surrounding him was ideal for the Jazz Age.

Ruth had many of the qualities necessary for an ideal hero in the 1920s. His rags-to-riches life caught the attention of a generation raised on Horatio Alger books. Ruth's skill in power hitting was phenomenal and signaled the change in baseball from the "dead ball" to the "live ball" era. As individual and team home-run totals climbed, Ruth led the way. Ruth's personality abetted his hero status. A poor and ill-educated urban lad with childlike mannerisms, Ruth posed no threat to the established customs of the game. He was at home with kids because in many ways he remained a child all his life. Many of Ruth's pecadillos—namely, his enormous sexual appetite and his alcoholic exploits—were concealed from the public by a sympathetic press before the age of candid journalism. What did filter through, especially information about his gastronomic feats and financial extravagance, excited more interest than outrage. Even Ruth's anti-hero qualities—rebellion against authority, carousing, and high jinx—endeared him to a public steadily becoming accustomed to roadhouses, short skirts, and the hip flask.

Ruth's popularity represented a broadening foundation for baseball's appeal. The darlings of the press during the "dead ball" era had been middle-class figures like college boy Christy Mathewson. This was perhaps normal during a period when afternoon baseball meant attendance by largely middle-class crowds. Ruth's urban, lower-class background, however, helped to draw new fans from the lower strata of society. This democratization of fandom would be greatly accelerated by the spread of Sunday baseball in the

1920s and 1930s and the development and growth of night baseball in the 1930s and 1940s.

Later, when the Jazz Age gave way to the Depression, World War II, and post-1945 international responsibilities, the successors to Ruth as baseball idols showed that the game was seeking to project a more serious, "All-American" type of image. Lou Gehrig, Joe DiMaggio, and Stan Musial, although suitably ethnic to boost box office appeal, were reflections of a growing tendency of baseball to stress a corporate appearance, blending with the team rather than emphasizing individual eccentricities and leading a life free of scandal. Examples of the change were numerous. Consider the impact in St. Louis as the irascible Rogers Hornsby and the unpredictable Dizzy Dean gave way in the 1940s to the non-controversial efficiency of Stan Musial and Marty Marion. As Richard Crepeau suggests, by 1950 the-man-in-the-grey-flannel-suit conformity had already been expressed by the new baseball heroes in their grey-flannel road uniforms.

During the 1920s baseball changed dramatically on the field. Pre-Ruthian baseball was aptly called "inside" baseball or the dead ball era. Pitching predominated, and games were low-scoring affairs where sacrifice bunts, hit-and-run plays, and stolen bases were the means employed to squeeze out runs. After Ruth, in the era of a livelier and more frequently replaced baseball, power hitting predominated as Ruthian-type teams won pennants and captured headlines. More home runs attracted bigger crowds, and teams flocked to employ a panoply of fence busters. A peak of sorts was reached in 1930 amid charges that the baseballs had been greatly juiced up. The entire National League had a batting average above .300, led by the N.Y. Giants' team mark of .319. The Philadelphia Phillies had a team batting average of .315 yet finished forty games behind the pennant-winning St. Louis Cardinals.

Although the game on the field changed dramatically during the period 1920 to 1950, success remained in the hands of a relatively small number of teams. Competitive balance, the idea that major-league teams should be and have been roughly equal, has been a persistent myth since the creation of the National League in 1876. During the period 1920 to 1950, this balance did not exist. In the American League the New York Yankees won over half the pennants during that time span, and three teams in each league (thirty-eight percent of the franchises) garnered over sixty percent of the pennants. The dominance of New York City teams since the turn of the century continued, but mainly through the American League franchise. The monopoly of success was reenforced when Branch Rickey of the St. Louis Cardinals devised the farm system, whereby the parent major-league team owned several minor-league clubs as an exclusive source of talent. Superb farm systems explained the dominance of the Cardinals and the Yankees in the 1940s, producing such stars as Joe Gordon, Tommy Henrich, Stan Musial, and Enos Slaughter. Yankee dominance continued at the end of the era as the club won five straight World Championships starting in 1949 and sixteen of the next eighteen American League pennants.

Much of baseball's hold over the American sporting mind resulted from its ability to exemplify two apparently contradictory sets of values. In one

Three members of the 3,000-hit club, Tris Speaker, Stan Musial, and Paul Waner, meet in 1958. *(St. Louis Post-Dispatch)*

sense baseball was rural, calling fans back to simpler pastoral America or to the unhurried pleasures of youth. The green field evoked images of the America of William Jennings Bryan or even that of Thomas Jefferson. In the 1920s the census for the first time registered that a majority of Americans no longer lived on the farm. Baseball offered a means of reacting to this change by looking backward. This nostalgic appeal was strengthened by those players who still hailed from rural America and by the game's tradition, its refusal to change its rules or dimensions.

On the other hand the growth of professional baseball had been clearly linked to the urbanization of America. Even before the turn of the century, Mark Twain had characterized the game as "the very symbol, the outward and visible expression of the drive and push and rush and struggle of the raging, tearing, booming, nineteenth century." Baseball had grown with the spread of trolleys and urbanization. From 1920 to 1950 it benefited from these continuing patterns of growth as well as by technological innovations such as the automobile, radio, and illumination. Thus, the sport was curiously the beneficiary of two seemingly contradictory trends and sets of values.

Literature also shows this strain between simple rural America and complex urban America. As Wiley Umphlett and Ralph Graber have written, baseball literature grew up in the period 1920 to 1950. Early baseball literature, typified by the Frank Merriwell stories of Gilbert Patten, had in effect been Horatio Alger on spikes. Selling over twenty-five million copies, these stories chronicled the accomplishments of ballplayer Frank Merriwell, whose hard work, diligence, and skill always paid off in last-minute triumphs over less noble characters. Despite stock characterizations and improbable situations, these novels reenforced the values expounded in the Alger books. Yet by World War I this type of baseball fiction was giving way to a more realistic, albeit more cynical type.

In his influential *The End of American Innocence* (1959), Henry F. May suggested that the period before, during, and after World War I witnessed a social and intellectual maturing of the United States as the country forsook the naiveté of the nineteenth century. Baseball fiction supports May's thesis. Heywood Broun and Ring Lardner had firsthand experience with the game as sportswriters. Works such as Broun's *The Sun Field* (1923) and Lardner's *You Know Me Al* (1916) and *Alibi Ike* (1915) said as much about the human condition as they did about baseball. Presenting players as real people with faults and virtues, they reflected on an America being transformed by urbanization and technological innovation. Lardner in particular satirized the Frank Merriwell genre by presenting ballplayers who were not larger than life and who suffered the same problems of social disorientation and insecurity encountered by ordinary mortals. The disorder of Lardner's world was made sharper by his placing his characters in a sport which put much emphasis on rules and tradition. The cynicism of these works anticipates the "all crusades fought, all Gods lost" tone of F. Scott Fitzgerald and Sinclair Lewis. More than seeking virtues for young boys to emulate, Broun and Lardner portrayed the conflict between the real and the ideal, the isolation of the individual in modern society, and the rural values in urban America.

Post-World War II baseball literature to a lesser degree also reflected the dominant mood. The self-satisfying triviality of a time that looked forward to the "American Century" was at ease with the tone of Valentine Davis' *It Happens Every Spring* (1949) and H. Allen Smith's *Rhubarb* (1946). These works became successful films that anticipated the complacency of the 1950s.

The status of blacks in baseball showed another, more painful way in which the sport embodied American life, for the segregation of professional baseball reflected the national racial dilemma. After some token black participation in the professional game in the 1880s, the game had succumbed to Jim Crowism by the 1890s. Black baseball shared the status of black schools, black churches, and black public accommodations—separate and in most ways unequal. The stories of the National Negro Baseball League, the Eastern Colored League, and the Negro American League from the 1920s to the 1940s constitute a significant pattern in black history and offer insight into the mode of life in segregated America. The Negro leagues together with boxing offered the major means for the black athlete to earn his way in pre-1950 America. Satchel Paige stood at the summit of athletic success, as his estimated salary during World War II ($40,000 per year) may have exceeded that of any white ballplayer at the time.

The Negro Leagues produced players of consummate skill and showmanship. Men such as heavy-hitting Josh Gibson, fleet-footed "Cool Papa" Bell, and others would be later honored by belated induction into the Hall of Fame. Prominent businessmen such as Rube Foster, Cumberland Posey, and Gus Greenlea found an outlet for their economic abilities—a not inconsiderable outlet, considering that the Negro major-leagues may have been the largest black-owned business in America by World War II. However, the Negro leagues were not all stardom and success. They suffered from team instability, scheduling difficulties, poor salaries, inadequate stadia and training facilities, and inattention from the white and black press. Despite the fact that black all-star squads compiled impressive records in match-ups with white major-leaguers, the black leagues were compelled to resort to showmanship to attract audiences. Clowns, dwarfs, and "Stepin Fetchit" routines abounded in an attempt to attract white and black fans. The impact of such antics in supporting racial stereotypes can only be guessed.

Baseball's reign as the national pastime was in no small way the result of its ability to survive the traumas of the Great Depression and World War II. In 1930 the major leagues experienced a record attendance, but the unsettling wake of the Wall Street Crash and the start of the Depression promoted the first talk of a reduction of salaries as a hedge against the prospect of hard times. By 1931 as the pall of depression spread and affected attendance, the owners reacted with a cut in the player limit from twenty-five to twenty-three and with salary cuts. Babe Ruth, the symbol of the game's prosperity in the 1920s, became the symbol of hard times with a six percent salary cut for 1932 and a seventeen percent reduction in 1933. After criticism from the players, who complained that they were bearing the brunt of depression economies, Commissioner Landis cut his salary by forty percent. The most dramatic example of the hardships of the Depression was the story of Connie Mack, who claimed that financial distress forced him to sell the key figures on his powerful 1929-1931 teams. Future Hall of Famers Al Simmons, Jimmy Foxx, and Lefty Grove were sold from Mack's Philadelphia A's, who drifted to the bottom of the American League barrel.

The worst depression years for baseball were 1931-1933, but by 1936 recovery was underway and a record attendance was reached in 1940. The damage of the Depression was offset by the potential of new methods in winning fans. Radio broadcasts spread rapidly, despite the misgivings of owners who feared their effect on attendance. Far from hurting attendance, radio seemed to encourage fans to come to the game, and, more importantly, it strengthened the loyalty of those unable to afford admission to games during the worst years of the Depression, leaving them eager to return to the stands once times grew better. By 1950 broadcasters such as Gordon McLendon and Dizzy Dean would be an important aspect of the game's appeal. Radio also enhanced the game's appeal to female fans, and efforts to attract them continued in the 1930s. Perhaps most dramatically, on May 23, 1935, the Cincinnati Reds introduced night baseball at the major-league level.

Games under the lights tapped the market of the laboring man, who had had no opportunity to see day games during the week. Although night baseball grew slowly, by 1940 only five teams abstained from it, and by the 1950s a majority of games played would be under the lights.

No sooner had baseball emerged from the Depression than it faced the challenge presented by World War II. Both baseball and the United States government drew on their experiences in World War I to meet the crisis more effectively than in 1917-18. Although no exemption from military service was granted for players, the majors were encouraged to continue their schedules, and unlike 1918 no season was shortened for the war. Eventually over 1,000 major-leaguers served, and organized baseball raised money for equipment to be distributed among military units. Bond drives and free admissions to servicemen in uniform served as other examples of baseball's attempt to play its patriotic part. On the field, play was not seriously affected until 1943, when many top players were drafted. The clubs made do with older players, Cubans, and players of lesser ability. The most vivid example of making do (although it was perhaps a bit of showmanship) was the St. Louis Browns' use of Pete Gray, a one-armed outfielder. Umpiring crews dwindled to two men, as men in blue succumbed to the lure of higher-paying jobs in defense industries or entered the service. Players again were asked to make sacrifices, as they suffered salary freezes in the midst of wartime inflation. This government directive failed to recognize the shortness of a player's prime earning years.

Still, the game remained the national pastime, aided by overseas World Series broadcasts by 1943 and abetted by the plots of some Hollywood grade-B war movies that assured audiences that World War II was a struggle to protect the right of kids to play baseball rather than carry a knife or engage in military drill. Also, the free admission to servicemen helped to create new fans in the postwar era.

Baseball emerged from World War II apparently as strongly entrenched as ever as the national pastime. The smooth surface showed record attendance, impressive stars, and the promise of further greatness. On the field, power continued to dominate, and total home runs increased. Most strikingly, more and more players swung freely with light-weight bats, meaning that the lowliest eighth-place-hitting shortstop might be going for a home run. Defense adjusted with bigger gloves and the increasing use of highly skilled relief pitchers such as Joe Page of the New York Yankees. These innovations marked a move toward specialization that would accelerate after 1950.

Yet, the postwar era was also a period of substantial change. In 1947 Jackie Robinson became the first black major-leaguer since the old American Association days of the 1880s. He was Rookie of the Year in 1947 and Most Valuable Player in the National League in 1949. Robinson inaugurated a profound change in the make-up of major-league rosters and sounded the dramatic first note of the Civil Rights struggle of the postwar era.

The integration of baseball provided both a preview of and a stimulus to the integration of American society. The process of breaking baseball's color line anticipated many elements of the national integration struggle in the

Jackie Robinson of the Brooklyn Dodgers in his prime during the early 1950s. He broke major-league baseball's color barrier in 1947. *(Los Angeles Dodgers Baseball Club)*

1950s, and its success served to open the doors to the integration of other sports and segments of American society. As early as the 1930s baseball segregationists had argued that only outside agitators wished to integrate the game and that the race question should be left to the South. Claiming that Negro players were inferiors who would suffer in competition with whites, segregationists predicted violence if the game were integrated. These very same arguments and dire predictions are familiar to any student of the efforts to desegregate public education in the United States after the *Brown v. Board of Education* decision of 1954. Also paralleling the national pattern were the active efforts of white supporters of integration. In this sense Branch Rickey of the Brooklyn Dodgers, Jimmy Powers of the New York *Daily News*, and Bill Veeck of the Cleveland Indians were baseball's equivalents to Senator Hubert Humphrey, Eleanor Roosevelt, and Chief Justice Earl Warren. Lastly, of course, the moral courage which would enable Jackie Robinson and other black ballplayers to endure insults on and off the field after 1947 would have countless imitators in the lunch counters of the southern United States in the 1950s and 1960s.

As another harbinger of the future, the Pacific Coast League in 1949 attracted over a million spectators. Indicating a demographic change in the United States, the potential market on the Pacific Coast provided a great stimulus to franchise expansion in the 1950s and 1960s. Equally important was the arrival of television, which would soon make profound changes in team revenue, salary structure, and the playing of the game. Still another postwar change was the rapid increase of automobile ownership and use as Americans became a nation on wheels. The automobile extended the market for major-league teams but threatened many minor-league clubs in nearby

62   cities with extinction. Moreover, the automobile facilitated the suburbanization of America, leaving old ballparks in the inner city while affluent fans moved to the outskirts.

Throughout the period from World War I to the Korean conflict, baseball had proudly maintained its status as the national sports pastime. It had done so by closely reflecting the nation that produced it. Baseball changed its pace of play to keep in step with an accelerating tempo of life during the 1920s, and later the game grew by adapting new technology to its purposes. The sport surmounted the disruption of depression and war. Baseball's heroes epitomized changing currents in the popular culture, and the sport demonstrated a remarkable ability to identify with changing and sometimes conflicting popular values. Even the American racial dilemma was reflected in baseball's racial failures and triumphs.

In 1950 baseball fanatics might be excused for believing that their sport's dominance would continue. However, the next three decades brought changes that both helped and hurt the game. Television and the automobile devastated the minor leagues and abetted the rise of other sports, which competed for the fan's dollar and overlapped the baseball season. Professional football seemed especially well suited to television and a more violent America. Expansion and television revenues sparked player demands for a larger share of the profits. Racial integration brought new talent but also left charges of continued discrimination within the integrated game. All in all, the years after 1950 were a mixed bag for baseball. These years saw a growth in revenues and attendance and a continued fan allegiance, but they also witnessed a strong challenge to baseball's claim as the national pastime.

Sources and Suggested Readings

Creamer, Robert W. *Babe: The Legend Comes to Life* (New York, 1974).

Crepeau, Richard C. *Baseball: America's Diamond Mind, 1919-1940* (Orlando, Florida, 1980).

Graber, Ralph. "Baseball in American Fiction," *English Journal, 56 (November, 1967), 26-45.

Guttmann, Allen. *From Ritual to Record: The Nature of Modern Sports* (New York, 1978).

Holway, John. *Voices From the Great Black Baseball Leagues* (New York, 1975).

Peterson, Robert W. *Only the Ball Was White* (Englewood Cliffs, N.J., 1970).

Roden, Donald. "Baseball and the Quest for National Dignity in Japan," *American Historical Review*, 85 (June, 1980), 511-535.

Seymour, Harold. *Baseball: The Golden Age* (New York, 1971).

Smelser, Marshall. *The Life That Ruth Built* (New York, 1975).

Umphlett, Wiley. *The Sporting Myth and the American Experience* (New York, 1975).

Voigt, David. *American Baseball: From Commissioners to Continental Expansion* (Norman, Oklahoma, 1970).

6

The College Sports Scene

Jack W. Berryman
Stephen H. Hardy

During the first half of the twentieth century, college sport continued a dual development which periodically brought to the surface serious questions about its ultimate purpose. On the one hand the administrators, coaches, promoters, and participants continued to champion a philosophy that espoused "educational values of athletics." On the other hand, these very same groups and their ever wider circles of allies, including the media and general public, fashioned their programs in concert with President Calvin Coolidge's memorable aphorism, "the business of America is business." While the worst instances of inconsistencies occurred at the level of big-time university programs, the ramifications were felt at all levels of intercollegiate competition.

Well before the First World War, college administrators developed a rationale for sports as a part of education. They were quick to explain that play, games, and sport promoted good health and hygiene, physical and mental fitness, citizenship, teamwork, sportsmanship, and character. They were "educational" under a revised definition which portrayed education "as broad as life itself." With sociologists, psychologists, recreation leaders, and educators emphasizing "sport as education," physical training became physical education, and coaches in every sport imaginable began to receive faculty status in what was soon to be a regular department of educational instruction on most college campuses. Supporting this administrative arrangement were the NCAA, various coaching groups, and the American Physical Education Association. So successful was the transformation of physical training that by 1917, physical education and sports were seen to be one and the same by laymen as well as professionals in the field.

In addition to the educational justification, college officials pointed to the "doctrine of good works." According to this theory, gate receipts were utilized to benefit the entire campus community. An example lay in intramural sports, in which the opportunity to compete was provided to students

64   who had high interest but limited ability. Further, the popularity and visibility of a successful collegiate team was emphasized in the rush for student recruits, alumni contributions, and continued patronage from local or state taxpayers. By World War I, the intercollegiate athletic enterprise was justified by most boards of trustees and regents as part of the accepted mission of the university. College officials succumbed to the lure of "free" publicity and the thrill of alumni concern for their alma mater. Victory in sports was viewed as a success for the entire university, and more often than not, the public identified sporting achievement as a vital hallmark of a quality institution of higher education. Community and state support, local pride, and boosterism all propelled college sports to greater heights.

Resting on a solid foundation of both educational and popular public support, college athletics after World War I grew stronger and more vibrant than ever before. Intercollegiate football with its star players, expert coaches, intersectional rivalries, large crowds, and all-star teams, joined with professional baseball, horse racing, and boxing as a dominant national spectator event in the 1920s. Recognized by historians as the "Golden Age of Sport," the decade of the twenties witnessed unprecedented growth in the intercollegiate spectacle. Underlying the growth was a continuing argument for the educational credibility of competitive sports. Developments like mandatory physical education requirements (sports skills) in many states assisted in this rationale, but the University of Illinois and the University of Oregon provided more telling contributions. The former instituted a four-year degree program of athletic coaching and physical education in the College of Education in 1919. A year later, Oregon formed its School of Physical Education, composed of four separate departments dealing with health, physical education for men and women, and intercollegiate athletics.

Testimony by military officials and college-age males that sport had played a vital role in winning World War I also spurred public support for sports as bulwarks of national defense, physical stamina, morale, and general patriotism. Not surprisingly then, both the U.S. Military Academy and the U.S. Naval Academy began to field high-calibre athletic teams, especially in football. In addition, Navy's rowing team represented the United States in the 1920 Olympics in Antwerp, Belgium, where they won the gold medal.

Although international competition was at most sporadic, intersectional competition became the standard. In their quest to prove regional superiority, colleges developed schedules which included opponents from all over the country. Dartmouth traveled to Seattle in 1920 for a football game with the University of Washington; New York University went to Atlanta, Georgia, to win the National Amateur Athletic Union's basketball championship the same year; and Ohio State's football team journeyed to Los Angeles to play California in the Rose Bowl the following year.

With the growing popularity of college football came the necessity for stadia with larger seating capacities. As Arch Ward of the *Chicago Tribune* noted at the beginning of the 1920 season, "giant stadia were rearing their steel and concrete contours high into the sky in the prairie cities and towns which were seats of the great universities." Georgia Tech enlarged Grant

Notre Dame's "Four Horsemen," as nicknamed by sportswriter Grantland Rice, 1923-24. Left to right: Don Miller, HB; Elmer Layden, FB; Jim Crowley, HB; Harry Stuhldreher, QB. *(St. Louis Post-Dispatch)*

Field to seat 25,000, Vanderbilt's horseshoe was expanded to 20,000, Illinois' stadium held 66,000, Ohio State's had room for 72,000, and the Los Angeles Coliseum held 75,000.

Highly skilled players and coaches, championship teams, media exposure, the lure of rival opponents, and the automobile all contributed to the availability and lasting appeal of college football. Skilled athletes were recruited to institutions of higher education from throughout the United States as part of a complex sport feeder system. Already by 1922, the National Federation of State High School Athletic Associations represented eleven states. Coaches like Fielding Yost (Michigan), Harold Miller (California), Amos Alonzo Stagg (Chicago), Bob Zuppke (Illinois), and Knute Rockne (Notre Dame) were hired on a full-time basis and earned very substantial incomes. The "Praying Colonels" of tiny Centre College in Danville, Kentucky, coached by Charlie Moran, achieved national recognition for themselves, their state, and the entire South in 1921 when they defeated national power Harvard. California had its "Wonder Teams," Princeton had its "Team of Destiny," and Notre Dame had the "Four Horsemen." Large metropolitan dailies and general-circulation magazines kept the action in the public eye on a regular basis with daily coverage, special reports, and assigned scribes to cover local teams. Writers like John Tunis, Ring Lardner, Grantland Rice, John Kieran, and Heywood Broun became household names throughout the United States. The radio, a new medium of communication, hit the public scene in 1921, and it was not long before Harold Arlin was broadcasting a college football game between Pittsburgh and West Virginia. Motion picture newsreels featured key football competitions from every region of the

66   United States. The popularization and expanded availability of the automobile also greatly assisted the rise and continued development of intercollegiate football. The car alone aided the increase in attendance and drastically altered recruiting practices.

While competitive sporting opportunities for male college students were rapidly expanding during the early 1920s, their female counterparts were severely restricted by the view which women physical educators took towards competition. Although female physical educators were basically in agreement with the educational components of sport participation, they objected to the overt emphasis on winning, gate receipts, and travel, and instead, chose to dwell upon the "socialization aspects" of sport competition. The 1920 Conference of College Women Directors of Physical Education went on record to disapprove intercollegiate athletics, and a survey of fifty colleges three years later revealed that only twelve percent were competing on the varsity level. With the formation of the Women's Division of the National Amateur Athletic Federation the same year and the publication of its resolutions in the form of a "creed" in 1924, member institutions were to abstain from competition which involved gate receipts, travel, or emphasis on winning. Further to seal the fate of high-level athletics for women in education, the National Association of Secondary School Principals came out in 1925 with its public disapproval of interscholastic sports for girls. Because of such actions, almost all sporting competition for high-school- and college-age females was sponsored by organizations outside the educational sector. Within education, women's sports were usually conducted in the form of intramurals, telegraphic meets, play days, and sports days.

While women were limiting competition, the participation of their male counterparts was expanding. By 1921 the NCAA had 102 member colleges participating in at least seven different conferences and by 1927 had official rules for football as well as other sports like boxing, wrestling, lacrosse, ice hockey, track and field, swimming, and gymnastics. As the major governing body, the NCAA enjoyed a direct affiliation with educational organizations representing teachers, principals, and college presidents. At the same time, the NCAA was actively promoting mandatory physical education legislation, formally organized departments of intramural athletics, departmental status for athletics, faculty appointments for coaches, and academic degrees in athletic coaching.

College sports and particularly intercollegiate football became a dominating influence in the 1920s and affected social values. Two individuals, one a coach and one a player, characterized collegiate football in that decade and epitomized the importance which Americans attached to victory. In the decade before his untimely death in a plane crash on March 31, 1931, Knute Rockne of Notre Dame amassed a record of 96-3-3. Rockne coached Grantland Rice's famed "Four Horsemen," produced innumerable All-Americans, brought thousands through the turnstiles in every town they played, and led the "Fighting Irish" to perfect seasons in 1929 and 1930. The other individual was Harold "Red" Grange, the "Galloping Ghost" or "Wheaton iceman," who enrolled as a freshman at Illinois in 1922 and went on to be an All-American the next three years. Every game he played was exciting, but the 1924 contest against undefeated Michigan in which he scored four touchdowns in the first quarter is probably the best remembered. His mystique and overall popularity became even more evident his senior year when Illinois played before a total of 370,000 fans, twice that of the previous year. The following year he became the first college superstar to participate in the young and "spurious vocation" of professional football. Many critics assumed that the image of the collegiate game would be hurt by Grange's enlistment in the sordid world of pro football. College football was harmed by the success of Red Grange, but not in the way university officials anticipated. As Paul Gallico noted in retrospect in *The Golden People* (1964):

. . . .in their frantic attempts to acquire similar attractions (to Red Grange), the universities impaled themselves front, back, and sideways on the horns of the dilemma that had been created—how to coax, lure, rent, hire, or buy football stars who would be drawing cards, while at the same time managing to keep their fingers off the swag. During this process they fractured amateur codes into so many pieces that no one has yet been able to put them together again.

The success of individuals like Rockne and Grange fueled an engine of emulation which carried college football further in the direction of big business.

College baseball players were also being lured to professional franchises in 1924 and 1925 and usually got bonuses and other special privileges not often provided the non-educated. Both professional baseball and football were increasingly perceived as viable careers by college graduates. This marked the beginning of an era when college teams began to be used as part of the farm-club system for professional baseball and the main supplier of professional football talent. By 1927, college men accounted for one-third of all starting positions in major-league baseball, and these talented players, sensitive to economic concerns, set new standards in salaries for playing a game. Oscar Lewis, writing the same year in *Independent*, recognized this new trend and remarked that "more and more, the possibility of lucrative professional contracts will occupy the minds of youths all over the country as soon as they begin to emerge as athletic stars." But, was this the mission for which collegiate sports were intended? Some suggested otherwise.

In 1927 the president of Oberlin College, Ernest H. Wilkins, admitted, "Intercollegiate football is at the present time an enormously powerful force in the life of the nation," interfering "to an intolerable degree with the attainment of the purpose of the American college." A year later, John Tunis, in a *Harper's* article titled "The Great God Football," recognized that college football was "at present a religion, sometimes it seems to be almost our national religion." Comments such as those of Wilkins and Tunis, combined with instances of scandal, cheating, ineligible players and recognition of the fact that college sport was much closer to business than education, culminated in the lengthy Carnegie Foundation for the Advancement of Teaching, Bulletin 29, on *American College Athletics*. The report, written by Howard J. Savage and distributed on October 23, 1929, the day of the

68   first big scare in the New York Stock Exchange, was very critical of the non-educative aspects of big time sports. The report was prefaced by the following negative remarks:

> The paid coach, the gate receipts, the special training tables, the costly sweaters and extensive journeys in special pullman cars, the recruiting from the high school, the demoralizing publicity showered on the players, the devotion of an undue proportion of time to training, the devices of putting a desirable athlete, but a weak scholar, across the hurdles of the examination—these ought to stop. . . .

Although it stimulated growth in intramural sports, the report had very little impact on the intercollegiate scene. Just three months after the release of the Carnegie Report, a *New York Times* writer, obviously agreeing with the findings of Savage, said, "The seed is working in the ground of academe, and it is to be hoped that in time the present overgrown oak of athletics will be uprooted by a saner and more graceful growth." In a 1934 issue of *Harper's Magazine*, John Tunis analyzed the meaning of the Carnegie Report and put it into perspective.

> "Bulletin 29" was the warning signal of the start of the deflation in sport, just as that first crash signaled more declines to come on the Exchange. The period from 1920 to 1930 had been beyond question the most spectacular era in our whole sporting history, the era in which everything was superlative: the best players, the biggest gates, the largest gate receipts, the greatest stadia, and so on. This period drew to a close early in 1930.

Although level-headed educators tended to sympathize with Tunis and other critics, the Carnegie Report could not detain the unprecedented rise of college football. Indeed, even a national emergency like the Great Depression had but a minimal impact on the overall record-setting pace of attendance figures and profits.

    Surveys taken after the 1930 football season indicate that the depressed economy was having some effect on college football, but the overall damage was minor. Game attendance at forty-nine of the reporting colleges was 3,289,078, a decline from 3,617,421 in 1929, and gate receipts for sixty-five reporting colleges totalled $8,363,674, a decline from $9,032,160 in 1929. Eight colleges, however, claimed receipts of more than $500,000, and thirty-three other colleges reported more than $100,000. In addition, as an Associated Press survey taken in 1931 verified, football attendance increased in some regions: "Depressed business conditions have not hit all of the major colleges by any means, notably in such sections as the Pacific Northwest, Rocky Mountain, and Southwest areas where football 'booms' were enjoyed last fall." Football attendance reached its lowest level in 1932, but each subsequent year brought a new record in attendance and gate receipts. Further, four new post-season bowl games were initiated between 1933 and 1937. The Orange Bowl began in 1933, the Sugar Bowl started in 1935, the Sun Bowl was instituted in 1936, and in the following year the Cotton Bowl had its first competition.

    Football was not the only collegiate sport to achieve financial success during the depression years. Basketball had traditionally enjoyed its greatest popularity among YMCA and YWCA patrons, female college students, and AAU competitors. During the 1920s, however, it began to receive more consistent attention in male collegiate sporting circles. Because of the petitioning of Forrest "Phog" C. Allen, coach at the University of Kansas, basketball received "exhibition" status at the 1928 Olympics in Amsterdam. Ironically the first rush of interest in the college games occurred during the depression years.

Fierce competition between New York City colleges like St. John's, New York University, City College of New York, Columbia, Fordham, Manhattan, and Long Island University showed that college basketball could draw crowds and support itself under the big business model previously standardized by football. In 1931 over 12,000 spectators crowded into New York's 106th Infantry Armory for a basketball game, and Mayor Jimmy Walker staged benefit games in Madison Square Garden for the Unemployment Relief Fund. One of the extravaganzas, a triple-header, brought 15,000 to the Garden. Although progress was being aptly demonstrated by larger attendance figures, fan interest, and newspaper coverage, the crucial turning point for college basketball came in 1934. The mayor and sportswriters of the city staged a marathon seven-game event in the Garden in the interests of depression relief. The card drew 20,000. One sportswriter, Ned Irish of the *New York World-Telegram*, realizing the potential of college basketball, eventually quit his job with the paper and began to promote the sport. He utilized Madison Square Garden as an ideal facility for basketball viewing, established intersectional competition, and encouraged radio coverage of the game, using announcers like Marty Glickman. In 1934, Notre Dame came to the city and played NYU. College basketball, as it began to be a recognized spectator event, had started its metamorphosis following in the football tradition.

Stanford University and its three-time All-American, Angelo "Hank" Luisetti, came east to play in 1936 and once again demonstrated the interest in intersectional competition. Luisetti, with his one-handed shooting, speed, floor play, and charisma, was a national hero by his senior year in 1938 and was basketball's first superstar. Signs of acceptance and permanency were clearly visible when the sport was granted a regular position in the 1936 Olympic Games. The following year, the sport had a national tournament when the National Association of Intercollegiate Basketball Championship (not officially organized until 1940) was started. Organized for small colleges, the tournament drew teams away from the previously popular National Amateur Athletic Union Tournament. In 1938, the New York Metropolitan Basketball Writers invited six teams to play at Madison Square Garden in the first National Invitational Tournament. That year Madison Square Garden drew over a quarter of a million spectators for college basketball. Not to be left out, the NCAA began its own basketball tournament in 1939. The sport was proving that it could compete in the entertainment market for spectators and their amusement dollar.

Football and basketball were not alone in generating heroes. Track and field, although never a money-maker on either the collegiate or professional level, received some attention during the 1920s and '30s, largely due to record-

Hank Luisetti: Stanford University's all-time great basketball player. His one-handed shot in the 1930s revolutionized the game. *(Stanford University)*

breaking performances. Charlie Paddock was a world-class sprinter at the University of Southern California in 1923, and Sabin Carr, a Yale undergraduate, polevaulted a record fourteen feet in 1927. But it was Jesse Owens of Ohio State who directed more attention to track and field than any other individual. At a Big Ten dual meet with Michigan at Ann Arbor on May 25, 1935, Owens broke three world records and equaled a fourth in the 100-yard dash, 200-yard dash, 220-yard low hurdles, and the long jump. His record in the long jump stood for twenty-five years. In 1936 he represented Ohio State and the United States in the Berlin Olympics, where he proved the superiority of American track by defeating world rivals in winning four gold medals.

College sports were successful as entertainment. At the same time, however, the educational justification for the place of sports in higher education was solidified and systematically entrenched in departments of physical education all over the United States. Elmer Mitchell's book on *Intramural Athletics* (1925) served as a reminder to skeptics that sports competition was being made available to all students, not just the gifted athletes. In 1930, Jesse Feiring Williams, Chairman of the Department of Physical Education at Columbia University, published in the *Journal of Higher Education* his article on "Education Through the Physical." That same year he co-authored the influential *Athletics in Education*. Williams was a staunch supporter of the view that participation in sports produced individual biological, social, and psychological advancements, the components of a general education. The following year President Thomas S. Gates of the University of Pennsylvania provided other colleges with a model of internal governance which clearly established athletics in the academic curriculum. He established the Department of Physical Education under the direction of a dean, with three directors of divisions dealing with student health, physical instruction, and intercollegiate athletics. The University of Pennsylvania model was reinforced by an article of J. H. Nichols of Oberlin College, which highlighted "The Inter-Relationship of Physical Education, Intramural and Intercollegiate Athletics." Full reports on both ideas were published in the May, 1932, issue of *Research Quarterly*, a journal widely read at the time by teachers, coaches, and administrators. Looking at developments in the following years, it is clear that other colleges began to adopt the new concepts and pointed to such arrangements as "proof" that athletics were indeed educational and belonged on all college campuses.

As education or entertainment, college sports reached an ever wider audience. The principal reason was radio. During the late 1920s and early 1930s, stations throughout the country began to broadcast high school and college football, baseball, and basketball games. By 1932 CBS estimated that 16,026,620 homes were equipped with radios, and listeners heard all sorts of shows, including college sports. This new method of distributing the college sport package was not always seen as favorable by the institutions concerned. They feared losing valuable gate receipts. The advertising fees generated by radio stations were usually not a great enough inducement to attract unhesitating support from college administrators or conference officials. For example, in 1932 the Eastern Intercollegiate Association passed a resolution banning all radio broadcasts of football games. Uncertain of radio's impact, other colleges and conferences went through similar trial-and-error decisions as the decade progressed. While institutions ranging from Harvard and Princeton to Western Reserve University of Cleveland, Ohio, refused to sell their radio rights in 1937, Yale sold a six-game home package for $20,000. In the same year, both the Pacific Coast Conference and the Southwest Conference arranged for exclusive rights packages. These deals were signs of things to come as other colleges quickly realized that profits were to be made with little or no influence on attendance figures.

Just as radio became an acceptable and profitable medium for college sports, a new communication device began in its experimental stages. A television crew with one camera broadcast a baseball game between Princeton and Columbia on May 17, 1939, and a little more than four months later televised a football game between Fordham and Waynesburg. Closed-circuit television was being used for basketball games from Madison Square Garden, and by early 1940, the sport was being broadcast on public sets in the city. On February 28, 1940, NBC televised a basketball doubleheader, and another new era of college sports was born. The success of these early ventures illustrated the potential for a close and profitable relationship between the television industry and the intercollegiate sports establishment. By 1949, a survey of sixty-four television stations revealed that football, boxing, baseball, wrestling, and basketball were filling anywhere from four to thirty-five percent of the station's total airtime. College presidents and athletic directors quickly utilized the new medium of television to their financial benefit.

While high-level sporting opportunities continued to escalate for male college students in the 1930s, the best competition for college women still remained outside the realm of educational sponsorship. AAU district and national championships in basketball, swimming, and track and field attracted high-calibre athletes. Similar opportunities to play for one's college, however, were severely curtailed by the grip of the Women's Division of NAAF. In 1931 the NAAF reinforced its power by affiliating with the American Physical Education Association and voting in 1932 against the participation of American women in the Olympic Games. A 1936 survey of seventy-seven colleges offering women's sports revealed that only seventeen percent provided competition at the varsity level. It was the heyday of the telegraphic meet and play day, where cooperation was substituted for competition.

Women's programs notwithstanding, college sports successfully weathered the throes of economic depression. World War II was hardly a serious impediment. From the first signs of the impending crisis, the necessity of physical fitness for national defense was emphasized in the sponsorship of sports for college-age males. Colleges encouraged intramurals, especially those endurance-producing sports like football, boxing, wrestling, basketball, ice hockey, lacrosse, water polo, soccer, speedball, handball, squash, track and field, and swimming. Educators and military leaders also emphasized the value of sports in the building of morale. Testimony such as that of Major Theodore P. Bank, writing about "Army Athletics" in 1941, abounded:

We Americans are all aware of the obvious physical benefits derived from participation in competitive athletics, but we sometimes forget the intangible benefits the soldier receives from competitive athletics. Sports like boxing, or other sports involving bodily contact, rapidly develop in the individual man the sense of confidence, aggressiveness and fearlessness that is always desirable in a trained soldier. Sports like football, basketball and other team-play sports also develop the principles of coordination between groups of men that are invaluable on the battle field.

Many campuses became training centers for various programs of the Armed Forces. Similarly, many college teams were largely composed of Navy personnel since V-5 and V-12 program trainees were eligible for intercollegiate competition. Football also produced another round of nationally recognized players and coaches during the war in the likes of Elroy "Crazy Legs" Hirsch at Wisconsin, Otto Graham at Northwestern, and Mike Holovak at Boston College. Colonel Earl H. "Red" Blaik coached his Army teams to a dominance of college football in 1944 and 1945, and in the latter year, his stars Glenn Davis ("Mr. Outside") and Felix "Doc" Blanchard ("Mr. Inside"), received constant public attention in the media.

The war did have a certain negative impact on intercollegiate sports. Competition diminished as most colleges either abandoned or limited their schedules. The depletion of manpower, lack of athletic supplies, and gas and tire rationing were chief causes. But, despite the troubled times, the *concept* of intercollegiate sport not only survived; it rose out of the conflict with revitalized support because of its direct connection with victory, nationalism, and general democratic ideals. Believing that college-age males displayed the same stamina, strength, and power on the battlefield as they had on the football field, Americans after the war welcomed a renewed emphasis on sporting competition of all kinds.

During the postwar years, veterans, colleges, and their sports enjoyed the educational benefits of the G.I. Bill of Rights, as schools admitted almost a million more students in 1946 than they had in 1940. In football, Michigan, Notre Dame, Ohio State, and UCLA played each of their games before crowds of over 50,000. The seventeen post-season bowl games the same year attracted 478,000 fans and generated receipts of $1,765,000. In 1947, two more bowl games, the Gator and the Tangerine, were added to a growing list of post-season contests. The University of Michigan was playing regularly before crowds of 80,000 by 1948, and the Army-Navy game took on such national importance that 102,000 saw the two teams battle in 1949.

College basketball also flourished after the war. Madison Square Garden continued its prominent role, featuring thirty nights of basketball in 1946 and hosting an expanded NIT field in 1949. Coaches such as Clair Bee of Long Island, Adolph Rupp of Kentucky, and Henry "Hank" Iba, who led his Oklahoma A & M team to NCAA championships in 1945 and 1946, added new life to the rapidly growing game. In addition, George Mikan, a three-time All-American at De Paul in 1944, 1945, and 1946 and Bob Cousy, an All-American from Holy Cross, went on to spectacular professional careers. Mikan as the "good big-man" at 6'10" and Cousy as a fast ball-handling successor to Hank Luisetti, epitomized the thrill, excitement, and obvious financial potential for college basketball and its participants. The merger in 1949 of the National Basketball League and the Basketball Association of America to form the NBA made the professional game available in seventeen different cities, thereby providing the talented college basketball star a career opportunity similar to that of baseball and football. In so doing, college basketball followed its predecessors into the entertainment arena and took on more and more of the characteristics of the professional big business model of competition. Not coincidentally, problems arose in the areas of recruiting, subsidization, professionalism, gambling, game fixing, and eligibility.

A gambling and game-fixing scandal hit college basketball in 1945 when Brooklyn College was the focus of point-shaving charges. Five players admitted taking bribes before a game with Akron, and the contest was then canceled. The event was "glossed over" by all concerned, but it was an indication of the real problems of college sports. Although still using athletes enrolled at colleges, still playing games on university campuses, and still hiring coaches as faculty members, the major college sport scene had a much closer affinity with business enterprise than with education. Concerned both with the allegations of illegal activities and with the maintenance of credibility, the NCAA held a conference in Chicago in July, 1946, to determine "Principles for the Conduct of Intercollegiate Athletics." Long overdue, the major issues of concern in the "Sanity Code" were amateurism, institutional control, academic standards, financial aid, and recruiting.

While enforcement of the "Sanity Code" was problematic, certain events immediately proved the need for such regulation. In 1950, it was revealed that the Manhattan District Attorney was probing the allegation that several Manhattan College basketball players had taken bribes. The following year saw another point-shaving scandal in basketball involving Long Island and CCNY. During the same year, more than thirty basketball players from seven schools admitted game-fixing, ninety West Point cadets were expelled for aiding football players in exams, and two coaches from William and Mary resigned when their tampering with student transcripts became evident. Just as the Carnegie Report had castigated college athletics at the close of the 1920s, the beginning of the 1950s found critics who felt justified in accusing universities of losing sight of educational ideals.

The principals directly involved with collegiate sports obviously viewed their activities in a positive light. Presidents and boards of trustees of major programs especially supported football and basketball, because they could make money for the university from gate receipts, concessions, radio and television contracts, and by increased alumni, public, and private giving. The visibility generated by the extensive coverage of athletics in the media was viewed as a positive factor in attracting prospective students. Further, it was assumed that sports would offer a common rallying point, thereby promoting school spirit and *esprit de corps*. For many male physical educators, sports became the central subject of their profession, to be taught and played as part of the educational and health curriculum in required gym classes throughout the United States. Highly skilled athletes viewed athletics as a way to get an inexpensive college education and, if good enough, a ticket to a career in professional baseball, football, or basketball.

For those indirectly involved with intercollegiate athletics as spectators, readers of the sports page, listeners of radio, or viewers of television, the events meant different things, usually of an intense personal nature. On one level, some fans enjoyed witnessing sports that were made exciting by physical contact, combativeness, violence, bloodshed, and man-against-man challenges. College sports offered diversion from everyday life, and especially in times of stress such as the depression years or the World War II era, they provided a "safety valve" for releasing the tensions of life itself. With their upsets, records, thrills, champions, surprises, and heroes, college sports had all of the components of any successful theater production or motion picture. Intercollegiate athletics also potrayed the classic manifestations of American democracy in their own ritualistic celebrations. Time-honored virtures such as citizenship, sportsmanship, and patriotism—the components of a national faith—were regularly attached to every contest between university students.

At the same time, college sports and their stars were cultural forms which reassured a nation fearful of losing its sense of individual achievement in the face of mass modes of production, transportation, and communication. Ironically, however, college sports were the epitome of middle-class WASP business values, identified by their impersonality and trend toward bureaucratization, rationalization, centralization, and organization along functional lines. With their records, scores, standings, statistics, national rankings, all-star teams, attendance figures, and gate receipts, the success or failure of college sports could be measured, counted, and analyzed just as any other business enterprise.

Additional elements supported the growth of collegiate sports. There was something very manly about college games, with football the embodiment of an autumn masculinity rite. They were further recognized as developers of men and vigorously promoted during war by analogies between the playing field and battlefield. With their female cheerleaders and admiring coeds, the contests were relished by thousands as important ingredients in the game of courtship. Finally, it was clear that the athletes represented not just the college and its alumni. The success or failure of the local college team became an important component of state and city pride and was often utilized as a form of boosterism whereby success in sport was transferred to all who lived and worked in that particular locale.

By 1950 college sports had weathered three decades of social, economic, political, and military turmoil and had emerged with a stronger commercial and ideological base. If some institutions viewed the "big time" as too costly, many more eagerly entered the fray. Moreover, on balance it was clear that Americans within and without the university had warmly embraced the attractions and benefits of collegiate sports. Critics would continue to emphasize the inconsistencies between entertainment and education, but they could only shrug their shoulders at the remarkable increases in participation, attendance, and revenues.

Sources and Suggested Readings

Allen, Frederick Lewis. *Only Yesterday: An Informal History of the Nineteen-Twenties* (New York, 1931).

Berryman, Jack W. "Historical Roots of the Collegiate Dilemma," *Proceedings*, National College Physical Education Association for Men (Hot Springs, 1976), 141-154.

Cozens, Frederick W. and Florence S. Stumpf. *Sports in American Life* (Chicago, 1953).

Crepeau, Richard C. *Baseball: America's Diamond Mind, 1919-1941* (Gainesville, 1980).

Danzig, Allison and Peter Brondwein, eds. *Sport's Golden Age: A Close-Up of the Fabulous Twenties* (New York, 1948).

Isaacs, Neil D. *All the Moves: A History of College Basketball* (Philadelphia, 1975).

Kaye, Ivan N. *Good Clean Violence: A History of College Football* (Philadelphia, 1973).

Lewis, Guy M. "Adoption of the Sports Program, 1906-1939: The Role of Accommodation in the Transformation of Physical Education," *Quest*, 12 (Spring, 1969), 34-46.

_____ . "Enterprise on the Campus: Developments in Intercollegiate Sport and Higher Education, 1875-1939." Bruce L. Bennett, ed. *Proceedings of the Big Ten Symposium on the History of Physical Education and Sport* (Chicago, 1972), 53-66.

Scott, Harry A. *Competitive Sports in Schools and Colleges* (New York, 1951).

Steiner, Jesse F. *Americans at Play: Recent Trends in Recreation and Leisure Time Activities* (New York, 1933).

7

The Athletic Hero in Film and Fiction

Charles T. Summerlin

An age that loves sports and idolizes athletes as ours does has a hard time believing it did not invent these passions. Actually, man has played and his play has intrigued the human imagination since ancient times. Furthermore, he has organized his play, defined it by rules, measured his achievements, and competed against others. The Greeks were devoted to competitive athletics, and the hero fit to wear the laurel carried immense prestige among them. Homer opens a door on ancient Greek athletic endeavor in both the *Iliad* and the *Odyssey*, depicting competition among the assaulters of Troy and the games of the Phaeacians in which the wanderer Ulysses participated. Although, as Edith Hamilton tells us, sport for the Romans was a much bloodier activity, it still had a high priority. Probably no era saw sport in a more aristocratic light than did the Middle Ages, in which competition at chivalric tournaments was reserved for the elite. But even then, perhaps especially then, contests on the field of play, as well as in more serious combat, fired the poet's imagination.

To explain why sports or athletic endeavor has interested so many of us for so long is far beyond the scope of this essay, but we should venture some generalizations. (Terms such as "sports," "athletics," "games," and "play," though they operate within the same field of meaning, are certainly not synonymous. Indeed, some of the points in this essay will hinge upon distinctions among such terms.) Games inevitably pattern themselves after and become images of the way we perceive and live our lives. In sports, as in life, we deem successful one who handles challenges, overcomes obstacles, perseveres, and excels. Perhaps the Biblical admonition to "run . . . the race that is set before us" captures this analogy most succinctly. Furthermore, our imagination's impatience with the ordinary and frustration with limits also find vehicles in athletic achievement. George Brett flirts with the magic .400 barrier, and we fix our dreams on him. After all, as Ted Williams said, hitting a baseball is the single most difficult athletic skill to master, and if a mere mortal can succeed in hitting it that well, what can't we do? Thus, athletic prowess teases us into grander dreams of ourselves, and on such stuff the imagination thrives. Whether it be the Man of La Mancha's "impossible dream," Tennyson's Ulysses, who vows "To strive, to seek, to find and not to yield," or the Star Trek explorers' mission "to go where no man has gone," our art, high- and low-brow, continues to create figures who probe or challenge human limitation. This questing spirit is also essential to the hunter, to the hurdler, and to the hockey star, and each in his own way is a model for us of the desire to excel and to transcend the norm.

Granted that sports have figured significantly in literature of the past, it is yet accurate to say that in the last century or so the athletic hero has assumed a more prominent role in our society and, correspondingly, in our literature. Very briefly, a number of influences—the British sporting tradition, an increasing concern for physical conditioning, growing prosperity and leisure, vastly improved means of communication and transportation, to name some prominent ones—contributed to a growth of interest in organized athletics in the nineteenth century and laid the groundwork for the multitude of amateur and professional sports Americans now watch or compete in. So great has become our love of, and perhaps obsession with, sports that when we break down the significant events of the world for our evening news, we create a sacred trinity of news, weather, and sports. Our presidents discuss the "game plan" by which they seek to "quarterback" and search the bench for "team players." The more we watch and play, apparently, the more we find sport a meaningful measure of value and the superior athlete a capable hero. We differ in what we admire, to be sure, and whom we admire, but we agree in valuing athletics as an essential metaphor for, or even a literal criterion of, human excellence.

An influential portion of nineteenth century literature leans heavily on athletics as a very *literal* measurement of excellence. Two nineteenth century literary figures loom large in this context. The first is a native American hero, not primarily a participant in organized sports, but an athlete of legendary proportions nonetheless. He is the lone outdoorsman, vigorous and sturdy, a worthy adversary of the wilderness or of any mortal foolish enough to challenge him. The legendary Daniel Boone helped cast the mold. James Fenimore Cooper's Natty Bumppo largely delineated his features in the Leatherstocking saga. *The Pioneers* (1823), *The Last of the Mohicans* (1826), *The Prairie* (1827), *The Pathfinder* (1840), and *The Deerslayer* (1841) depicted the frontier hero from youth to old age. Plain of speech and pure of heart, Bumppo embodied our yearning to be healthy, innocent Adams in Paradise—but Cooper's series reminds us that such dreams are contradicted by experiences. Admirable as he is, this noble savage is doomed by progress and civilization. In Davy Crockett and his kind the frontiersman developed a comic braggadocio. But whether tragic or comic, this American hero could run, shoot, paddle, or wrestle with mythic prowess. At his most sublime he is a grand, god-like individual who towers over his fellow men. The frontiersman has spawned offspring too numerous to account for, but figure among them all the Virginians, the Shanes, and the Hipshot Percussions, those soli-

The American Frontiersman: Athlete of mythic proportions. *(National Archives)*

tary warriors who follow their rugged codes with fierce innocence. As we shall observe later, our own century has created its versions of this hero, nature's athlete, who relies on his strength, speed, and wits to survive.

For the other dominant nineteenth-century image we turn from wilderness to society, in particular to the English public school. The Duke of Wellington's linking of victory at Waterloo to the playing fields of Eton is a well-known testimony to British respect for organized sport. In schools like Rugby, John Locke's ideal of "a sound mind in a sound body" was developed into a militant credo that encompassed both physical and moral well-being. A result was the concept of "muscular Christianity," strength of character accompanied by strength of body, which found its most famous expression in Thomas Hughes's *Tom Brown's School Days* (1857). Hear Hughes as he defends Brown's readiness to box with the ruffian Williams:

After all, what would life be without fighting, I should like to know? From the

80 cradle to the grave, fighting, rightly understood, is the business, the real highest, honestest business of every son of man. Every one who is worth his salt has his enemies, who must be beaten, be they evil thoughts and habits in himself, or spiritual wickedness in high places, or Russians, or Border-ruffians, or Bill, Tom, or Harry, who will not let him live his life in quiet till he has thrashed them.

Tom Brown fostered a number of spiritual progeny in American fiction. Indeed, Americans, with their famous devotion to rugged individualism, increased attention to the "strenuous life" popularized by Teddy Roosevelt and writers such as Richard Harding Davis, seem especially appropriate heirs of this tradition. The most famous of these characters, probably, was Frank Merriwell, the creation of Gilbert Patten (alias Burt L. Standish). Merriwell was as honorable as he was quick, strong, and spunky, as he demonstrated in hundreds of stories and novels from 1896 to 1913. His contemporaries were Dink Stover of Yale and the Rover Boys, all youthful heroes who, in the words of historian John Betts, "inspired the fair play on the fields of sport and good conduct in the game of life." Not surprisingly, juvenile literature of this sort, immensely popular, offered a largely uncritical and highly idealized portrait of the athletic hero. This archetypal hero of early American sports fiction is, then, essentially a juvenile character. He has been perpetuated in our time in hundreds of novels involving football, baseball, track, fishing, hunting, and many other sporting activities. Nowadays, this hero is less exclusively Anglo-Saxon and male and much more likely to confront social issues such as racism and sexism, but while the faces vary, the profile remains essentially the same.

Sports literature of eighty to one hundred years ago, increasingly interested in competitive athletics, thrived largely on such characters. It was not that the public and writers were so naive as to believe in the universal purifying power of sports. Journalists and cartoonists of the late nineteenth century railed against ignorant ballplayers, greedy club-owners, and bogus student athletes. A belief in the spiritual properties of sports, however, was a dominant force in the literature of the era, literature of admittedly less than classic stature.

A different note is struck in some early twentieth-century fiction. Jack London's *The Game* (1906), for instance, offers a curiously ambivalent look at boxing. Until the last few pages it reads like a typical Merriwell story— clean-cut Joe Fleming fights a brute for one last purse before he marries his dream girl, who in disguise is watching the sport she loathes. But the familiar scenario does not work out, for a lucky punch and a fall crush Fleming's skull, leaving his Genevieve to ponder the "irony and faithlessness" of the blood game and "the grip it laid on men's souls." Ring Lardner's athletes, portrayed vividly through their own idiom, are a far cry from muscular Christians. Lardner gives us not heroes but ordinary characters, certainly not much better, and frequently worse, than ourselves. Alibi Ike is a mixture of self-deprecation and conceit. Jack Keefe in *You Know Me Al* (1916) is a semi-literate blowhard. Midge Kelly is a vicious sociopath. Lardner begins his story of this ring champion laconically: "Midge Kelly scored his first knockout when he was seventeen. The knockee was his brother Connie, three years his junior and a cripple." In Lardner's work, then, athletics begins to be scrutinized less sympathetically and, probably, more honestly. His stories are a precursor of a body of literature and film that has become a growth industry in our more consciously cynical times. This industry thrives on "the way it is" narrative which reveals, it likes to believe, the world of sport frankly and without false piety. Lardner's work is a harbinger of our times in another way as well: in its attention to the professional athlete. The two facts are not unrelated, for apparently it is hard for athlete and artist to discover the heroic ideal in the professional sports world.

Sports literature that is critical more than adulatory and that depicts anti-heroic behavior is not unique to our time. Augustus Longstreet's *Georgia Scenes* (1835) makes hay of the clownish and vicious rural sports of gander pulling, shooting, and gouging. But undoubtedly the critical or satirical approach has become more familiar, even expected, in our century. In this respect, sports fiction reflects a movement in literature generally. It has been the continuous tendency of literature since Renaissance times to move toward a low-mimetic (miming or depicting man in his less ideal state) attitude, to use critic Northrop Frye's terminology. Our century certainly has witnessed a willingness to emphasize the darker side of human nature. Understanding this corrosive skepticism and irony in our age may provide us perspective on the changes that Lardner signals. Some of the most familiar instances of this shifting point of view are non-fiction works. Jim Bouton's *Ball Four* (1970), Gary Shaw's *Meat on the Hoof* (1972), Dave Meggysey's *Out of Their League* (1970), and Jack Scott's *The Athletic Revolution* (1971), are popular examples of the kind of exposé journalism focusing on American athletics, professional and amateur. They dispose us in general to see athletes as vulgar, egotistical skirt-chasers or as hapless victims of rapacious systems.

Fiction has avidly entered this arena as well, in the short story, the novel, the play, and the film. Consider some representative sports films of the last forty years. Few sports have presented a readier target for the anti-heroic approach than boxing. *Champion* (1949) tells a version of Midge Kelly's story, one which softens some of the boxer's sharp edges, but which gives ample evidence of his sadism. *The Harder They Fall* (1956) indicts the whole seedy boxing scene. A British import, *This Sporting Life* (1963), portrays a miner-turned-rugby-star whose values are as empty as the satisfaction he ultimately derives from athletic success. On the far reaches of athletic endeavor is Fast Eddie Felson of *The Hustler* (1961), another who leaves human carnage in his wake, though Eddie has a kind of barely articulate sensitivity most of his ilk lack.

Felson's late change of heart and the stature he achieves when he defies a gambler who "owns" him signal a modified judgment of the modern athlete. Often the downbeat sports film will concentrate its criticism on the athlete's milieu and permit some measure of stature to the individual. Boxing, again, offers worthy examples of this genre. In *The Set-Up* (1948) double-crossed Stoker Thompson wearily maintains his integrity in the ring. Terry Malloy in *On The Waterfront* (1954) is brutish and ignorant, but he has the courage to stand up to labor racketeers. In *Body and Soul* (1947) Charlie Davis suc-

82 cumbs to the garish life of the champion until the deaths of two friends
through the machinations of the mob move him to refuse to take the dive he
has been paid for. The rodeo, subject of a number of competent movies,
seems to specialize in contributing characters who are outsiders or losers
with redeeming qualities. There is an almost tragic dimension to *The Lusty
Men* (1952), in which Robert Mitchum plays an over-the-hill bull rider who
teaches a younger man his profession, revealing his own humanity in the
process. Eventually, however, he is goaded by the younger man's taunts into
one final, fatal ride. *Golden Girl* (1979) gives us a particularly current varia-
tion on this theme, with its story of genetic manipulation and commercial
exploitation of a gifted athlete. Football has offered a fertile field for criticism of the inhuman "system." In *The Longest Yard* (1974), the prison setting of an incredibly brutal football game between inmates and guards is
clearly a metaphor which reminds us that organized sports, corrupt and
repressive, may be the villain itself. Little that is admirable remains in this
film but the jaunty spirit and sense of humor of some of the participants.

Few movies have attempted to condemn more thoroughly the institution
of professional sport than *North Dallas Forty* (1979), based on ex-Dallas
Cowboy Pete Gent's novel. The football team's owners are cold despots, its
coach is a Bible-quoting hypocrite, and the organization seems almost more
devoted to abusing its participants than to winning. The players themselves
are animals or easy marks for the dark forces that control them. They are
"whores," one suggests, or perhaps merely part of the equipment. Predict-
ably, it is a devil-may-care wide receiver, wisecracking and contemptuous of
authority, who alone salvages much from the sordid scene. Pure sensation,
the physical high of athletic performance, provides his redemption, at least
until he is made the scapegoat in a drug-related witch hunt and canned.

In these latter films, the relationship of the athlete to his sport and those
who control it closely approximates the human plight in existentialist philosophy. The existential being cannot discern reliable authority in the universe
outside him, only the alien or absurd, and must construct ethical meaning
from within. To be fully human is to take that radical individual responsibil-
ity. The existentialist theme has nourished many in the twentieth century
as muscular Christianity did in an earlier time, and it has found in athletics
a ready vehicle, particularly in the lonely competitor who finds no solace in
the bands and bright lights and little satisfaction in victory, if victory is his
lot. What little value he retains is likely to be personal satisfaction in his own
integrity, in a job well done, or in the sensuous pleasure he can share with
few, if any, others. Thus, Fast Eddie Felson confesses that only in those
moments when he makes everything click, when he has "oil in his arm," is
he truly himself.

The melancholy common to this sort of movie takes another shape in
stories which emphasize the ex-athletic hero's failure as a human being. Irwin
Shaw's Christian Darling, whose vision of himself is captured in one eighty-
yard touchdown run in a college scrimmage, is such a failure. Another is
Rabbit Angstrom in John Updike's *Rabbit Run* (1960), who conducts a
desperate, futile search as an adult for the satisfaction he found as a high-

school basketball star. The former hero is at times ingratiating and often repulsive. He is classically immature and irresponsible. As Wiley Umphlett has ably demonstrated, this variety of the anti-hero is a persistent one in our literature. And it is one which insists that athletic excellence may be a metaphor for human excellence, but it is hardly a satisfactory substitute.

Another version of the hero that has been propagated in film relies on a yoking of the sturdy values of the traditional athlete to a gritty realism. Biographical films commonly take this approach. They vary widely, of course, in quality (in depth and vividness of characterization, narrative coherence, thematic development), but they tend to be alike in being less willing than clearly fictional sports films to surrender the older, heroic motif. Swallowing the myth whole, as in *The Babe Ruth Story* (1948), is probably less common now than it once was, but the highly successful *Brian's Song* (1970) is a comparatively recent film which adroitly combines tough candor in some situations with careful editing of fact in others to build toward a sentimental conclusion which depicts a domestic harmony in the Piccolo family that unfortunately did not exist. Of course, this film should not be blamed for the excesses of a host of other to-an-athlete-dying-or-at-least-getting-maimed-young films that have become staple TV-movie fare in the last decade. Such films may seem to reverse the Frank Merriwell success pattern, for they often end with the ultimate athletic failure, death; but in spirit they are closer to the verities embraced by the traditional heroic model and are light-years removed from the brutal image conveyed in movies like *North Dallas Forty*, *This Sporting Life*, or *The Longest Yard*.

A twisted version of the old derring-do is present in another category of contemporary sports film as well. Are not *Rocky I* and *II* testimony that the spirit of Tom Brown is alive in the 1970s? Rocky Balboa, a loan shark's collector, is no choirboy; but, when challenged by fate, he becomes a bright light in a shady business, a dedicated believer in himself, who willingly accepts the discipline his battle demands of him. Consider *The Bad News Bears* (1976). The "low-mimetic" characteristics of these contemporary heroes are apparent. The kids are foul-mouthed, unruly beer-drinkers, but they positively reek of the never-say-die spirit which sees impossible odds as another incentive. Their triumphant rebelliousness is a bubble-gum blend of the anti-establishment attitude of our time and the true-blue dedication of an earlier day.

To speak of *The Bad News Bears* is to move into the comic mode, of course. A considerable amount of modern sports writing is in this lighter satiric vein, one which is likely to combine tart candor with a genuine feeling for the object of satire. George Plimpton's recitals of his experiences as an amateur dallying with professional boxing, football, hockey, and baseball may be placed in this category. His *Paper Lion* (1966), for instance, is a pre-Bouton exposé of life in an NFL training camp, but one that is clearly affectionate, not bitter or downbeat. Dan Jenkins' *Semi-Tough* (1972) is somewhat similar in tone. Its approach is Lardneresque (a pro quarterback is taperecording during Super Bowl week for a book he will write) and suitably raunchy, but the book is at least semi-tender and quite probably sentimental. Our hero clearly has a heart. He is a good guy in spite of himself, as

Sports has always been a major theme in American films. Bob Lemon of the Cleveland Indians shows future President Ronald Reagan how to grip the ball for the 1952 film "The Winning Team." Reagan played Grover Cleveland Alexander, and Doris Day was Aimee Alexander. *(St. Louis Post-Dispatch)*

he shows by the disclaimers of racism that accompany his zestful use of derogatory ethnic terms. Another example of this more amiable hero of our time can be found in Mark Harris' trilogy *(The Southpaw, Bang The Drum Slowly, A Ticket for a Seamstich)*, supposedly the notes of one Henry Wiggen, major-league pitcher. Wiggen is unlearned, and he and his comrades are no models of virtue or decorum, but Wiggen is a more traditional hero in that he learns and grows ethically through his experiences. Though far from being a blue-eyed paradigm, he possesses not only athletic skills but also genuine character.

Much of the preceding survey of the modern sports hero has dealt with motion pictures, light fiction, and journalism, examples of popular culture that entertain, while frequently making little pretense to aesthetic greatness. One of the most striking characteristics of the sport motif in our century, however, is the degree to which it has interested the "serious" artist, which, for instance, a Mark Harris seeks to be. The concept of the sports hero has undergone complex and fascinating changes in the hands of some of the literary craftsmen of the twentieth century. Consider the way athletics, primarily baseball, with its long preëminence as "national pastime" and its rich history, has been invested with mythical garb and used to dramatize our dreams and fears. Douglas Wallop's *The Year the Yankees Lost the Pennant* (1954)—*Damn Yankees* on stage and screen—is a lighter example of baseball as myth. A middle-aged Washington Senators fan sells his soul to the devil in exchange for the athletic prowess to lift his cellar-dwellers to the pennant. Only last-minute intervention saves Joe Hardy's soul, and he must score the winning run on his own fifty-year-old legs—with no help from Mephistopheles. Wallop's story is pleasant escapism; Bernard Malamud's *The Natural* (1952) is something more. Raw-boned Roy Hobbs aspires to lift his team to glory, but his plans, portrayed in imagery drawn from Christian, Jewish, and pagan traditions, do not meet Hardy's happy fate. Hobbs is both savior and *schlemiel*, and he is a natural both in his instinctive grace, skill, and power (which he readily acknowledges) and in his mortality (which he prefers to ignore). For Malamud, the hero is dazzling in his brash willingness to take on all comers and pitiful in his inability to come to terms with his own humanity.

The borders of fantasy Malamud touches on are crossed over in two remarkable novels, Robert Coover's *The Universal Baseball Association, Inc., J. Henry Waugh, Prop.* (1968) and Philip Roth's *The Great American Novel* (1972). Coover's *Association* is the complex creation of a fifty-six-year-old accountant who has breathed life into over half a century of a private baseball league, whose games he plays with charts and dice, and into its players, whose lives on and off the field are far more real and satisfying to him than his own. Waugh's hold on his daily life is both enhanced (his sexual potency, in particular) and destroyed by his mania for the private baseball world. Eventually, he imagines his players to be reënacting religious rites as they rehearse ancient games their great-grandparents had participated in a century before. For Coover's central character baseball is the stuff of "heroes and history" that gives meaning and order to an otherwise chaotic world.

Roth constructs his wild Melvillean story through the memoirs of a veteran sportswriter, "Smitty" Word Smith, who pleads for recognition of the long-suppressed Patriot League, victim of the Communist witch hunts of the late 1940s. In so doing he unfolds the story of athletic demigods (Gil Gamesh, Frenchy Astarte, John Baal) in consciously, perhaps too self-consciously, mythic terms. Roth's athletes, who run the gamut from hero to scoundrel, dramatize the ancient human struggle between passionate desire and control, between individual expression and recognition of authority. It is a vivid testimony to the power of popular sports to provide an accessible framework for the imagination to build upon.

The great majority of examples we have surveyed has illustrated artists' interest in organized sports, particularly professional sports. But athletic activity, as we were reminded in the figure of the American frontiersman, is not limited to professionalism nor even to the playing field. The impulse to find satisfaction in the exercise of physical skills transcends organized sports. Athleticism in this more general sense is dramatically portrayed in James Dickey's *Deliverance* (1970), one novel that has not been betrayed in its film version. The leader of Dickey's weekend canoeists, Lewis Medlock, is a modern counterpart of the frontier hero, driven by the need to prove himself through his body, to handle all risks life hands him, and to court others. At the root of his craving for self-sufficiency, says his friend Ed Gentry, is the fact that "Lewis wanted to be immortal," and his strenuous life is a means of perpetuating that illusion. None of the participants in the grisly Cahulawassee canoe trip proves immortal, but Ed is able by means of his sudden courage and quiet heroism to wrest a kind of "deliverance" from the mundane that is the nearest approximation to immortality, perhaps, that the flesh can offer.

No twentieth-century writer has been more haunted by this notion of the stark challenge of life and of the necessity of the individual to look within himself for the courage and code to behave "well" than Ernest Hemingway, who not only wrote of athletes but acted out the rugged life personally. For him "grace under pressure" became the ultimate virtue. Pedro Romero, tenacious young matador of *The Sun Also Rises* (1926), furnishes a kind of salvation for himself which contrasts with the unredeemed life of the "lost-generation" pleasure-seekers around him. He has a meaningful craft; they have nothing so solid. Hemingway, however, is another writer who is interested in more than the professional athlete. In the short story "Big Two-Hearted River" (1925) he recounts how Nick Adams deals with the physical and emotional trauma of war through a careful return to the ritual of fishing in a Michigan stream. His old Cuban in *The Old Man and the Sea* (1952), eighty-four days without a fish, is a vivid symbol of the virtues of quiet fidelity and tenacity. In *The Sun Also Rises* Hemingway's Jake Barnes scoffs at Robert Cohn's pride in collegiate athletics—a way of scoffing in general at the rah-rah spirit of organized sport—but for Hemingway, the boxer, the hunter, the bullfighter, and the fisherman always remained images of courageous commitment.

Another compelling vision of life that relies on athletic metaphor is that found in William Faulkner's "The Bear" (1942). Faulkner's story is a complex telling of the alternately anguished and comic history of the McCaslin family. For Isaac McCaslin, who learns through his family's ledgers of the inhumanity of his slave-abusing grandfather, hunting trips into the Mississippi delta become a cleansing ritual. The wilderness, demanding competence and self-reliance, offers him an alternative to the human world of manipulation. Ike is especially fascinated as a boy by the mammoth emblem of the wilderness, Old Ben the bear. But Ike, though a hunter, does not seek to kill Old Ben. Instead he deliberately eschews gun, knife, and compass and pits his vulnerable wits and body against nature—and only then does he find his quarry. (Norman Mailer's *Why Are We In Vietnam?* (1967) also touches on the necessity for the human being's abandoning the instruments of his power over nature before he can experience the wild.) Ike's goal is deliverance, for his repudiation of power over nature and nature's creature is analogous to his repudiation of the land and dominion of the McCaslin family. If Ike McCaslin's renunciation is not entirely satisfactory to Faulkner, his courageous acceptance of physical challenge and desire to prove himself worthy rather than to acquire domination at the expense of others are compelling. Faulkner shows us something extraordinary in that dimension of athletics which is so easily forgotten in a world crowded by competitive sports and their trappings. Perhaps this is the most truly heroic version of the athlete after all.

American artists have given us a variety of athletic heroes. They have idealized the rugged, honorable competitor, and they have satirized organized sports as a degrading and inhuman institution. They have treated sports sentimentally, and they have unflinchingly exposed its vices. While our burgeoning interest in organized sport has been amply reflected in literature and film, our artists have not forgotten that athletic prowess involves more than successful competition in games. We may not have the simple faith in public heroes we once had, but undoubtedly the desire to locate heroism in athletes and athletics, defining those terms in the widest sense, has not disappeared from our world.

Sources and Suggested Readings

Chapin, Henry B. *Sports in Literature* (New York, 1978).

Coover, Robert. *The Universal Baseball Association, Inc., J. Henry Waugh, Prop.* (New York, 1968).

Higgs, Robert J. and Neil D. Isaacs, eds. *The Sporting Spirit: Athletes in Literature and Life* (New York, 1971).

Holtzman, Jerome. *Fielder's Choice: An Anthology of Baseball Fiction* (New York, 1979).

Hughes, Thomas. *Tom Brown's School Days* (London, 1857).

Lardner, Ring. *The Portable Ring Lardner.* Ed. Gilbert Seldes (New York, 1946).

Malamud, Bernard. *The Natural* (New York, 1952).

Roth, Philip. *The Great American Novel* (New York, 1973).

8

The Black Athlete in American Sports

William W. MacDonald

Someday the following question will grace the pages of some sports trivia book: What college football team was the last one to win the national championship without a single black on its roster? The answer, an astonishing one in this age of black prominence, is the University of Texas, which, having defeated Notre Dame in the Cotton Bowl, was crowned football's National Collegiate Athletic Association champion on January 1, 1970. That was just ten years ago, a decade, merely a few months in the long history of American sports. It is essentially an astounding revelation, for even to the casual observer, not to mention the dedicated fans, it is obvious that black Americans are a dominant force in American sports.

Black Americans comprise approximately eleven to twelve percent of the American population, but consider the following: more than seventy-five percent of the National Basketball Association's players are black; almost all of the superstars in that league are black; and one team, the New York Knickerbockers (significantly located in the most important communications center in the U.S.), has no white players at all. In the National Football League, almost fifty percent of the players, most of them "skilled" athletes like running backs, linebackers, and defensive backs, are black, and, more importantly, more than sixty-five percent of the 1981 "all-pro" players are black. In baseball blacks comprise *only* twenty percent of the major-league players, but those twenty percent exert an influence on the game exaggerated by their *meager* numbers. Moreover, blacks dominate college athletics as well, in numbers far out of proportion to the percentage of black students on campuses. Most of the records in the major sports, records in rushing, scoring, slugging, once held by such legendary white athletes as Red Grange, Babe Ruth, Ty Cobb, and Bob Pettit, have been broken, surpassed with a vengeance it should be added, by such potent black athletes as Earl Campbell, Henry Aaron, Lou Brock, and Kareem Abdul Jabbar. Black athletes, finally, have been responsible for many of the records of the Olympic

Games since Jesse Owens raced and leaped into history in the 1936 Berlin Olympics. As one envious European track coach observed at the 1976 Olympic Games in Montreal, "Without the blacks, the United States team would finish somewhere behind Ecuador."

Clearly one of the dominant themes in American sports since World War II has been the emergence of the black athlete. It is obvious that the black community in America is not just contributing more than its share of participants to sports; it is, in fact, contributing immensely more than its share of sports stars, such as the Reggie Jacksons, the O.J. Simpsons, the Jim Rices, the Hershel Walkers, the "Magic" Johnsons—the list is almost endless. An American would have to be color-blind not to see that blacks, on the surface, are superior athletes. This fact has not escaped the attention of white America, for it has been proclaimed in many national news publications, sanctified by sports magazines, whispered in sweaty locker rooms, and violently condemned in local taverns across the nation. Sports enthusiasts see what executives in Madison Avenue advertising agencies are just beginning to observe: black athletes are the new idols of American culture, superstars nonpareil, the dominant factor in American sports life. Blacks are the athletes who make the most money, lead their teams to victories and glory, set the style, and make the slang that somehow filters down to their less talented, less influential white teammates.

The image of the star athlete is increasingly the black image on a color television. But it is not just the black dominance that both fascinates and frightens white Americans; it is the way they dominate. It is not simply that blacks are superb athletes, for that is an obvious observation, but it is their flair, their style, their individualism in team sports that floats across the ambiguous images of blacks in white America. *Time* magazine recently wrote:

To say that Julius Erving jumps is to describe Beethoven as a guy who wrote music. Dr. J. ascends. He springs into the air at the foul line, floats down the side of the lane, holding the basketball in his right hand. Still airborne, he swivels, turns his back to the basket, switches the ball to his other hand and cleanly flips a soft, lefthanded hook shot into the net. On the floor, play resumes at a dazed half-speed as opposing players stand in disbelief.

When asked to comment on the inordinate number of blacks in professional sports, Lynn Swann, the gifted wide-receiver of the Pittsburgh Steelers, commented, "If I said that blacks were not athletically superior, I think I'd be kidding myself. There is something there. It seems like the black athletes are just able to do more things than the other athletes." Joe Morgan, the National League's Most Valuable Player in 1975 and 1976, has echoed Swann's thoughts, observing that blacks have more speed, quickness, and agility. Baseball, basketball, and football, said Morgan, "put a premium on those skills. I don't know the reasons why, but we are clearly superior in that way." And the extraordinary Julius Erving, the subject of *Time's* breathless prose, argues that jumping, an integral aspect of basketball, is an ability that can be developed by practice and that Bobby Jones, his teammate on the Philadelphia 76ers, is an exceptional jumper "for a white guy." Erving quickly adds, however, that most basketball players who cannot jump well suffer from "white guy's disease," and that whites simply aren't comparable to blacks "like myself who can jump and do something else while they're in the air."

Despite *Time's* adulatory prose, despite the good Doctor's congratulatory hyperbole, the fact remains that black Americans are *the* force in American sports as never before. It is important here to point out that when we speak of American sports, we are speaking of baseball, basketball, and football. For despite Lee Elder, Arthur Ashe, and Althea Gibson, blacks have had little impact on golf or tennis, the other two highly profitable sports in America, and virtually no significant influence on skiing, swimming, ice hockey, and a host of lesser participatory sports—perhaps because of economic, cultural, and environmental factors. But does the obvious superiority of so many black athletes in the more visible major sports mean that blacks are better athletes than whites, and, if so, why? The fact that little research has been done on the questions has not stopped fans from giving answers, from the blacks' inverted racism, like that of Swann, to white coaches' images of blacks having the ability to relax, to hang loose—"you know, they hang everything loose. They walk loose, they are loose, they dance loose. You can see it easily in their dancing." Sometimes simple, succinct comments appear to resolve the problem. For example, Jerry West, perhaps the greatest white basketball player ever, said of black dominance in college and professional basketball: "They're quicker, faster; they jump better; they seem to do everything a little bit better."

On a more scholarly level, sociologists, economists, psychiatrists, anthropologists have seriously analyzed the black phenomenon but arrived, at best, at tentative or contradictory conclusions. L. L. Holloman, a white psychiatrist, has suggested revenge, compensation, and a desire to identify with the white race as the motivating factors behind the black's success in athletics. Alvin Pouissant, black psychiatrist and Dean of Students at Harvard Medical School, on the other hand, views the dismal Darwinian selectivity of slavery as responsible for the black phenomenon in sports. First of all, Pouissant argues, "they selected for slavery only those with a lot of brawn and ability to work hard: only the best. Second, only the strongest survived the long voyage. We may already have a very selected group of blacks in this country." There is, indeed, a grim element of fact to Pouissant's theory, for it has been estimated that five percent of the slaves captured in Africa died on the harsh marches to the coast; another fiteen percent died during the passage on the slave ships; another thirty percent died during the "seasoning" process, the three- or four-year period during which a slave was broken in to work in the fields. Thus for every two blacks condemned to slavery, only one survived to labor in the New World.

Even after slavery ended with the Civil War, a black had very little to which he could aspire. Sports have always been a great leveler, a great equalizer, a tool used by all minorities in the U.S. to fight their way out of the ghettoes and into the mainstream of American life. In *Organized Sports in Industrial America* (1965), J. R. Betts has persuasively argued that nowhere has the process of American egalitarianism been more prevalent than in American sports, and nowhere has Betts's dictum been better exemplified than in black America. As one black coach expressed it so well in "The Black Athlete—A Shameful Story" *(Sports Illustrated)*, "A white kid tries to become president of the U.S. while a black kid tries to become Willie Mays."

Black sociologist Harry Edwards, author of an astute critique of racism in American sports and leader of the black athletes' revolt that culminated in the much-publicized open rebellion of black athletes in the 1968 Olympic Games in Mexico City, has correctly observed that for the white athlete the alternatives have obviously been greater, and thus whites do not have to channel all of their energies into one particular area. With the channeling of black athletes disproportionately into sports, the result is the same as it would be if blacks were taught and studied nothing but the English language. Suppose that only blacks, Edwards argues, attended the University of California at Berkeley "as a result of some ruthless recruitment process where everyone who couldn't read or write well was eliminated at elementary level from age six all the way through junior college. It would only be a short time before the greatest prose—the greatest innovations in teaching, learning and writing English—came out of Berkeley. It is the inevitable result of all this talent channeled into a single area. The white athlete who might be an O.J. Simpson is probably sitting behind a desk."

Research scientists, though reluctant to tangle with the controversial subject in this volatile age of black rebellion in the inner cities of the U.S. and increased klan activities in rural America, have nevertheless discovered measurable differences between whites and blacks that might account for the black dominance in American sports. Modern scholars, basing most of their research on the pioneering work of Dr. Eleanor Metheny, who conducted careful anthropomorphic studies of American blacks more than forty years ago, have discovered that the black American tends to have a shorter trunk, a more slender pelvis, larger arms (especially forearms) and longer legs (especially from the knees down) than his white counterpart. His bones are denser and, therefore, heavier than those of whites. He has more muscle in the upper arms and legs, less in the calves. His fat distribution is patterned differently from that of the white man, that is, lesser in the extremities but not much different in the trunk. And there is a trace of evidence, but just a trace, because this aspect has been studied so little that it is still in the highly speculative state, that the black man's adrenal glands, a vital factor in many sports, are larger than the white man's. Subsequent research, while severely limited, has essentially confirmed Metheny's conclusions. In the 1960 Olympic Games, Dr. J. M. Tanner used x-rays and photographs to study more than 125 black athletes, and his findings, published in *The Physique of the Olympic Athlete* (1961), concluded that "amongst competitors in both track and field events there were large significant racial differences in leg length, arm length and hip width." Dr. Allan Ryan, editor of *The Physician and Sportsmedicine*, has studied the problem thoroughly, and his conclusions have demonstrated that black athletes have a greater leg-to-trunk-length ratio than

The Harlem Globetrotters playing an outdoor game in Austria. *(National Archives)*

whites, a ratio which gives them an advantage in activities requiring explosive force, such as sprinting and jumping.

The debate rages and will undoubtedly continue to rage. Whatever the reasons for black excellence in athletics, the surpassing skill is evident. It is especially evident to young black males. For most of them sports are their way out of the despair of the slums, a route to special privileges among their peers, and sometimes a way to fabulous wealth. Few other roads to fame and financial rewards have been open to the young black American. But sports in recent years, especially the last thirty years, have opened some very special doors. Every black male child, no matter how much he might be discouraged from a professional career with a Wall Street brokerage firm or IBM or General Motors, knows that he has a sporting chance in baseball, football, and basketball.

That sporting chance, that uniquely American concept of the American dream, has not always been there for black Americans. Indeed, professional sports are still a novelty to blacks, and blacks are still a novelty to professional sports. For several decades after their legal emancipation from slavery in 1863, black athletes plodded along in relative obscurity, mere oddities in white America's sporting life. In football and baseball, the two popular new

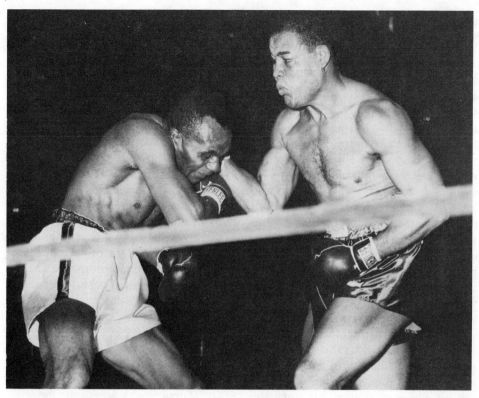

Joe Louis fighting Jersey Joe Walcott in Madison Square Garden in 1947. *(National Archives)*

sports of the late nineteenth century, a few sons of wealthy black families in the North managed to play for college varsities. But these young men, like W. C. Matthews who played for Harvard or George Jewett who played for Michigan, came from a rare and privileged class of blacks. Other black athletes were reduced to entertaining whites who paid to watch the "darkies" clown around just as the plantation slaves had done in the ante-bellum South. Nearly all the best Eastern summer resorts had teams of such performers, composed of busboys, gardeners, and waiters from the hotel staff. Black waiters of the Argyle Hotel in Babylon, Long Island, formed the first team, calling themselves the Cuban Giants and speaking a gibberish on the field that was supposed to pass for Spanish. "They are comical cusses with a natural sense of mimicry," observed a writer for *Munsey's Magazine* in 1882. "They are managed by a darkie, Frank Thompson, and they give a fine performance, worth the price of admission. They do not take the game of baseball as seriously as white folks do, but they are very innovative and they amuse." The Cuban Giants amused by rolling their eyeballs, flashing their teeth, and strutting about shamelessly. "We hated some of the shameful things that circumstances forced us to do," wrote George Johnson of the Giants at the turn of the century. "But there was no real choice. To survive, we often gave the white public exactly what they wanted. We also played some damn good baseball." The same words would be used to describe the antics of the Harlem Globetrotters, but they would be used after World War II!

Only two black athletes achieved success and fame in America prior to World War I. The first was Jack Johnson, the flamboyant, audacious, provocative heavyweight boxing champion who outraged white America for almost two decades simply by insisting on his full rights as a human being when most blacks, like Booker T. Washington, thought it best to be discreetly submissive. Johnson flaunted his success, taunted his white opponents in the ring, and destroyed a host of "great white hopes" who were pressed into service to restore white supremacy in boxing. Johnson acted just as if he were a white champion, a factor that produced an astonishing hatred that would intensify until it destroyed not only the boxer but the man as well. He made no secret of his tastes: he liked white women, and rather than just sleeping with them, he married them. It was the marriages to the white women that did Johnson in, for he was eventually arrested on charges of immorality, jumped bail, spent years in exile in Europe, lost his championship to the white boxer Jess Williard in Havana, and, finally, spent a year in Federal prison upon his return to the U.S. in 1920. He ended his career in failure as an exhibit in Hubert's Celebrated Museum and Flea Circus, amusing tourists who wandered through New York's Times Square.

Jack Johnson was the most notorious black athlete of his era; but he was not the most successful one. That athlete was Isaac Murphy, the greatest jockey of his day, the man who rode three winners in the Kentucky Derby, setting a record that stood until the 1960s. Murphy was accepted, indeed, honored by white America; he became rich, owned horses; he died wealthy and respected. His success undoubtedly inspired many other blacks, for thoroughbred racing was dominated by black jockeys during the late nineteenth century. In the first twenty-five runnings of the Kentucky Derby, black jockeys brought in fifteen winners. Willie Simms, a black jockey who was a two-time winner of the Derby and a three-time winner of the Belmont Stakes, was the first American to win a race in England. But just as quickly as black jockeys rode to fame, they departed. By the 1920s it was rare to see a black face in a jockey's quarter. "They came and they dominated," said another famous black jockey, Jimmy Winkfield in 1923. "Then colored kids just stopped thinking about horses. That's all there was to it." It wasn't quite as simple as Winkfield described it, for blacks' history in American sports has always been a reflection of blacks in American society as a whole. Between 1890 and 1920, for example, the "Jim Crow" laws, which effectively segregated blacks from whites in American society, drifted into American sports. "Separate but equal" became the law of the land in the South and the unwritten law in American sports; the fact that it was separate but unequal, unjust, and unconstitutional bothered only black Americans. Nowhere was this inequality more apparent than in the most important sport of all, American baseball.

Although it may surprise many Americans, black participation in major-league baseball goes back to the 1880s. When Jackie Robinson's features

were cast in bronze and the bust fastened to the wall at the Baseball Hall of
Fame in Cooperstown, New York, it was necessary to note that "Robinson
was the first *modern* black to play in the major leagues." The Walker brothers, Fleetwood and Welday, had preceded Robinson by some sixty years.
Both were members of the Toledo Mudhens of the American Association, at
that time ranked as a major league. There were approximately twenty black
men earning their living in professional baseball at this time, the Walkers in
the major leagues and the rest in the minors. After winning more than thirty-
five games for the Newark Giants, a black club, George Stovey, a black
pitcher, was purchased by the all-white New York Giants. It was here that a
pivotal event occurred that entrenched black-white relations in American
sports for more than half a century. Adrian "Cap" Anson of the Chicago
White Stockings, a legendary figure in American baseball history, strongly
and loudly denounced the Giants' signing of Stovey and threatened to boycott baseball. The National League surrendered to Anson's prejudices, and
Stovey was banned from baseball. When the Chicago team came to play
Toledo, it was Anson again who doomed the Walker brothers, for he refused
to take the field until they were banished. The Walkers did not play that
day, and in less than a week they were gone from baseball entirely. No one
has ever really adequately explained why Anson, born and reared in an all-
white town in Iowa, harbored such hatred for blacks. But his influence on
baseball and on black-white relations in organized sports in the U.S. in the
1880s was enormous, for by the 1890s the color line had been drawn in
major-league baseball.

The antipathy of white ball players toward blacks was a significant factor in the eventual elimination of blacks from the major leagues. The following, though undoubtedly exaggerated, is a fairly good, if not harrowing,
description of how most whites viewed black ballplayers. White ballplayers,
wrote shortstop Ed Williamson in 1891:

. . . do not burn with a desire to have colored men on the team. It is, in fact, the deep-
seated objection that most of them have for an Afro-American professional player that
gave rise to the 'feet-first' slide. You may have noticed in a close play that the base-
runner will launch himself into the air and take chances on landing on the bag. Some go
head first, others with the feet in advance. Those who adopt the latter method are prin-
cipally old-timers and served in the dark days prior to 1880. They learned the trick in the
East. The Buffaloes—I think it was the Buffalo team—had a negro for second base. He was
a few lines blacker than a raven, but he was one of the best players in the old Eastern
League. The haughty Caucasians of the association were willing to permit darkies to carry
water to them or guard the bat bag, but it made them sore to have the name of one on
the batting list. They made a cabal against this man and incidentally introduced a new
feature into the game. The players of the opposing team made it their special business in
life to 'spite' this brunette Buffalo. They would tarry at second base when they might
easily have made third, just to toy with the sensitive shins of the second baseman. The
poor man played in two games out of five perhaps; the rest of the time he was on
crutches. To give the frequent spiking of the darky an appearance of accident the 'feet-
first' slide was practiced. The negro got wooden armor for his legs and went into the
field with the appearance of a man wearing nail kegs for stockings. The enthusiasm of
opposition players would not let them take a bluff. They filed their spikes and the first
man at second generally split the wooden half cylinders. The colored man seldom lasted

Fritz Pollard, a member of the 1916 Brown University Rose Bowl team. He was the first black to coach in what became the National Football League.
(Brown University)

beyond the fifth inning, as the base-runners became more expert. The practice survived long after the second baseman made his last trip to the hospital.

This hatred of blacks, this antipathy toward black Americans, fanned by white politicians in the South and eventually legalized in the infamous "Jim Crow" laws, set in throughout the nation, and blacks were driven from baseball as well as from such diverse occupations as horse racing and barbering.

Banned from the major leagues, American blacks formed their own baseball league. The Cuban Giants became so famous that nearly every black club borrowed their nickname—the Mohawk Giants, the Page Fence Giants, the Baltimore Elite Giants, the Lincoln Giants, the Brooklyn Royal Giants, and many others. Most of these teams barnstormed throughout the nation. Some of the black ballplayers were paid well, but most were not. The really great black baseball clubs, like the Homestead Grays and the Kansas City Monarchs, received little publicity. White sports writers, when they deigned to write at all about the Black Leagues, referred in print to the "coon" and "nigger" leagues. But the black clubs had some brilliant ball players on their rosters, men like "Cool Papa" Bell, an outfielder, Josh Gibson, reputed to be the greatest catcher ever, and the legendary Satchel Paige. Some of these players are familiar to American sports fans, primarily because there is at present a special committee of baseball writers who vote to allow these former black stars to enter baseball's Hall of Fame. But most of the blacks who played in the old Negro leagues are just names, men who played in relative obscurity, faceless players in the history of American sports. There are, however, plans to build a Baseball Hall of History for black players who were barred from playing in the major leagues. The Hall will be housed in Ashland, Kentucky, where a million-dollar building has been donated.

Certainly many of the black stars in the Negro leagues would have been stars in the majors. Walter Johnson, one of the greatest pitchers in the history of baseball, told reporters in the 1920s that he had seen black pitchers better than he, like "Cyclone" Joe Williamson, a huge right-handed pitcher from Texas, and "Red Ant" Wickware of the Mohawk Giants. "If his hair wasn't curly and his skin too bronze," Johnson said, "this fellow Williamson would be the very best there is. . . . It is a shame these fine fellows do not get a chance to show their wares in the same competition as the rest of us." Shameful as it was, few people in white America really paid much attention, and thus several generations of brilliant black players were lost to baseball and almost to history. It made no difference to baseball that other sports survived from what can best be described as "token" integration of their sports. Fritz Pollard of Brown University, for example, played for Akron in 1920, the first year for what would become the National Football League. "Rube" Marshall also played in 1920 with the Cleveland Indians. Paul Robeson, of Rutgers University, the future great opera star, is credited with a 1920 start, but he did not actually play for Akron until 1921. Pollard, incidentally, was the first and only black head coach in the NFL, with the Milwaukee Badgers in 1922 and the Hammond (Indiana) Pros in 1923-25.

The long hiatus for blacks in professional sports came to an end after World War II. In 1946 William "Dolly" King, star basketball player for the all-black New York Rens, signed with the Rochester Royals and became the first black to play in the National Basketball Association. The flood of black players in the NBA followed. In that same year, the Los Angeles Rams, just moved west from Cleveland, signed black stars, Kenny Washington and Woody Strode; a couple of weeks later the Cleveland Browns signed Marion Motley and Bill Willis. Literally thousands of black superstar football players in the NFL followed. And, finally, in 1947 Jackie Robinson, perhaps the most important black athlete in the long history of black Americans in American sports, took the field for the National League's Brooklyn Dodgers and became the first modern black to play baseball in the major leagues; in that same year, Larry Doby was signed by the Cleveland Indians and eventually became the first black to play in the American League. Robinson's signing was certainly the single most important event in the history of the black athlete, for it broke (destroyed would be a better word) the color barrier in American sports, and, as they say, the rest is history. The Negro leagues were quickly "raided" of their baseball stars, and a deluge of superbly talented black athletes followed Robinson's trailblazing path. When Dr. J. B. Martin, president of the Negro American League, was asked if he felt bitterness that the major leagues were taking his players and thus helping to destroy his league, he replied, "When Negro players got into the big leagues, people said it would hurt Negro baseball. I said, 'Let it hurt it.' When we had an entire Negro outfield—Henry Aaron, Frank Robinson, Willie Mays—on the National League team in the All Star game, well, my chest kind of poked out. I was happy to know it." White owners and white fans alike were happy as well, for they quickly discovered that when it came to winning, black was indeed beautiful. Segregation of black Americans on the playing fields of American sports is dead, gone, finished; but segregation where the real power resides in American sports, ownership and management, is still prevalent, despite the occasional signing of blacks, like Bill Russell, Maury Wills, and

Frank Robinson, to coach and manage professional clubs.

The success of the black athlete in America is undoubtedly greater than Branch Rickey, Brooklyn's general manager in 1947, could have conceived on that day in the 1940s when he was inspired to introduce to baseball's cloistered world the talents of Jackie Robinson. But there is the rub, for the very success of the black athlete has created very special problems for black Americans. Black athletic success has served to focus aspirations of the black community on athletes, a trend that many scholars and black athletes themselves believe is severely limiting the potential of many young black Americans. The most influential black spokesman for this conviction is tennis player Arthur Ashe, the present captain of the American Davis Cup team. In a recent open letter to all blacks in the *New York Times*, Ashe explained the bleak prospects of a young black earning a living as a professional athlete, pointing out the chances are worse than one thousand to one. Unfortunately, Ashe wrote, the blacks' most vividly recognized "role models are athletes and entertainers—runnin' and jumpin' and singin' and dancin'." While blacks are more than seventy-five percent of the NBA, they are less than four percent of the doctors and lawyers in the U.S., less than two percent of the engineers, less than ten percent of construction workers. Ashe urged black parents to instill a desire for education alongside the desire to be Julius Erving and issued a challenge to young blacks to spend two hours in the library for every hour on the athletic field. Ashe concluded that blacks have won their fight, a long, arduous fight to be sure, to compete equally on the playing fields of America with white athletes. But "we have been on the same roads—sports and entertainment—too long. We need to pull over, fill up at the library and speed away to Congress and the Supreme Courts, the unions and the business world." If young blacks consider Ashe's advice, the race to success, if the race in sports is indicative, may very well result in some major black victories in middle-class white America.

Sources and Suggested Readings

Batchelor, Denzil. *Jack Johnson and His Times* (London, 1956).

Bontemps, A.W. *Famous Negro Athletes* (New York, 1964).

Chalk, Oceana. *Pioneers of Black Sports* (New York, 1975).

_____. *Black College Sport* (New York, 1976).

Edwards, Harry. *The Revolt of the Black Athlete* (New York, 1969).

_____. *The Sociology of Sports* (Homewood, Ill., 1973).

Henderson, E.B. *The Negro in Sports* (Washington, 1949).

_____, editor. *The Black Athlete: Emergence and Arrival* (New York, 1976).

Nelson, R.B. *The Negro in Athletics* (New York, 1940).

Ribalou, H.U. *The Negro in American Sports* (New York, 1954).

Robinson, Jackie. *I Never Had it Made* (New York, 1972).

Young, A.S. *Negro Firsts in Sports* (Chicago, 1973).

_____. "The Black Athlete in the Golden Age of Sports," *Ebony* (Oct., 1969 to Dec., 1971).

Part III

Changes and Challenges

1950 to present

From the time that North Korean soldiers crossed the 38th parallel, sparking a major international conflict, until ex-President Carter flew to Germany to greet the recently released American hostages returning from Iran, America has experienced the strains and tensions of a nation that has assumed the role of leader of the Western World. Since 1950, the U.S. has expanded its influence and power around the globe in response to what it has perceived to be a Soviet attempt at world conquest. As leader of the so-called Free World, America has accepted challenges and responsibilities which have tested not only its economic and military might but also its domestic institutions and way of life. Many nations look to America to set standards of equality and justice in domestic affairs which will offer an attractive alternative to the communist system. In addition to these international pressures, the accelerated pace of industrial life in recent years has created new problems or intensified old ones. Advances in communications, transportation, technology, and business management have transformed and, in some cases, destabilized American society. The combination of increased responsibilities abroad and dramatic changes at home has forced Americans of this generation to meet new challenges and seek solutions to the recurring problems of industrial society.

Since 1950 the American economy has expanded and changed rapidly. In the first essay of this section, Harry Jebsen, Jr., a social historian, traces the impact of this rapid business growth on professional athletics. He maintains that pro sports have followed the general trends of expansion, collective bargaining for labor, increased corporate control, and government subsidies, which are apparent in the larger society. Jebsen concludes that by any standards professional sport is big business.

In the second essay, Joan S. Hult and Roberta J. Park, professors of Physical Education, examine the role of women in sports. They trace the evolution of the place of American women in athletics, focusing most of their essay on the recent era when women's rights has become a potent political issue. Hult and Park conclude that a variety of social forces crystallizing after World War II forced government and women's athletic organizations to accept a more competitive role for women in sports. They also highlight courageous individuals such as "Babe" Didrikson Zaharias and Billie Jean King, who led the movement for women's rights in sports.

One of the great problems of modern mass society has been the increase in violence and disrespect for the law. In the third essay, Douglas A. Noverr and Lawrence E. Ziewacz, specialists in American studies, focus on the subject of violence and sports. Drawing on research for their forthcoming book, *The Games They Played: American Sports and Culture, 1865-1980* (Nelson-Hall), they examine the forces that have caused sports violence both on the field and in the stands. Sports violence, they conclude, is only symptomatic of the prevalence of violence and aggression in American society as a whole. Perhaps the solution to the problem of athletic violence is self-regulation within the sports establishment spurred on by threatened Federal regulation in that area.

The concluding essays in this section place emphasis on sports and America's expanding international activity in the last three decades. William J. Miller, a sports historian and Far Eastern specialist, examines how U.S. sports, particularly baseball, basketball, and volleyball, have helped to shape America's image overseas. He concludes that the impact of "America's sports empire" has had both positive and negative results with regard to U.S. prestige abroad. Finally, William J. Baker and John M. Carroll analyze America's role in the modern Olympic movement. While politics have always been a part of the Olympic Games, the authors maintain that since the beginning of the Cold War this tendency has increased. In recent years, the Olympics have become as much politics as sport.

9

The Big Business of Sports

Harry Jebsen, Jr.

In the film version of Pete Gent's *North Dallas Forty* (1979), Phil Elliott, the disillusioned wide receiver, is having a conversation with team owner, Conrad Hunter. The owner proudly shows Elliott a mosaic tree on the office wall. The symbolism of a tree (Hunter Enterprises) and its branches (the individual family businesses) is not lost on the wide receiver. Along with separate branches for electronics, oil, and construction is a football team, the North Dallas Bulls. Hunter proclaims that "There is not one damned corporation I own which means as much to me as my football team," and viewer and Elliott quickly realize that while the team is only a small part of the huge conglomerate, it is the most glamorous.

William Wrigley, chewing-gum millionaire and owner of the Chicago Cubs, said often that "Baseball is too much of a business to be a sport, and too much of a sport to be a business." His cross-town rival, Bill Veeck, who twice owned the Chicago White Sox as well as two other American League clubs, ridiculed the illusion that sport is sport and business is business. In *The Hustlers' Handbook* (1965) he wrote: "No one really believes that baseball isn't a business, not you or me or Anna Maria Alberghetti. What we really believe is that baseball is entitled to its special exemption because of its special character and the special position which it holds in national life." Veeck's unromanticized view of sport challenges the preconceived notions of many Americans who believe that sport deserves a privileged status in society. However, sport as a vital part of contemporary society has continually interacted with the various forces which have molded modern America.

A cursory look at sports journals and daily newspapers convinces the reader that the tensions which exist in modern team sports derive from the incredible influence which big business has had on professional athletics. Several themes dominate the contemporary sports pages together with the box scores, game reports, and player transactions. For example, franchises have been bought and sold frequently. Owners, therefore, have become a

102   dramatic part of the game. Leagues have found it profitable to expand into markets which previously had been considered too small to support a team. New leagues have challenged the supremacy of Major League Baseball, the National Football League, the National Hockey League, and the National Basketball Association. The rapid proliferation of franchises across the nation has become the most salient theme in the business of sport.

The expansion of modern professional sports brought several side effects which have caused considerable changes in the structure of modern athletics. Television has created more fans and larger sources of money for owners and players. The athletes, realizing the special regard which the public holds for them as well as the general trend toward the protection of individual rights, have achieved higher salaries and greater freedom. Owners have been able to coax, coerce, and sometimes bludgeon local governments into building new facilities in "better" neighborhoods in order to keep or obtain a sporting franchise. The business element in sport has effectively stimulated greater interest in the sports as well as profits for the owners while at the same time greatly altering modern sports.

Twentieth-century Americans tried to curtail the influence of big business during the early 1900s and in the 1930s, but neither attempt fully succeeded. Large corporations and conglomerates, which combined activities from several fields of production under one organization, became the dominant element in American business. These corporations made use of mass advertising campaigns and the ability to sell a quality product at a cheaper price to weaken regional or small competitors.

Congress as well as the executive branch, fearing the concentration of power in the hands of large businesses, increased its own regulatory power. Judicial decisions, legislation, and executive orders appeared to counterbalance the influence of big business. Government played an increasing role as arbiter in the conflicts which existed between adversary elements of the business world.

Sport has in fact experienced the same process. Roger Noll, editor of *Government and the Sports Business* (1974), defines a professional sports league as "a cartel, with the purpose of restricting competition and dividing markets among firms of the industry." This allows three of the most vital aspects of league operations to be directly controlled by central management: the acquisition and disposition of players, the direct control of marketing rights, and the location of franchises. Baseball's internal control over these aspects of business has been more complete than in the other sports. By winning the *Federal Baseball* case (1922), baseball gained complete exemption from antitrust law and thus became a self-regulating monopoly. Since then court cases, including *Flood* v. *Kuhn* (1972), have upheld this special status. In these cases, the courts generally point out that legislation is required to correct *Federal Baseball*. In two cases in the 1950s, the *United States* v. *International Boxing Club of New York* (1955) and *Radovich* v. *NFL* (1957), the court refused to extend to boxing and football respectively the same antitrust exemption which baseball had. Thus other professional

Bill Veeck, one of the most colorful and imaginative clubowners in major-league history. *(Chicago White Sox Baseball Club)*

sports, though operated in a manner similar to baseball, have been subject to antitrust law.

The thriving postwar American economy combined with ample leisure time to allow citizens to become avid consumers of professional sports. The availability of fans eager to spend money to attend games prodded investors into the formation of new leagues and an expansion of existing ones. Although only fifty-two franchises existed in 1950, ninety-six have survived the frantic expansion of the 1960s and 1970s. At the end of World War II, professional sports were confined largely to the East and Midwest, but the growth of franchises in the Sunbelt and along the West Coast followed the tremendous rush of people and business activity into those areas.

When the war ended, baseball with its two eight-team leagues still dominated professional sports. Franchises ranged from Boston as far west as St. Louis. Teams still traveled by train and played most games during the day. The return of stars from the war, notably, Ted Williams, Joe DiMaggio, and Stan Musial, brought people back to the ballparks. For example, the Yankees' attendance jumped from 800,000 in 1945 to 2,000,000 in 1946.

Professional sports began its shift into new regions immediately after the war. The All-American Football Conference, a challenger to the National Football League, established franchises in Los Angeles and San Francisco. Major-league baseball, however, still avoided the West Coast, though the troubled St. Louis Browns made an attempt to move there in 1942. Because of daily play and long travel time to the West Coast, major-league baseball delayed its western migration until 1957.

Baseball had not moved a major-league franchise in fifty years when in 1953, the Boston Braves, who had won a pennant as recently as 1948, shifted to Milwaukee. Bill Veeck then tried to move his Browns from St. Louis to Baltimore, but American League owners, who disliked Veeck's promotional activities which included using a midget as a pinch hitter, refused to approve a shift until he sold the team to Baltimore investors in 1954. Another weak American League franchise, the Philadelphia A's, shifted to Kansas City the next season. Three cities which had supported two franchises were now left with one each. Still, the biggest franchise shift was not orchestrated until 1957. Walter O'Malley, owner of the Brooklyn Dodgers, attempted to convince New York authorities to build a new stadium to replace venerable Ebbets Field. After four fruitless years of negotiations, O'Malley announced in February of 1957 the purchase of the Los Angeles territory and its minor-league team from William Wrigley. Knowing that the National League would not approve his unilateral shift to the West Coast, he convinced his friend, Horace Stoneham, owner of the New York Giants, to move to San Francisco. New York, which had had three teams since the early 1900s, opened the 1958 season with only the Yankees.

By the 1960s team shifts became common. In 1961 two franchises were added to each league. New York received the Mets, a team which the city immediately took to its heart despite its inept play. Houston also obtained a National League franchise. The American League moved the Washington Senators to Minneapolis and then replaced them in Washington with an expansion "Senators" in addition to moving a team into the Los Angeles market. The American League has added four new teams since 1961 and has moved several others. In the late 1960s the National League shifted a franchise from Milwaukee to Atlanta and then expanded to Montreal and San Diego. As air travel increased the number of sites available for franchises and as profitable new markets seemed ready for major-league clubs, the status quo which had prevailed between 1903 and 1953 was shattered. The major leagues eagerly took advantage of new opportunities and resolutely fought their detractors. They quickly stifled any hopes which the abortive Continental League had in the mid-1960s. Baseball offered the public more night games during the week, expanded television coverage, and moved into commodious new stadia. Thus, while baseball faced challenges to its dominance seriously, it reacted strongly to maintain its profitability. Other sports played primarily in fall and winter acquired strong followings, and baseball ultimately had to share the spotlight and sports dollar, but it did so begrudgingly.

Football, basketball, and hockey tapped the wave of enthusiasm for spectator sports. When new leagues challenged the supremacy of the existing leagues, the latter did not take the challenge lightly. The threat of new organizations taking over prime markets caused the older leagues to expand. The resultant proliferation of leagues caused a rush of new franchises, many of which failed. The steady growth indicated in Chart 1 does not show the number of franchises which failed to survive through the decades. It also does not show the many franchises in the North American Soccer League, which has become a viable part of American sport.

CHART NUMBER 1

NUMBER OF PROFESSIONAL SPORTS FRANCHISES

	1950	1960	1970	1980
National Basketball Association	17	8	12	23*
American Basketball Association			11	
National Football League	13	14	26**	28
American Football League		8		
American League	8	8	12	14
National League	8	8	12	12
National Hockey League	6	6	12	21***
	52	52	85	98

*Includes four teams merged from the American Basketball Association.
**Includes all teams from the American Football League.
***Includes four teams merged from the World Hockey Association.

The sport which prospered and expanded most rapidly since 1945 was professional football, which now challenges major-league baseball as the "national pastime." Several plausible explanations for football's exceptional growth are possible. The hard-hitting, controlled violence of the game has been attractive to a society taught to be nonviolent. Allen Guttmann in *From Ritual to Record* (1978) finds that football is more attuned to modern urban society than the more passive baseball, which appealed to small-town society. One simple yet seemingly credible explanation is the tie between football and American education. Football is the key game of the high schools and colleges, and that relationship carries over to the professional game.

The expansion of professional football began in 1946 when the All-American Football Conference challenged the National Football League

106   (NFL). In 1949 three franchises from the All-American Conference, two from the West Coast, joined the established league. The sport grew steadily throughout the 1950s with the aid of limited television coverage. By the late 1950s, expanded telecasting by the networks stimulated fan interest. The 1958 championship game between the New York Giants and the Baltimore Colts marked a turning point in the professional game. The overtime victory of the Johnny Unitas-led Colts on a cold, snowy December afternoon in New York proved the qualities of the game to modern Americans. It became so popular that by 1961 Lamar Hunt spearheaded a group of investors, many of whom had been unable to purchase an NFL team, who organized the American Football League (AFL). Television's thirst for more football, the wide-open style of play in the AFL, and the 1961 Federal Sports Broadcasting Act, which allowed leagues to sell all rights as a package through the league office, enticed the ABC network to pick up AFL games. Since 1970 all three major networks have telecast NFL games to a public which eagerly supports franchises with overflow crowds and high television ratings. This television monopoly became a primary factor in preventing the World Football League from successfully challenging the NFL in 1974-1975.

Professional basketball had yet to achieve a solid organization when World War II ended. The public's desire for more professional sport was met by investors willing to field basketball teams. The National Basketball Association (NBA) came into existence in 1949 when the National Basketball League and the Basketball Association of America merged. Professional basketball had been loosely organized with teams from Sheboygan, Wisconsin, and Fort Wayne, Indiana, competing with teams from New York, Boston, and Chicago. The league struggled through the 1950s, averaging less than 3,000 fans per game. AAU basketball, which was then sponsored entirely by large corporations such as Phillips Petroleum, Peoria Caterpillar, Vickers Petroleum, and Goodyear Rubber, challenged the professional circuit in popularity and the quality of players. By 1959, the NBA had only eight teams, and all were located in large cities. The league solidified in the 1960s and expanded to cities across the nation. Since then two leagues have challenged the NBA. The American Basketball League survived only two years in the early 1960s, while the American Basketball Association withstood many franchise problems until four of its teams were absorbed into the NBA in 1976. While both challengers had many quality players, they lacked consistent attendance, a television contract, and the dominating centers which have been an attraction of NBA play.

The National Hockey League (NHL) failed to expand until the late 1960s when it began a rapid multiplication of new franchises. The six teams which had comprised the league since 1942 allowed no expansion until 1967, when membership doubled. Competition from the World Hockey Association convinced NHL leaders to continue expansion and finally to absorb four franchises in 1979 from the rapidly fading World Hockey Association. This brought the number of NHL franchises to twenty-one in the United States and Canada.

CHART NUMBER 2
NEW SPORTS LEAGUES SINCE 1945

NEW LEAGUES	FATE OF THE LEAGUE
All-American Football Conference, 1946-1949	Three teams merged with NFL
American Football League, 1961-1970	All teams merged with NFL
American Basketball League, 1961-1962	Disbanded
American Basketball Association, 1967-1976	Four teams merged with NBA
World Hockey Association, 1972-1979	Four teams merged with NHL
World Football League, 1974-1975	Disbanded

The rapid multiplication of franchises failed to dampen the value of teams in any of the sports. In fact, franchise values increased tremendously through the 1960s and 1970s. The rapid escalation of team values has narrowed the range of potential owners, concentrating activity in the portfolios of those with established wealth. Ownership of teams by sportsmen, families, or those with limited resources has become difficult. Calvin Griffith, whose family has owned the American League Minnesota Twins (previously Washington Senators) since 1903, runs a family business without additional investments. He now finds it difficult to compete with franchises supported by corporate wealth. Successful family-owned franchises, most notably the O'Malleys' Los Angeles Dodgers and the Halas family's Chicago Bears, were purchased prior to the rapid escalation in franchise values.

Corporate ownership has become far more common. Conglomerates which own major sports franchises include Gulf and Western, Anheuser-Busch, and Warner Communications. Some investors directly tie their franchises into their other businesses. Ted Turner, owner of the Atlanta Braves and Atlanta Hawks, for example, bought the baseball and basketball teams to anchor his cable television station, which is marketed nationally. Often ownership of franchises by business magnets reflects their desire to be in the national spotlight. As Conrad Hunter, the fictional owner in *North Dallas Forty* noted, the modern sports team is a most glamorous investment which provides exposure unavailable to the average corporate executive. Ownership of a franchise has become as much a gratification of vanity for the rich as an investment of their wealth.

Owners have not been the only ones who have profited from the expansion of modern professional sports. Players have obtained a larger share of team profits for themselves and have gained greater control in terms of their contractual rights as well. *Sports Illustrated* estimated that basketball players get forty percent more of the teams' gross revenue than they did in 1967, while football players receive ten percent more, baseball players receive thirteen percent more, and hockey players twenty-six percent more. While the average National Football League player in 1946 earned $4,000, he made $63,000 in 1978.

Inflated salaries and players' rights are not new issues. When William

Hulbert engineered the coup which led to the formation of the National League in 1876, owners secured control over the players, whose "excessive" salaries and freedom to move from team to team had caused franchise instability. In several phases beginning in 1879, the reserve clause, which allowed owners to sell and trade a player but left the player with absolutely no right to bargain for his own services, was added to baseball's standard player contract. Since baseball provided the model upon which other professional sports were structured, this control system became the standard method of operation. Players in all sports have been controlled by a draft of amateur players, standard player contracts which must be signed by the commissioner, and the reserve system. Since 1945 professional athletes have more frequently organized players' associations to gain greater freedom from these restrictive practices.

Players' associations, competing leagues, and law suits have been the main weapons used by players to increase salaries and to reform the old system of player control. The first attempt at post-World War II sport unionism came in 1946 when many major-league baseball players joined the American Baseball Guild. The union failed to gain recognition, but players did get a pension plan, a $5,500 minimum salary, severance pay, and expense money. The players obtained a stronger voice in the late 1950s when the Major League Players Association organized with former Judge Robert Cannon at its helm. Cannon, who craved the commissioner's job, failed to accomplish much; and in 1966 the players hired Marvin Miller, a labor economist, to head their association. Miller set out to gain higher salaries, an improved pension plan, and most significantly, freedom from the absolutism of the reserve system. In response baseball hired a professional negotiator, and since 1967 the contractual relationship between players and owners has been hammered out between hired negotiators. By 1970 all professional leagues had associations with hired executives who negotiated on behalf of the players.

Football, basketball, and hockey players took advantage of competing leagues to increase their salaries. In football the AFL caused salaries to escalate rapidly. Bonus contracts offered by the new league frequently exceeded $250,000, an unheard-of figure before 1960. Even the abortive World Football League pushed NFL salaries from an average of $27,500 in 1973 to $42,000 in 1975. Basketball players, who earned $8,000 in 1960 prior to the formation of the American Basketball League, had an average salary of $46,000 in 1970. By 1976 before the NBA absorbed four American Basketball Association teams, professional basketball salaries averaged over $110,000. The creation of the World Hockey Association drove up hockey salaries. The average NHL salary in 1967, when expansion began, was $19,133. The competition for players caused by the WHA drove the average salary in the NHL to $96,000 in 1977.

Baseball players increased their salaries without a competing league. The establishment of free agency caused owners to compete for players with huge salary offers. Although baseball won the 1972 *Flood* v. *Kuhn* case, which upheld the validity of the reserve system, the contractual arrangement fell apart within three years. James "Catfish" Hunter received his freedom

Marvin Miller, Executive Director of the Major League Players Association, gained many benefits for the players, including higher salaries, during the 1960s, '70s, and '80s. (*St. Louis Post-Dispatch*)

in 1974 when Charlie Finley, owner of the Oakland A's, failed to meet all the terms of Hunter's contract. The next year, two pitchers, Dave McNally and Andy Messersmith, challenged the system by playing a year without a contract. An arbitration panel, headed by Peter Seitz, ruled in favor of the pitchers. Though McNally subsequently retired, Messersmith signed a million-dollar contract with Atlanta. Since that ruling, players have freedom to move at specified intervals which have been determined through the negotiation process between players and owners.

Football never had blanket immunity from antitrust law. In recent years it has had a modified free-agency program which provides compensation to teams that lose free agents in the form of draft choices or other players. The compensation plan has been voided by two court cases. Joe Kapp, a quarterback with the New England Patriots, signed a nonstandard contract, which

110   the commissioner voided. Kapp sued, and the court ruled in 1974 that the standard player contract violated federal law. In 1975 the National Football League Players' Association sued to generalize the ruling of the Kapp case. The resulting *Mackey* case voided the compensation plan while the amateur draft had to be modified because of the *Yazoo Smith* case (1976).

The relationship between players and owners in sports became more strained during the 1970s. Player agents negotiated most individual contracts, and free agency, higher expense money, and increased participation in auxiliary revenue dominated negotiations between owners and players. A new militancy, which led to a baseball strike in 1972, an umpire's strike in 1979, and threats of several other strikes, has become indicative of the athlete's desire to achieve a wage equal to the financial worth which society attaches to his services. While some Americans find player demands to be excessive, advocates for the players point out that in professional football in 1979, the average payroll for players, coaches, and trainers was less than $3,500,000; yet, each team received $5,600,000 from television revenue alone. George Steinbrenner, often accused of overspending for players, feels that players traditionally have been underpaid. But he is "inclined to think they're close to where they ought to be now."

Much of the increased sums of money in modern sport comes from television. Sports franchises have profited increasingly since televised sports became a primary method of selling beer, gasoline, automobiles, and insurance. Although some feared that telecasting might diminish attendance, more people, particularly women, come to games because of their exposure to sports on television. Skilled producers, led by Roone Arledge of ABC Sports, "packaged" sports, captured their inherent drama, and convinced many of the fascination of high-quality athletics.

When the first sporting events were telecast in 1939, New Yorkers with receivers saw a boxing match and a college baseball game. Through the late 1940s and early 1950s dramatic episodes, particularly Bobby Thomson's home run in the 1951 Giants-Dodgers play-off game, led to expanded coverage. In 1954 the NBA signed a television contract. Baseball teams sold their local rights while the leagues adopted a "game of the day" format for Saturday and Sunday for those not in major-league markets. In 1961 after the passage of the Federal Sports Broadcasting Act, the NFL sold its exclusive rights to CBS. Since 1961 sports executives have concluded that the telecasting of many games is clearly advantageous to the leagues. At one time or another in the past two decades, all four major leagues have had national television contracts. By 1978, football teams earned $5,600,000, baseball teams $990,000, and basketball teams $880,000 from network contracts.

Hockey, which lost its network contract in 1977 because of poor ratings, has been hurt by this loss. Though local television revenues tend to be small in football, hockey, and basketball, this money has been quite large in baseball. Teams in larger markets, particularly Los Angeles, New York, Chicago, Boston, and Philadelphia, receive a few million annually; but teams in smaller markets, such as Dallas, Milwaukee, and Kansas City, receive far less.

The ability of sports to sell merchandise is unquestionable. NBC, for

Roone Arledge, President of ABC News and Sports, an innovative television executive. *(American Broadcasting Company)*

example, profited in 1969 when the New York Jets defeated the Baltimore Colts in Super Bowl III. The victory allowed NBC to raise advertising rates for AFL games by forty percent. Local television promoters, moreover, enabled the Philadelphia Phillies to sign Pete Rose in 1978. As Rose negotiated with several teams, the Phillies obtained his services when WPHL, a local station, guaranteed the club an extra $600,000 per year as the club's share of increased advertising revenue. Also in 1978, the three networks offered football $656,000,000 for telecasting rights. The phenomenal advertising rates which networks charge sponsors (as high as $325,000 per minute for the Super Bowl) indicate clearly that sports programs sell products.

While television generated significant new income, public ownership of playing facilities has been a kind of subsidy for professional teams. Minimal rents (most pay less than ten percent of their gate), no property taxes, and minimal maintenance fees have allowed the seventy percent of all franchises who play in public facilities larger potential profit. The last major stadium built with private money, Dodger Stadium in Los Angeles, was built in 1962. Since then, the public sector has built multi-use facilities in order to attract teams and to prove their city's "major-league status." Today, this costs urban Americans an estimated $25,000,000 annually in interest, mainte-

Chavez Ravine, home of the Los Angeles Dodgers, is an example of the new stadia that attract overflow crowds. *(Los Angeles Dodgers Baseball Club)*

nance, and upkeep. But most city officials place a high priority on such construction or renovation. Lila Cockrell, mayor of San Antonio when the basketball Spurs moved to that city, clearly justified an incredibly low rent for the team when she stated: "We have a great opportunity in this city through the gaining of national stature on the sports scene. This will help attract industry and assist our economy."

That major-league teams attract industry is doubtful, but they do generate tourism and some new jobs and contribute to civic pride as well. These incentives have led cities to raze older facilities and build new multipurpose stadia at the public's expense. Cincinnati, Pittsburgh, and St. Louis all erected stadia in the late 1960s at the cost of approximately $500 per seat. Owners of Mile High Stadium in Denver donated the facility to the city, then demanded $265,000 in new lighting in order to telecast Monday Night Football games from Denver. The most highly criticized stadium transaction has been the construction of the New Orleans Superdome, which was to cost $35,000,000 but eventually cost $163,000,000. Since that city has neither a major-league baseball team nor an NBA basketball franchise and annual interest payments are in excess of $1,300,000, it costs taxpayers an amazing amount to support the New Orleans Saints plus special events.

New facilities do not guarantee fans an opportunity to attend games. Of the 55,031 seats in Robert F. Kennedy Stadium in Washington, D.C., for example, less than 15,000 persons own all season tickets to Redskins games. Corporations purchase seventy-eight percent of all season tickets to major-league baseball games. When President Carter tried to eliminate the tax deductions for season tickets purchased by companies, organized sports and business leaders defeated the proposal. These new facilities, though clean, large, and commodious, have been a mixed blessing for the average fan.

Sports in the 1980s differed greatly from what they were in 1945. But American society does not drive a Hudson automobile, depend on sulfa drugs to cure ills, listen to Harry James records, or wear silk stockings. The business alterations in modern sport have companion shifts throughout the economy. All of the changes in sport may not be, in Bowie Kuhn's favorite euphemism, "in the best interest of the game," but most have created greater profits for the owners. Whether professional athletics is a sport or a business does not seem relevant today; it is clearly both. Even Anna Maria Alberghetti must realize that sports have become a dependable tax advantage for people with high incomes. Sports also provide glamour and profit for the wealthy who crave national attention. Since sports have become less profitable for those with limited capital, family ownership has declined. But because of America's insatiable demand for professional sports, they have become a highly successful corporate venture. Professional sports have prospered and grown because they have participated in the business trends which have governed the modern economy.

Sources and Suggested Readings

"Contemporary Issues in Sport." *The Annals of the American Academy of Political and Social Science* (September, 1979).

Davidson, Gary. *Breaking the Game Wide Open* (New York, 1974).

Lowenfish, Lee and Tony Lupien. *The Imperfect Diamond* (New York, 1980).

Michener, James. *Sports in America* (New York, 1976).

"Money in Sports: A Special Report." *Sports Illustrated* (July 17, 24, 31, 1978).

Noll, Roger, ed. *Government and the Sport Business* (Washington, 1974).

10

The Role of Women in Sports

Joan S. Hult
Roberta Park

The 1970s witnessed an unprecedented growth in women's sport in the United States. New conceptions of equal rights and privileges for all citizens, regardless of race or sex, changing cultural values regarding women, and the enactment of federal regulations joined to create a social climate which fostered a rapid rise of interest in opportunities for women to engage in sports of all kinds: intercollegiate, amateur, professional, and recreational. American girls and women are now performing athletic feats which a mere decade earlier would have been thought impossible. The changes have been rapid and dramatic, and if equality of opportunity for women in sport is still not yet completely achieved, the possibilities are infinitely greater than they were one hundred years ago.

Sport, as we now think of it, is largely a phenomenon of the twentieth century. A variety of folk games existed during the Colonial Period, and horse racing often attracted considerable attention. After 1865, there was a growing tendency to transform informal games into highly organized and regulated sport. By the end of the nineteenth century substantial numbers of American boys and men had begun to engage in sporting contests. It was not until the middle of the twentieth century—and especially the decade of the 1970s—that American girls and women began to participate in sports in anything resembling similar proportions.

The prevailing attitudes of the nineteenth century severely limited the types of activities deemed appropriate for women. Women were believed to be physiologically and psychologically weaker than men. A pale complexion, delicate health, and spiritual high-mindedness were the ideal. Tight corsets, heavy petticoats, and long, full skirts accentuated these ethereal qualities and effectively limited movement. Walking, riding, archery, and croquet were the types of moderate activities which might be approved for members of the "fair sex." In the late 1800s and early 1900s some American women began to participate in sports like golf, boating, bowling, fencing, basketball, swimming, track and field, tennis, and field hockey. Such opportunities as did exist were available largely through colleges and universities, programs of various athletic clubs, and at the increasingly numerous elite country clubs. The safety bicycle, introduced in the late 1800s, had an important impact on women's clothing in general, as cycling safety demanded an abbreviated (yet modest) costume. In the 1890s basketball became a popular sport among college women, and by the early 1900s there was varsity-type competition in such sports as tennis, basketball, and field hockey. Women's college sports programs were, in general, carefully controlled; publicity was shunned, and male spectators were frequently prohibited.

During World War I (1914-1918) tens of thousands of American women were employed in industry, while others served overseas in the Red Cross and as military nurses. The nineteenth amendment, which in 1920 granted women the right to vote in national elections, was prompted by and also contributed to changing attitudes regarding the place of women in American society. During the 1920s and 1930s, urbanization, an increasingly mobile population, more leisure time, and a relaxation of the restrictive standards of the previous century contributed to the creation of a climate which favored greater, yet still limited, opportunities for women in many spheres of life. Sport was no exception. For example, in 1926 Gertrude Ederle, winner of a gold and two bronze medals at the 1924 Olympics, became the first woman to swim the English Channel. Glenna Collette captured her first national amateur golf title in 1922. Helen Wills, winner of eight Wimbledon tennis titles between 1927 and 1938, won her first Forest Hills championship in 1923 at the age of seventeen. There was a decided tendency to look more favorably upon those sports which were considered to be "more feminine," such as tennis, golf, swimming, and archery. Field hockey was considered to be a "ladies' game" in America. Moreover, in general, it was the wealthier woman, who had both the time and the money, who was likely to be able to pursue sports to any extent.

There were many notable female athletes in the 1920s, 1930s, and 1940s, yet it is generally agreed that the greatest of all was Mildred "Babe" Didrikson. Winner of gold medals in the javelin and 80-meter hurdles and a silver medal in the high jump at the 1932 Olympic Games, Babe was also an All-American basketball star, the winner of many national and international golf championships (both as an amateur and a professional), and an accomplished bowler, tennis and baseball player. The Associated Press named her Woman Athlete of the Century in 1950.

In the early 1920s a number of women physical educators became concerned about what they perceived as a growing overemphasis on varsity-type athletic competition for girls and women. Criticisms leveled against men's intercollegiate athletics (commercialization, recruiting abuses, exploitation of the athlete), as well as a fear that women might lose control of their own programs, precipitated what Ellen Gerber has aptly termed "The Controlled Development of Collegiate Sport for Women, 1923-1936." In place of varsity-type competition, which could accommodate only small numbers of players, play days and sports days, which were intended to make it possible

Babe Didrikson Zaharias on the pro tour in the 1950s. *(Babe Didrikson Foundation, Beaumont, TX)*

for all girls and women to enjoy the benefits of the sports experience, were instituted. The play-day, then sports-day, format prevailed in educational institutions until the late 1950s and 1960s, when extramural and varsity-type competitions for female students again began to receive attention. Not all women physical educators, however, were in agreement with the official policies of the professional physical education organizations, and varsity sports for high-school girls and college women did sometimes occur during the decades between the two wars. Moreover, church leagues, industrial leagues, clubs, the AAU, and various associations provided substantial opportunity for many girls and women to engage in such activities as softball, swimming, gymnastics, volleyball, basketball, tennis, track and field, and bowling—an extremely popular sport among women in the 1950s and 1960s.

World War II (1939-1945) caused further alterations in traditional beliefs, as large numbers of women took formerly all-male jobs in heavy industries or joined various branches of the women's armed services. The options available to American women in the 1950s, while still far fewer than those available to men, were, nonetheless, more numerous than in previous decades. In sport, indications of change were beginning to be seen. In 1951, the journal *School Activities* declared that in spite of the policies advocated by various physical education organizations, high-school girls in several states were competing in state tournaments in track and basketball. The Iowa State Girls' Basketball Tournament, one of the more popular annual events among Iowans, was televised in 1951. At the Pan-American Games, established in 1951, American women usually dominated in basketball and swimming. Gretchen Frazer won America's first gold medal in skiing at the 1948 Winter Olympics. Andrea Mead Lawrence won gold medals in the women's slalom and giant slalom in 1952. Tenley Albright, who in 1956 was the first American woman to win a gold medal in figure skating, subsequently entered Harvard Medical School and became a successful surgeon. At the age of sixteen Maureen Connolly won the 1951 U.S. Women's Singles Championship at Forest Hills and two years later became the first woman in history to win the world's four major tennis tournaments—Wimbledon, United States, French, Australian. In 1950 Althea Gibson became the first black tennis player to compete in the U.S. Nationals. In 1957 she won both the Wimbledon and the U.S. titles and was named Associated Press Woman Athlete of the Year. Patty Berg, who was instrumental in the organization of the Ladies' Professional Golf Association (LPGA) in the late 1940s, turned from amateur to professional golf in 1940. Her prize for winning the 1941 U.S. Women's Open was a $100 savings bond. Babe Didrikson won seventeen successive major golf tournaments during the 1946-47 season. In 1961 Mickey Wright captured golf's "grand slam": the LPGA Championship, the U.S. Open, the Titleholders. Yet, until 1969 no woman golfer had earned as much as $50,000 on tour in one year.

Whereas tennis, golf, figure skating, and skiing tended to be expensive, perhaps elitist, sports, bowling was within the reach of a majority of American women. Founded at St. Louis in 1916, the Women's International Bowling Congress claimed a membership of nearly three million in 1966. Marion

Ladewig, who dominated bowling in the 1950s and early 1960s, was the first woman to win the Bowling Proprietors' Association of America Women's All-Star title. At the height of her career, her annual earnings from bowling exceeded $25,000. Dottie Fothergill, whose application for membership in the all-male Professional Bowlers' Association in 1970 was rejected, accumulated nearly $40,000 from tournament earnings in 1973.

In comparison with men's professional sports, women's professional sports in the 1950s and the 1960s were poorly funded and given little attention. An article which appeared in *Holiday* magazine in 1952 exemplified the manner in which the press most frequently treated women athletes, particularly those in sports like baseball, softball, and basketball. In 1943 Philip Wrigley, owner of the Chicago Cubs, had founded a professional American Girls Baseball League. (Players' salaries never seem to have exceeded $6,000 a year.) The article devoted considerable attention to "femininity"—players were shown combing their hair and applying lipstick—and "high moral tone"—the team supposedly went nowhere without a woman chaperon. The baseball skill of the players was hardly mentioned.

Track, swimming, and gymnastics were three women's sports which received increased attention after the 1960 Rome Olympics. In track, American women captured five of nine first-place medals. Wilma Rudolph won the 100-meter and 200-meter dashes, anchored the 400-meter relay, and gained the admiration of millions at home and abroad. Once crippled by a childhood illness, she had overcome adversity and become the first American woman athlete to win three Olympic gold medals in track. This outstanding young black woman and the rest of her team were loudly applauded throughout the successful tour of Europe which followed their Olympic triumph.

America's women had done well in swimming at the 1920, 1924, 1928, and 1932 Olympics and had dominated in diving between 1920 and 1956. Chris von Saltza won three gold medals and one silver at the Rome Olympics. During the 1960s and 1970s American women again assumed a commanding position in Olympic competition. Television coverage helped popularize the exciting and graceful movements of women's gymnastics, a sport which was dominated by performers from Eastern Europe, and during the 1960s a growing number of American girls began to participate in gymnastics. America's Kathy Rigby placed tenth overall at the 1972 Olympics, the Games at which Soviet Russia's Olga Korbut captured three gold medals and one silver medal and the attention of millions of admirers.

Because a nation's medal record was determined by the combined scores of men's and women's victories, the large number of medals won by Soviet women athletes posed a serious threat to America's domination of the Summer Olympics. In a climate which saw the United States locked in an ideological and technological race with the U.S.S.R. (Russia's Sputnik was successfully orbited in 1957), international sport became more highly politicized. It was clear that organized efforts were needed if the level of women's athletics in the United States was to be improved—and continued American Olympic dominance was to be insured. Between 1963 and 1969 the Women's Board of the Olympic Development Committee and the Division for

120   Girls' and Women's Sports of the American Association for Health, Physical Education, and Recreation sponsored five National Institutes on Girls' Sports. These institutes were intended to provide participants with the most current coaching and training information in several international sports. The participants, in turn, were expected to disseminate this information in their home states. *The Final Report of the President's Commission on Olympic Sport, 1975-1977* called for greater emphasis on well-run sports programs for women.

There were other signs of an increasing interest among women in competitive athletics. By the mid-1960s many high schools and colleges across the nation had established varsity sports for girls and women. The National Association of State High School Associations assumed control of girls' high-school varsity sports in 1964, the same year that college women from thirty-four states attended the United States Lawn Tennis Association (USLTA) national tournament. The syndicated *This World* reported in July, 1963, that "a small band of determined co-eds this spring stunned the male sports world by winning varsity letters on men's teams at several major U.S. universities." Although there were numerous objections, exceptionally good female swimmers, golfers, and tennis players did occasionally earn a place on formerly all-male high-school and college teams. In 1969 a New York ruling which prohibited girls from competing on boys' teams was challenged, and by 1973-74 girls were competing on boys' high-school teams in non-contact sports in more than a dozen states; in some instances they were also participating on boys' teams in sports like soccer and basketball. The decision to open at least some male athletic teams to girls and women prompted the vexing question, "If boys' teams are open to girls, must girls' teams be open to boys?" There was some apprehension that in an effort to reduce program costs institutions might field only one team, and all but a few very able female athletes would be excluded. The net result would be a *loss* to those girls and women who were interested in sports. There was also a concern that if women were denied an opportunity to develop their own programs, women would be quickly relegated to subordinate positions in well-established male interscholastic and intercollegiate athletic departments.

Recognizing the need for expanded sports programs for college women, the Division for Girls' and Women's Sports and the National Association of Physical Education for College Women established a Commission on Intercollegiate Athletics for Women (CIAW) in 1967. Although the concept was not entirely new (a National Women's College Golf Tournament had been initiated in 1941, and a national college tennis championship had been held for several years in cooperation with the USLTA), prior to the establishment of the CIAW no single national organization existed to guide and control women's intercollegiate athletics. Within a few years the CIAW had sponsored national collegiate championship tournaments in gymnastics, track and field, golf, swimming, badminton, and volleyball.

The Association of Intercollegiate Athletics for Women (AIAW) was formed in 1971-1972 to replace the CIAW. The first AIAW championships were held in 1973; by 1977-78 the organization sanctioned national intercollegiate championships in thirteen sports. The ideological roots of the AIAW may be traced to the 1899 national women's Basketball Committee of the American Association for the Advancement of Physical Education. For more than seven decades the official policy of women's physical education organizations had insisted that athletic programs conducted under the auspices of educational institutions were to be broad-based and for the educational benefit of the participant, not for the entertainment of spectators. As interest in more extensive and more intensive athletic competition for women increased in the 1970s, the AIAW was increasingly confronted by issues which challenged this standard.

Although an interest in insuring greater equality for members of the female sex can be traced back to the early nineteenth century, the 1960s ushered in the modern era of the women's liberation movement. The Employment Opportunities section of the 1964 Civil Rights Act placed a ban on sex discrimination. A 1965 Executive order demanded that federal contractors, which included many colleges and universities, comply with equal opportunity practices in hiring and promotion. The National Organization of Women (NOW) was formed in 1966, and the Women's Equity Action League (WEAL) in 1968. In the modern struggle for equality two concepts have functioned: *social* access to equality; *legal* access to equality. In 1971 the proposed Equal Rights Amendment to the U.S. Constitution was passed by Congress and sent to the states for ratification. The single most powerful piece of legislation affecting athletics for girls and women to date has been Title IX of the Education Amendments Act of 1972, which required institutions which received federal financial assistance to provide equality in the area of physical education and athletics.

Following the passage of Title IX, a surge of articles dealing with women and sport began to appear in various magazines. Whereas those few articles which previously had appeared in the public press stressed individual sports and the "femininity" of the participants, the competitive skills of the woman athlete now began to receive attention. The three-part series on "Women in Sport," which appeared in *Sports Illustrated* in the Spring of 1973, opened with the message: "There may be worse [more socially serious] forms of prejudice in the United States, but there is no sharper example of discrimination today than that which operates against girls and women who take part in competitive sports, wish to take part, or might wish to if society did not scorn such endeavors." The article rejected traditional arguments that women are biologically incapable of high-level athletic performance, pointing out that the data did not support the contention. It also pointed to an issue which would receive considerable attention during the 1970s: By being denied an opportunity to engage in competitive sport, American women had been "programmed to be losers." One of the implications of this argument has been that since competitive sports teach "winning" or success, sports offer an important means for learning strategies which will help with other aspects of life, and women had suffered many types of losses due to restrictions which had been placed on their opportunities to compete in sports. The September 1974 issue of the newly established *WomenSports* magazine, co-published by Billie Jean and Larry King, summarized the effects of Title IX on the development of women's intercollegiate athletics, noted the existence of conflicting philosophies regarding the direction such programs should take, and described the growing struggle between the NCAA and AIAW over which organization would control women's inter-collegiate programs: "Part of the answer is that outstanding athletes, even women, are saleable, profitable and manipulable. The organizations that control them reap profits from TV rights and enjoy the power and prestige of governing national and international competition." The financial issue was paramount. Athletic budgets at major universities often exceeded a million dollars; some exceeded four and five million dollars. Control of pro-gram meant control of finances and how monies would be allotted. Moreover, the NCAA, which represented only male athletes, had long been at a dis-advantage to the AAU and other national associations which represented both male and female competitors when it came to the selection of athletes for international competitions and the Olympics. The NCAA would be in a much stronger position if it represented women as well as men.

In the years immediately following the passage of Title IX, much un-certainty existed concerning the directions which expanding programs of women's intercollegiate athletics should take. At the same time that the *Chronicle of Higher Education* published articles on expanded athletic pro-grams for women, it also included articles which criticized and called for remedies for the exaggerations and abuses associated with many men's pro-grams. (There was, in fact, sufficient concern over men's intercollegiate athletics to prompt the American Council on Education to undertake an investigation of the subject in 1974.) Some women physical educators and coaches favored patterning women's intercollegiate athletics after the exist-ing men's model. The majority, at least initially, believed that women should and could develop an entirely new concept of intercollegiate athletics—one which would provide the female athlete with better competitive experiences yet avoid the abuses of recruiting and commercialization. It was clear that immediate action was needed, as large numbers of colleges and universities were fearful that if they failed to meet the specifications of Title IX by the implementation deadline of July 21, 1978, they might lose millions of dollars in federal funds.

In an effort to avoid some of the difficulties which overzealous recruiting practices had brought to men's programs, the AIAW initially prohibited both recruiting and the award of "athletic scholarships" but was forced to aban-don its position when tennis players in Florida brought suit on the basis of unequal treatment. By the 1973-74 school year, over fifty colleges offered scholarships to female athletes. There were other instances of resort to legal action. One example concerned the refusal of the New Jersey Little League to permit girls to join its baseball teams on the contention that as a *private* organization it was not subject to Title IX regulations. After considerable debate, Little League Incorporated decided in 1974 to permit girls to join baseball teams. The issue of equal access was, however, far from over. In 1976 Westport, Connecticut, decided to allow boys to play on its girls' Little

League Softball team and won the State Championship with a team composed of ten boys and four girls. In the ensuing uproar, the team withdrew. While it appeared that there was support for girls to join boys' teams, the reverse did not seem equally acceptable.

In 1974, at the urging of the NCAA, Senator John Tower (Texas) introduced into the U.S. Senate an amendment which would have exempted football and basketball, two sports which were claimed to be "revenue-producing," from the provisions of Title IX. The Tower amendment was killed in a joint House-Senate Committee, but not until various women's groups had vociferously protested what they believed was a clear attempt on the part of the NCAA (which since its inception in 1906 had never registered an interest in women's intercollegiate athletics) to weaken developing women's programs. At its 1975 annual meeting, the sixteen-member governing Council of the NCAA announced that it had instructed its "women's committee on sports" to plan a pilot program of national championships for women in track and tennis. The AIAW was outraged, considering this action a clear attempt on the part of the NCAA to capture control of the women's program. A joint NCAA-AIAW committee was subsequently formed to make recommendations for the development of women's sports and the conduct of national championships, but after scarcely more than a year the committee was dissolved. The NCAA persisted in its efforts, however, and by 1979-80 a number of women engaged in the conduct of women's intercollegiate athletics looked with favor at some type of merger. At its January 1981 annual meeting the NCAA voted by a slim margin in favor of sponsoring national intercollegiate tournaments for women.

The women's collegiate game which received the greatest media attention was basketball. A series of rules changes in the 1960s and early 1970s and more highly skilled players had made it an exciting spectator sport. Immaculata College outscored Queens College before 12,000 fans at Madison Square Garden in February 1975, and a *Chronicle of Higher Education* article headlined "Women's Basketball: Too Good to Put Down" reported the 1975 national AIAW championship game between Delta State and Immaculata College. The contest was taped for rebroadcast by the Public Broadcasting Service—the first time women's basketball had received such extensive television coverage. Street and Smith's 1975 *Basketball Yearbook* included a preview of women's basketball, and Kodak picked its first All-American women's basketball team in 1975. Nancy Lieberman, the youngest member of the 1976 United States silver medalist women's Olympic basketball team, now plays in the women's professional league.

Although women's *professional* sport was not subject to the mandates of Title IX, it was nonetheless influenced by many of the same attitudes which were transforming women's intercollegiates. In 1969 golfer Carol Mann became the first woman to earn $50,000 in prize money. The 1972 Colgate-Palmolive Women's Circle Tournament was broadcast on national television. By 1973 television ratings for the event were among the top ten for *all* golf tournaments. Movie and television celebrity Dinah Shore lent her support to the tournament, and women golfers appeared in the company's commercials.

Kathy Whitworth won the Colgate Triple Crown in 1975 and earned over $550,000 in prize money. Although television had begun to pay some attention to women's athletics, the coverage was minimal.

There can be little doubt that the player who had the greatest impact on women's professional sports in the 1970s was Billie Jean King, who had experienced her first of a long list of Wimbledon tennis victories in 1961. In 1968 she signed a professional contract with the National Tennis League and began an active campaign to obtain greater financial recognition for female athletes. By 1971, King had become the first woman athlete to win over $100,000 in a single year. She amassed an impressive record of victories in the world's major tournaments, played World Team Tennis, and became the first woman to coach a team which included male professionals. On September 30, 1973, surrounded by a circus-like atmosphere of pageant and spectacle, twenty-nine-year-old Billie Jean King defeated fifty-five-year-old Bobby Riggs (Wimbledon and Forest Hills champion of the 1930s) at the Houston Astrodome in three straight sets. Riggs was cast as the exemplar of traditional "male chauvinist" attitudes, while King represented the "feminist movement" of the 1970s. The match, which was viewed by a television audience estimated to be fifty-nine million, was followed by a one-hour special on women athletes. During the 1970s several other outstanding American women tennis players shared a part of the sport's center stage with King. Sixteen-year-old Chris Evert lost in the finals of the 1974 U.S. Indoor Championship to King but went on to capture the French, Canadian, Wimbledon, and several other major titles that year. At the age of fourteen, Californian Tracy Austin became the youngest player to capture a professional title—the 1977 Avon Futures. Two years later Austin became the youngest player to win the U.S. Championships.

Tennis and golf were by no means the only professional sports in which women made advances. In addition, the "sex barrier" was broken in several which had previously excluded women. Diane Crump became the first licensed female jockey to race against men on February 7, 1969. In June 1971 Mary Bacon became the first to ride one hundred winners. Janet Guthrie entered the Indianapolis 500 in 1976, the first auto racer of her sex to do so. Women gained positions on the sports staffs of newspapers and magazines, and a few were hired as sports commentators on television. After considerable struggle, women reporters were permitted access to press boxes and, with some restrictions, to men's locker rooms.

The Tokyo Olympics had demonstrated that women's volleyball could be an exacting and exciting game. In 1975 movie producer David L. Wolper announced the founding of a professional coeducational International Volleyball Association, yet until Mary Jo Pepler (former UCLA intercollegiate star and winner of the first Women's Superstars competition in 1975) was made "setter" on her team, women were relegated to back-row play. For decades, considerable numbers of American women had played amateur softball. When the Raybestos Brakettes won the Women's World Softball Tournament in 1974, the United States garnered its first world title in the ten-year history of the tournament. A women's professional softball league

Helen Stephens, the "Fulton Flash," won two gold medals at the Berlin Olympics in 1936 in the 100-meter dash and women's 400-meter relay. She was named number-one woman athlete of the year in 1936 by the Associated Press. In the late 1930s, she headed a women's basketball team which toured the country. *(St. Louis Post-Dispatch)*

was established the following year; among its founders were Billie Jean King, Jim Jorgenson, co-founder of World Team Tennis and Women's Superstars, and Joan Joyce, outstanding Brakettes pitcher. The first games of the newly formed league were played in May 1976. Players' annual salaries ranged between $1,000 and $4,000, minimal in comparison with the figures earned by male baseball players.

Women's professional basketball developed more slowly than the women's intercollegiate game, in part because a pool of sufficiently skilled players was needed before a league could be established. An All-American World's Championship Girls Basketball Club (subsequently renamed the All-American Red Heads) had been established in 1936, and over the next four decades the team traveled hundreds of thousands of miles playing exhibition matches against men's teams before paying audiences. Iowa high-school star Denise Long was drafted by the San Francisco Warriors in 1969 but was prohibited from playing for the men's professional team by the NBA Commissioner. The first game of the newly established Women's Professional Basketball League (WPBL) saw the Chicago Hustle defeat the Milwaukee Does by a score of 92-87 in December 1978. The owners of the eight-team franchise maintained that it would be necessary to average 3,000 fans per game over a thirty-four-game schedule if the league were to become solvent by the target date of 1981. Whereas in 1978-79 a WPBL franchise had cost $50,000, by 1979-80 the cost had risen to $100,000, and there were hopes that by the end of the decade a franchise would be worth at least a million dollars. WPBL salaries in 1979 ranged between $5,000 and $15,000 in contrast with the men's NBA "average" of $143,000. In professional sports, women would have to *prove* that they could attract fans and be money-makers, for they could not rely upon the same Title IX legislation which had so rapidly converted women's intercollegiate programs.

During the 1960s and 1970s an increasing number of women became involved in every kind of sport, including three which had long been considered traditional male bastions—football, ice hockey, and boxing. A Women's Football League had been organized in the 1960s; the New York Fillies, formed in 1972, disbanded after a few losses. In 1974, however, there were women's tackle football teams in twelve cities. Canadian women had played competitive ice hockey for decades, but few American women had tried the game before the early 1970s. (When Brown University formed a women's team in 1964, it could find no team to compete against.) By 1976, the American Girls Hockey Association claimed a membership of 750 players. The first Annual Ivy League Hockey Team Tournament was also held in 1976. *Ms.* magazine reported that the first all-girls' boxing club was established in 1968 in Dallas.

Encouraged by a changing social climate, more coverage of sports and exercise for women in the media, a concern for health and fitness, and the models of success provided by top-level women athletes, greater numbers of American girls and women of all ages turned to amateur sports and exercise programs. Aerobics and jogging enjoyed almost overnight success, and jog-a-thons attracted female participants from eight (or younger) to eighty years of age. The women's 800-meter run had been dropped after the 1928 Olympics on the grounds that women were physiologically incapable of running long distances; it was not reinstated until the 1960 Olympics. In 1975 Francie Larrieu set world records in the one- and two-mile races. The International Olympic Committee rejected a proposal to include a 3,000-meter event for women in the 1980 Olympics, even though races of that distance had been part of the European Championships since 1974. For years the few opportunities which women had to run longer distances were in events sponsored by various local track clubs. Kathy Switzer registered as K. Switzer in 1967 in order to run in the traditional all-male Boston Marathon; her 1972 entry, however, could be in the sanctioned women's division. The first AAU national women's marathon was held in 1974, and before long women were running 50-kilometer races with ease, demonstrating that with proper training women were physiologically capable of heavy endurance tasks. In one sport men may have benefited from changes which were occurring. Field hockey had been popularized in the United States in the early 1900s by Miss Constance M.K. Applebee. For over seven decades it had been considered a "women's game" in America—but not elsewhere. Recently the game has begun to gain some popularity among male college students. The first joint AIAW-United States Field Hockey Association tournament was held in 1975, and a women's team was scheduled to participate in the 1980 Olympics.

During the 1970s women also entered the previously male-dominated world of crew, both by forming all-woman boats and by serving as coxswains of men's crews. Whereas in 1969 the number of women's crews in the United States was estimated to be less than thirty, by 1974 the number had risen to seventy-five. The Radcliffe crew finished two seconds behind the winning boat at the 1974 European women's championships, and each year competition at the National Women's Rowing Association Championships became more intense. By the mid-1970s several magazines reported that women rowers thrived on early-morning work-outs and intense training regimens. It became increasingly acceptable for women—athletes and non-athletes alike—to engage in weight-training and vigorous exercise programs. Tens of thousands turned to activities like jogging, swimming, and cycling for reasons of health and also for the pleasures and new sense of freedom which participation in sports and physical activities brought. As the United States entered the decade of the 1980s, larger numbers of girls and women than ever before—perhaps than ever dreamed of—were finding new satisfactions in competitive athletics, amateur sports, recreational activities, and physical education programs.

Sources and Suggested Readings

Gerber, E., J. Felshin, P. Berlin, and W. Wyrick. *The American Woman in Sport* (Philadelphia, 1974).

Hoepner, B.J., ed. *Women's Athletics: Coping With Controversy* (Washington, D.C., 1974).

Hollander, P. *One Hundred Greatest Women in Sports* (New York, 1976).

Killanin, Lord and J. Rodda, eds. *The Olympic Games* (New York, 1976).

Lichtenstein, G. *A Long Way, Baby* (New York, 1974).

Oglesby, C.A., ed. *Women and Sport: From Myth to Reality* (Philadelphia, 1978).

Sabin, F. *Women Who Win* (New York, 1975).

Twin, S.L. *Out of the Bleachers, Writings on Women and Sport* (Old Westbury, N.Y., 1979).

Violence in American Sports

Douglas A. Noverr
Lawrence E. Ziewacz

American sports have always included violent participants and featured acts of violence of an individual or group nature. After all, professional sports in the late nineteenth century and early twentieth century became avenues of upward mobility for lower- and middle-class youths who were aggressive, tough, and manly. Opportunities in sports brought immigrant ethnic groups visibility and acceptance as a cult of athletic ruggedness developed to compensate for the loss of frontier values and opportunities for individual glory and fame. The violence of the frontier and its code of confrontation and decisive conflict were transferred to the playing fields, where it could be more contained and controlled for social purposes and even for mass entertainment and spectator recreation.

Sports, then, became a training ground for the male leaders of the nation, a place where a model of masculine virtues could be featured and reinforced. Rough and even disreputable sports like football and baseball could be regulated and organized so as to emphasize fair play, controlled competition, and restrained but directed physical force. The rules of the game and the direction of stern, authoritarian coaches could mold unruly boys into "god-fearing men" and "useful citizens." However, an element of roughness was, within limits, desirable so that the strong, aggressive athlete or team could demonstrate physical superiority. Occasional fistfights, brawls, or one-on-one confrontations outside the structure of the game or rules could be tolerated and even excused as "boys will be boys." However, collegiate and professional sports in the period from 1865 to World War I had to restrain and limit violence in order to prove their useful purpose to society or to validate their legitimacy as worthy leisure pursuits in a culture that valued utilitarian ends and work. Professional sports had to develop an image of respectability if they were to attract younger fans or families to their games and to create an establishment that was above the disruptions or melees that might cut contests short or involve the police.

In the pre-World War I era sports violence was not a great social concern, nor was it seen as a threat to the existence of a sport, with the noteworthy exception of college football. Sports figures were not seen as violent but rather as aggressive and manly, accepting the dangers and risks of a sport as the spirit and code of the game.

Mass participation in sports, which would develop dramatically in the 1920s and as a result of service sports during the two world wars, meant a greater acceptance of sports as a means of conditioning the body, testing one's strength and skills, and meeting the demands of competition. Participation, then, was more important than winning, and the democratization of sports provided a cultural value orientation that made violence a violation of the discipline and rules. The competitive edge could be gained by innovations of play, the development of new skills, the discipline of training and conditioning, and the development of team play. Sports were a legitimate means of channeling and controlling aggression or potentially violent behavior, as well as a means of building character.

However, after World War II the levels or incidents of violence in sports began to increase or at least to become more noticeable and prominent. With the sports boom brought on by the postwar prosperity, sports had arrived and no longer had to legitimize themselves or prove their social and moral value. With the increasing professionalization of sports and the emphasis on winning as a measure of success, competition became more intense. Athletes became more mixed and diverse in backgrounds as racial barriers fell and as collegiate experience was no longer the main avenue to a professional sports career. Team or school dynasties became more commonplace, making certain teams the object of competitive envy or even animosity. Urban violence related to economic competition, racial or class conflict, or frustrations caused by the complexities of modern life provided a context for possible fan violence that might easily and readily carry over into the sports setting. Younger generations of fans came to sporting contests in their own crowds, rejecting the tradition of one generation's initiating the next into the ritual of and respect for a sport. An appreciation of the traditions, history, and continuity of a sport was often supplanted by a desire for vicarious excitement or emotional involvement in the charged atmosphere of the drama of winning and losing. Modern-day sports crowds became more diverse and intense, seeing the game as an individual moment rather than part of an ongoing continuity or heritage. As athletes became more individualistic as stars or personalities, fans divided along the lines of loyalties to individuals and could even find subjects to abuse on their own hometown teams.

All these factors tended to break down a prevailing consensus with its built-in restraints. The potential for disruptions or violence was increased as cities became places of conflict as a result of social and racial divisions. Ballparks and arenas were no longer special places where the sporting traditions continued untouched and unaffected by modern developments. As sports became big business, at both professional and collegiate levels, the real world impinged upon the sports world and disrupted it, indeed changed its very character. With the advent of television and the mass media, sporting events took on a significance far beyond the original purposes of the sport, and the sports industry provided a context for the increasing tensions and complexities of modern life.

Most recently sports, particularly professional sports, have witnessed an increasing number of well-publicized violent incidents both between players on the field or court and among fans in the stands. In 1975, Henry Boucha suffered a severe beating from Dave Forbes during a Boston-Minnesota hockey game, causing Boucha to lose seventy percent of his sight in one eye. Although Forbes was cleared of assault charges in a Minneapolis court in 1975, Boucha filed a $3.5 million suit in August of 1980, challenging "hockey's fundamental premise that violence on the ice is not subject to laws governing violence elsewhere in society." Alan Eagleson, executive director of the National Hockey League Players Association, called the suit "damaging to hockey." He further commented that "there is no way a trial of this kind cannot be harmful to the sport when players end up in court over some injury suffered in a game." The Boucha lawsuit was recently settled out of court with Boucha receiving a multi-million-dollar settlement. Thus, the serious legal issue of possible criminal prosecution for game situation violence was not settled.

In pro basketball, on December 9, 1977, Los Angeles Laker Kermit Washington literally shattered the face of forward Rudy Tomjanovich of the Houston Rockets with a devastating punch. On August 18, 1979, newspapers reported that a jury had awarded Tomjanovich $3.3 million in damages. He had been asking for $2.6 million. One of the jurors reported that the jury "reacted to the violence of the blow. That sort of thing does not belong. This game is basketball, not boxingball." Eleven days later, on August 29, 1979, newspapers would report that the judge had dismissed the jury because a settlement had been reached out of court, but that part of the agreement was not to disclose the amount of the award. In 1977 also, Kareem Abdul-Jabbar broke his hand by roundhousing rookie pivotman Kent Benson of the Milwaukee Bucks. Newspapers carried a picture of the incident with a caption noting that Benson was "Kareemed."

In pro football, which had seen many stars such as Gale Sayers end athletic careers prematurely because of injury, several quarterbacks began wearing flak jackets for protection. Football fans were shocked by the crushing blow Jack Tatum gave receiver Darryl Stingley in an exhibition game between the Oakland Raiders and New England Patriots on August 13, 1978. The result was that Stingley became a quadriplegic. Tatum would later extol the virtues of his hitting prowess in a book entitled, *They Call Me Assassin* (1980). Tatum stated that "I like to believe that my best hits border on felonious assault."

Even in baseball, where skill and not physical strength predominates, violence escalated. The "brushback" pitch has become part of the hurler's arsenal of pitches, used to move hitters off the plate, to retaliate for an opposing pitcher's use of the same tactic, or to settle old scores between antagonists. In 1980 *The Detroit News* noted thirteen incidents in which fights or all-out melees resulted from hit batsmen, and one case resulted in

132   the filing of criminal charges by the Chicago White Sox against Al Cowens, outfielder for the Detroit Tigers, who had charged Ed Farmer on the mound. Cowens had had his jaw broken by Farmer the previous season, and, even though he was not thrown at a second time, Cowens charged Farmer from his blind side, and a brawl involving all the players ensued. Because there was a warrant out for his arrest in Chicago, Cowens did not accompany the Tigers to that city for the next series, and again a legal action or determination was avoided.

Yet, violence in sports was not limited solely to the players on the field. In 1969, overly exuberant New York Mets fans celebrated their team's "miracle" World Series triumph by breaking seats and ripping up the turf, causing extensive damage to Shea Stadium. When the Oakland Raiders threw an open-ended victory party after their triumph in Super Bowl XI (1977), an all-out melee rather than a joyful celebration was the result, with beatings, muggings, thrown bottles, and general riot conditions.

In 1974, the Cleveland Indians staged a ten-cent beer night in Cleveland, which resulted in hundreds of fans battling one another and players from both the Cleveland Indians and Texas Rangers. In 1979, a disco record burning exhibition in Chicago between games of a doubleheader between the White Sox and the Detroit Tigers saw a full-scale riot ensue. The grounds were so badly torn up that the second game was cancelled and a forfeit awarded to the Tigers. Only a phalanx of Chicago's "finest" could sweep the field of an ugly crowd of destructive rioters.

Baseball players in particular have been the targets of rowdy fans' behavior. In the summer of 1980, Dave Parker had a nine-volt radio hurled at him. Pete Rose has had paper clips and bottles thrown at him. Leo Cardenas once had a bag of flour, presumably dropped from an airplane, explode near his position between second and third base. In 1976, Chris Chambliss had to fight off fans with the help of police in order to run the bases after hitting a decisive homer against the Kansas City Royals. Similarly, in 1977, Reggie Jackson, the World Series Most Valuable Player who had smashed five home runs, was captured on television as a frightened, desperate man, who sprinted from the outfield at the conclusion of the final play of the series, swinging and karate chopping at the swarms of fans who stormed the field, as he sought the sanctuary of the clubhouse. Ballparks and sports arenas have become settings for unruly, anarchic behavior rather than places where a respect for the game and its traditions imposes a certain degree of decorum and gentlemanly behavior. The increase in fan rowdiness and almost uncontrollable wildness have been attributed to such factors as the easy availability of beer, the tradition of cheap bleacher seats and sections known for brawlers and toughs, and the problems of providing adequate police enforcement. But these have always been problems in ballparks and sports arenas, which have always been places where healthy and energetic males "let off steam." Many fans seem to believe that the price of admission brings immunity from laws governing dangerous or threatening behavior and that to restrain fan enthusiasm and involvement is to deny freedom of speech and expression. Some fans, such as a certain element among the New York Rangers fans at

The infamous 1974 cheap-beer-night riot at Municipal Stadium in Cleveland saw the game halted in the ninth inning when drunken and unruly fans jumped onto the field and charged Jeff Burroughs of the Texas Rangers. Rangers rushed to the field with bats to protect their teammate, and as Texas players made their way to the relative safety of the dugout, they were showered with beer and refuse as well as taunted and verbally abused. The Indians were forced to forfeit the game as the umpires determined that the crowd was out of control. *(United Press International)*

Madison Square Garden, seem to delight in their reputation as "animals."

Sports management has not faced the problems of crowd control energetically either because of its desire for profits or because of its recognition that crowds can incite a team to play more ferociously and can intimidate an opposing team. The reputations of certain stadia as "snake pits" are in fact real and tangible factors in the sports environment. Rivalries between cities like Pittsburgh and Cleveland become, in the sportscaster's terminology, "wars" or "shootouts" or "street brawls" where the designated warriors carry the honor and reputation of their cities onto the playing field. "Grudges" are carried over from game to game and year to year, and rivalries assume a significance that is partly media "hype" and partly the local desire for recognition and a feeling of dominance. All of these factors serve to increase the potential for crowd violence or disorder as the opposing team becomes a focus for abuse, animosity, and hatred, even if only momentary. Fans are supposed to be "fanatical" about their teams, but the fine line between enthusiastic support and dangerous, threatening behavior is difficult to draw, especially in heated, excited circumstances. Police efforts to control fan rowdyism are often met with hostility, outrage, and even resistance. As crowd sizes have increased dramatically, people who behave violently are more difficult to spot or isolate.

A number of reasons or explanations have been given for this reaction of fan violence. In an article in *The New York Times* in its July 27, 1980 issue, Bill Veeck, the owner of the Chicago White Sox, maintained that "possibly as a result of the '60s and early '70s there is less respect for the law, for people in authority. 'Do your own thing' is the quote, I believe."

However, another, more academic authority quoted in the same article, Ronald Kamm, a New Jersey psychiatrist who is a specialist in the psychology of sports, blames the owners who treat fans with disdain by switching franchises and trading players without consideration of fan loyalties. He believes that most of the disruptive behavior has been instigated by "disenfranchised people feeling the most impotent in terms of inflation" who seem to enjoy "seeing the effects of their destruction on television." According to Kamm, "they're lonely, isolated people trying to make a dent."

Another psychiatrist (often consulted on the subject by major-league baseball), Dr. Arthur Beisser of Los Angeles, had come to the same conclusion five years earlier. Quoted in the May 20, 1975 edition of *The New York Times*, Dr. Beisser stated, "We're seeing a new use of violence. It's being used not as a means to an end, but for recreational purposes, for pleasure. It's an end in itself."

However, Stanley Cheren, an associate professor of psychiatry at the Boston School of Medicine, in an article in *The New York Times*, January 13, 1980, attributed much of the cause of fan violence to the players. According to Cheren, "It is not the amount of violence in sport that creates violence in the crowd. If that were the case, boxing matches would be very dangerous to attend. In fact, they're O.K. for spectators. However, let the rules get broken enough and the crowd gets ugly. The fans take sides not only in a metaphoric sense but in a real sense. They become participants."

He cited an example in tennis, a noncontact sport, when in a match between Ilie Nastase and John McEnroe, the players "engaged in rewriting the structure of the contest." The crowd became unruly because "they had confused themselves with the contestants." Only when play had been resumed, despite the commotion and uproar, did the crowd become controlled. According to Cheren, it was "the acknowledged structure of the game" which worked to restore order.

His conclusion was:

The rules of the game dictate who may do what to whom. That holds aggression in some sort of control. The dramatic structure of the game gives the opportunity for resolution of that aggression. Resolution may take the form of exultant satisfaction (winning) or dejection (loss). But it is resolved, decided. The tension is gradually undone.

Players, coaches and officials can help to prevent madness in the stands by preventing madness on the field. They can keep dangerous situations to a minimum by an awareness of the group dynamic implication of their behavior. The rules and structure of the game itself are their tools and are powerful tools at that.

Some five months later, however, Dr. Cheren had modified his position somewhat. In an article entitled "Spectators and Violence: A Vicious Cycle Grows," in the October 26, 1980 issue of *The New York Times*, he asserted that "as the population becomes more experienced with violence, the need for more extreme violence to satisfy the wish for violent stimulation grows" and that we "have become accustomed to violence and injury" and "need increasing doses to get a rise out of us." He indicates that there is now a "jadedness" to the spectators and that "we just will not accept anything less than authentic horror, and when we have seen enough of that we will need something still more extreme." Thus according to him, the following situation now prevails among sports spectators:

For fans to respond in 1980, the fallen player has to demonstrate something more impressive and gruesome than pain. If he does not move a muscle, in other words looks dead, then some ripple of reaction runs through us; otherwise we just want the guy off the field and out of the way so that the game can go on. It takes that hushed sense of an ultimate stroke to make us tense up. A broken bone won't do it anymore.

Cheren concludes that there is no easy solution, since the pattern of fan reaction becomes a "self-supporting cycle." He calls for "some sort of social action" which will "interrupt the cycle" and which would "put a clear limit on how far the process of increasing levels of violence will be allowed to go." He suggests that league managements, players' associations, and the media can all play a role in setting a limit to spectator violence. Cheren's conclusions on the insatiable appetite and tolerance for sports violence are supported by Don Atyeo in *Blood and Guts: Violence in Sports* (1979).

The opinions of Dr. Cheren and other authorities may well explain why fans react violently. They do not explain precisely why the nature of the games being played has changed in the last ten to fifteen years. A number of other factors help to explain more adequately the dramatic increase of brutality and mayhem in the arenas and on the playing fields.

First, the major spectator sports have become a "Big Business." They have grown in attendance, in revenues, in number of franchises, and the amount of salaries they pay to players. Huge new indoor stadia such as the Houston Astrodome ($45 million), New Orleans Superdome ($163 million), and the Pontiac Silverdome ($55.7 million) have been built to accommodate larger audiences and to increase revenues for owners who find themselves in an increasingly expensive business. Often the average taxpayer is left to shoulder the burden of the building debt and frequent operational deficits. (The Pontiac Stadium receives an annual $900,000 subsidy from the state of Michigan and was financed with twenty-five million dollars of revenue bonds plus a city appropriation and loans.) On September 22, 1969, *U.S. News and World Report* published an article reporting that attendance at professional football games had doubled. Almost six years later, on September 8, 1975, the same publication reported that from 1965-1974 attendance at major sports events had increased from 206,007,000 to 273,247,000. Also during that period, the number of major-league teams in professional sports had increased from 57 to 173. Below is a table of comparative attendance for the major American spectator sports from 1961-77.

TABLE OF COMPARATIVE ATTENDANCE

(Attendance in millions, including all playoffs; number of teams in parentheses.)

	BASEBALL	PRO FOOTBALL	PRO BASKETBALL	COLLEGE FOOTBALL
1977	39.5 (26)	——	10.7 (22)	——
1976	31.8 (24)	11.5 (28)	10.8 (25)	32.0 (637)
1975	30.4 (24)	10.7 (26)	10.7 (28)	31.7 (634)
1971	29.7 (24)	10.5 (26)	8.7 (28)	30.5 (618)
1966	25.3 (20)	7.6 (24)	3.0 (9)	25.3 (616)
1961	18.9 (18)	5.1 (22)	2.0 (8)	20.7 (616)

(Attendance per game, approximate.)

	BASEBALL	PRO FOOTBALL	PRO BASKETBALL	COLLEGE FOOTBALL
1977	20,000	——	11,200	——
1976	16,300	57,000	9,700	10,300
1975	15,600	57,000	8,600	10,300
1971	15,200	56,000	7,100	10,300
1966	15,600	45,000	7,700	9,100
1961	13,000	37,500	5,800	7,700

Source: *New York Times*
October 21, 1977

According to Robert C. Yeager, author of *Seasons of Shame: The New Violence in Sports* (1979), by 1973 pro football attendance averaged 58,891 per game, which was ninety-six percent of the seating capacity. In addition, by 1980, baseball had added 868 games to its schedule; basketball, 614 games; hockey, 510 contests; and football, 124. The total gross revenues for the four major sports had exceeded 700 million dollars per year.

Salaries had increased astronomically by 1980. Top women tennis stars were grossing anywhere from $100,000 to $500,000 a year. A number of top male golfers hit the $100,000 mark annually. In team sports, salaries soared skyward also. Joe Namath's signing for $400,000 in 1965 was looked on as phenomenal. By 1980, journeymen free-agent baseball players secured themselves extremely lucrative contracts, while established stars such as Pete Rose, Dave Parker, Rod Carew, Jim Rice, and George Foster could haul down million-dollar-a-year (or close to that figure) contracts.

In football, O. J. Simpson, obviously not the runner he was as a rookie with the Buffalo Bills, was paid over $700,000 to play for the San Francisco 49ers in 1978. Other top runners and quarterbacks also received salaries that reflected their importance to their franchises.

In pro basketball, Rick Barry received $500,000 per year, and in 1981 Earvin Johnson, the Los Angeles Lakers' sensational guard who led them to the NBA championship, signed a renegotiated contract that guaranteed him an estimated $1.5 million per year. Robert Yeager points out in his *Seasons Of Shame* that:

Average player pay in the four major American professional sports more than quadrupled in the 1967-77 decade, from $20,783 to $92,659. Taken separately, basketball paychecks soared 715 percent; hockey, 502 percent; baseball, 400 percent; football, 221 percent.

But Yeager has also noted that all players do not benefit equally from the largesse. For example, he points out that an "average" defensive back receives only $47,403 and that an "average" NBA player is paid $30,000. Yeager notes, "Indeed, the wide variance in player salaries is thought by some experts to contribute to playing-field violence." This kind of conjecture or supposition is hard to prove. One could just as easily argue that the highly paid stars are the source of a sport's popularity and box-office draw and that their health is vital to a sport's well-being. Thus, the high salaries provide for restraints on violence as players recognize that healthy, playing stars insure benefits for all.

With big money at stake, the emphasis is on winning, because winners produce profits and get into playoffs, which produce more profits. Winners are paid more; losers simply do not make money. Losing coaches get fired, losing teams lose fan support, and more importantly, losers are not featured on Monday-night television. Therefore, the profit motivation has undoubtedly contributed to the win-at-any-cost syndrome that encourages violent play. Players see shorter careers facing them because of injuries or replacement by younger, more skilled players or better box-office draws. The conditions of the game dictate a psychology of self-sacrifice and assertive individualism, thus negating traditions of sportsmanship or mutual concerns for well-being and health after the sports careers.

Television and the other media have also contributed, often in hidden ways, to the increasing violence in sports. The increased coverage of professional football by television and photojournalism cameras has made the documentation of violence graphic, specific, and sensational. Now millions can view instant replays of vicious and illegal tackles, "trench" violence at the line of scrimmage with punches and head slaps, injured quarterbacks, and unconscious players who have "had their bell rung" or "their lights put out," in the popular sportscaster lingo. Certain announcers, notably former players like Merlin Olsen or John Brodie, emphasize the cult of manly violence in their "color" commentary on the game. Pre-game interviews often become a litany of boasts, threats, and promises of violence, notably against the key performers of the opponents. On the field boom microphones record the audio violence of the two teams pounding each other, although the profanity and verbal abuse are usually filtered out.

The atmosphere of the professional game is charged with violence or its potential. Violent men make better stories for sports journalists because these players are seen as more complex, colorful, or quotable. The violence becomes part of the new legends and myths of the sports as fans learn how these giants "psych" themselves up into a rage or angry frame of mind to wreak havoc or intimidate to gain an edge. Meanness becomes a norm of the game—"to get them before they get you." Players may even exult in inflicting an injury with an open display of celebration as an opponent lies unconscious or writhes in pain.

Thus, the sports media have often taken an ambivalent and inconsistent attitude toward unnecessary or excessive violence on the field, celebrating it on one hand and condemning its worst excesses (those that result in serious injuries) on the other. For the most part, the violence of pro football is accepted uncritically and matter of factly as part of the game, and players are applauded or admired for "playing hurt," which often means playing with injections of pain killers or resorting to drugs. Roger Staubach suffered ten concussions, three in his last season, before he saw the wisdom of retiring. The sports press rarely reports on the hospitalization, treatment, rehabilitation, or disabilities of injured players. The casualties are paid off and ignored by the press. Thus, the media help to reinforce the prevailing violence by lionizing the "hitters and hurters," by accepting the violence as a necessary and inevitable consequence of the game, and by failing to report fully on the casualties and victims. A CBS *60 Minutes* segment on violence in pro football is quickly forgotten in the hype and excitement of next week's play-off game. The manly code of toughness, gritty determination, brawn over brain, and unflinching acceptance of pain is constantly reinforced in the ritual of the physical confrontation.

Another factor that has contributed to the increasing popularity and physical violence of pro football since the mid-1950s has been the technical sophistication of the game and play execution, as strategy and game plans become the keys to success. In 1950 pro football instituted the free substitution rule, which was to have enormous impact upon the game. This change was in direct opposition to the move that the colleges would make in 1953, when they returned to one-platoon football. With two-platoon football, the pro teams could utilize specialists better and could concentrate in training on various facets of execution. The result was a better, more polished game. Finesse on offense could now be met with finesse on defense. In addition, the platoon system extended the longevity of players' careers— thus allowing football to develop perennial stars, just like baseball—and fans could talk about pro-football players' feats year round.

Thomas B. Morgan, in an article entitled "The American War Game" in *Esquire*, October 1965, has noted that specialization

... gives the game a tougher basis—tougher because individual players are better at what they do and likely to be better able to do it throughout the game. Nowadays, one is more likely than ever before to see blocking and tackling as crisp and brutal in the last minute of play as in the first. Sixty minute players, working both offense and defense would be annihilated in such a game.

In regard to specialization on offense, the quarterback became dominant. With a flick of a wrist an adroit flinger could sling salvos of passes downfield to fleet-footed receivers, thus negating the impact of oncharging defensive linemen or "red-dogging" linebackers. Thus, specialization of the quarterback, who became essentially a nonrunner who either handed off or passed and did not have to play defense, called for an evolution of a new type of player—"the linebacker."

To avoid being stung by the offense's throwing to a back coming out of the backfield, teams began dropping back the middle guard to protect against the pass. Soon two other linemen joined him to form what would become the standard 4-3 pro-defense. So quickly did the importance of this position become apparent that when the Detroit Lions defeated the Cleveland Browns 59-14 in the 1957 NFL Championship game, middle linebacker Joe Schmidt was carried off by knowledgeable Detroit fans at Briggs Stadium.

Specialization meant that players could be physically developed so that they could increase their own skills to a higher level than before. Coaches became specialized, and separate defensive and offensive coordinators were introduced. The specialization spread to the special teams or so-called "suicide" squads, that, according to one expert, will "in a few fractions of a second they will collide" cause "more sheer violence, and more injuries, than from any other part of the game." Punt and kickoff returns have also produced more penalty situations than any other phase of the game as clips, face-mask grabbing, and unnecessary roughness take their toll of injuries and increase animosities between players who have hyped themselves up to manhandle each other.

In recent years players began to make their physical training a twelve-month-a-year job. This meant they were in better condition than their predecessors to physically carry out their assignments. Sid Gillman, former San Diego Charger coach, stated in 1965 that football was a rougher game than ever before "because we have been replacing potbellies with a new breed of bigger, stronger, quicker, faster young men in top condition—you can't get ready for the season in a steam bath anymore."

Specialization meant that larger-sized physical specimens played the game. Linebackers became a breed unto themselves. Generally they were

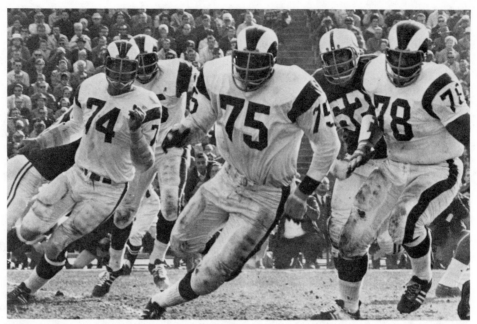

The development of the front four in professional football added to the physical violence of the game as defensive linemen became agile and quick to complement size and weight. The war in the "trenches" (on the line of scrimmage) became a key to victory or defeat as quarterbacks became hunted game and sometimes victims of the passrush and "sacks." The Los Angeles Rams' "Fearsome Foursome," led by David "Deacon" Jones, was an awesome unit of physical power and mobility. *(Pro Football Hall of Fame)*

well over six feet tall, weighing between 220 and 240 pounds. Joe Schmidt of the Detroit Lions, Sam Huff of the New York Giants, Ray Nitschke of the Green Bay Packers, and Bill George and Dick Butkus of the Chicago Bears were just some of the stellar standouts at the middle linebacker position. Butkus's play earned him such terms of endearment as "Animal," "the Enforcer," and the "Maestro of Mayhem." Ironically, Butkus was forced to retire from pro football in 1973 after a relatively short career, numerous knee injuries putting an end to his playing days. Eventually an out-of-court settlement of $600,000 from the Bears allowed him to search for another "meaningful" career.

At the same time defensive linemen became larger. It was not unusual to see linemen who were 6'4" in height and weighed close to three hundred pounds. Roosevelt Grier of the Los Angeles Rams was 6'5" and 290 pounds; Roger Brown of the Detroit Lions was 6'5" and 300 pounds; and Ernie Ladd of the San Diego Chargers and Kansas City Chiefs was 6'9" and 311 pounds, teaming with Buck Buchanan, who was 6'7" and weighed 275 pounds.

Not only was this new breed of linemen gargantuan in physical size, but they were remarkably quick in pursuit. Alex Karras, former lineman for the Detroit Lions, in his book *Even Big Guys Cry* (1977), notes that Roger Brown was quicker than a former Olympic dashman. A phrase coined by the television commentators came to describe the new pro-defenders in the trenches: "mobile, agile, and hostile"—and they were.

Quarterbacks and running backs also grew larger, but there was a limited advantage in this since at these positions a loss of mobility and speed usually accompanies a larger body size. It is no wonder that quarterbacks and running backs generally suffer the most injuries. A report commissioned by the National Football League Players' Association and the owners' management council has found that every professional football team runs a fifty percent chance of losing a running back because of surgery each year. The report indicated that "a running back had greater than twice the likelihood of sustaining an injury of the kind described here than any other player on the team, excluding quarterbacks."

N.F.L. INJURIES REQUIRING SURGERY

NO. = number of players requiring surgery;
PCT. = percentage of injuries requiring surgery.

	1978		1979		TOTAL	
OFFENSE	NO.	PCT.	NO.	PCT.	NO.	PCT.
Center	1	1.7	1	1.3	2	1.5
Guard	6	10.3	5	6.5	11	8.1
Tackle	4	6.9	2	2.6	6	4.4
Tight End	2	3.4	4	5.2	6	4.4
Quarterback	6	10.3	2	2.6	8	5.9
Running Back	12	20.7	16	20.8	28	20.7
Wide Receiver	3	5.2	8	10.4	11	8.1
TOTAL	34	58.5	38	49.4	72	53.1
DEFENSE						
Line	7	12.0	7	9.1	14	10.4
Linebacker	6	10.3	12	15.6	18	13.3
Back	2	3.4	12	15.6	14	10.4
TOTAL	15	25.7	31	40.3	46	34.1
SPECIAL TEAMS	6	10.3	8	10.4	14	10.4
OTHER	3	5.2			3	2.2
TOTAL INJURIES	58		77		135	

Source: National Football League Players' Association
Published September 21, 1980, *New York Times*

Thus with the evolution of the modern professional football game, the elimination of key offensive personnel could mean the difference between winning and losing. Detroit Lion tackle Bob Miller was quoted in the October 24, 1955 issue of *Life* as saying, "We're not trying to hurt anybody, but it's no secret that star pro passers are a bad insurance risk. They get hit even after they get rid of the ball."

In 1956, the Detroit Lions asked that the Chicago Bears defensive lineman Ed Meadows be banned for life for his blind-side hit of star passer Bobby Layne in the Western Conference championship game. An investigation was made, but the Lions did not get their wish. However, it was disclosed that "a 1951-53 member of the Los Angeles Rams was anonymously quoted as saying that the Rams had a get-the-quarterback cash pool, which went to the player who knocked the rival quarterback out of the game."

Joe Namath, whose celebrated gimpy knees were often the target of the NFL's most infamous hit artists, had his career of playing with the violence and pain featured in an article in the October 1976 issue of the *Saturday Evening Post*. The article concluded that:

There are all kinds of legal and illegal ways to mangle, mash, and mutilate a quarterback. Joe's tried them all from the wrong end of the action—proving that the best way to break up a play is to break up the players.

With this fact evident, the infliction of pain became a strategic weapon. In his "The American War Game," Thomas B. Morgan has documented his theory about pain as an attrition factor. "Tackled again and again, twisted, stomped, gouged, and repeatedly buried under a half ton of flesh, even the best may be discouraged by the fourth quarter. The pressured quarterback may begin throwing too soon or the aching halfback may falter, especially on faking assignments . . . roughly one-fourth of scoring in the NFL Championship games since 1933 has occurred in the fourth quarter. If, as may be assumed, players are at their physical peak in the earlier period, scoring in the fourth quarter probably should be lower. That it isn't, indicates, I think, that the strategy of pain works."

Aspiring defensive players, eager to get a share of the big bucks, soon earned reputations as intimidators. Included among them were such impresarios of mayhem as Fred "The Hammer" Williamson, who had boasted of his infamous arm chop until he was neutralized by the Packers in the first Super Bowl. Dick Butkus and his heir apparent with the Chicago Bears, Doug Plank, were notorious late-hitters. "Mean" Joe Green of the Pittsburgh Steelers dynasty did not win his nickname for being "Mr. Nice Guy" but for his devastating head slaps. And of course, Jack Tatum, the man responsible for paralyzing Darryl Stingley, recalls with gusto in his autobiography how he enjoyed hitting a receiver and then emitting a train whistle. As long as the "bad ass" image is romanticized, glamorized, and more importantly, rewarded, then excess violence will exist in pro football or any other sport.

Another major factor in the escalation and proliferation of violence has been the "new breed" of coaches. For example, college administrations tolerate men like Woody Hayes and Bobby Knight, who despite violent outbursts and ill treatment of their own players continue to coach because they are "winners," unless an "incident" occurs which is too big to ignore—as in Hayes' case when he slugged a player who had intercepted an Ohio State pass and sealed a Buckeye bowl defeat.

In pro football Vince Lombardi, who supposedly stated that "winning isn't everything, it's the only thing" and who emphasized playing with pain,

Violence in the National Hockey League saw an unexpected development in December, 1979, when members of the Boston Bruins, led by Terry O'Reilly, went into the stands at Madison Square Garden and scuffled with fans. Fortunately, security personnel prevented a wholesale riot. *(Wide World)*

and George Allen, who once said "losing is worse than death," embodied the win-at-all-cost syndrome. Yet Dr. Thomas Tutko, co-founder of the Institute of Athletic Motivation at San Jose State University, has found in pro sports that victors are ruthless and unhappy because "Most Americans truly believe that they're going to walk on water if they win. But winning is like drinking salt water. It's never saleable."

To reduce injuries and to open up the offenses and make the game more popular, the NFL has recently made several rule changes. In 1978, the so-called "chuck" rule was revised. Defensive backs were restricted to one hit of pass receivers within five yards of the line of scrimmage. Also, offensive linemen were allowed to open their arms while fighting off charging-behemoth defensive linemen, lessening the amount of holding penalties and allowing the quarterbacks additional time to pass. The result was that from 1977 to 1979 average points per game increased by seventeen percent, and 286 more touchdowns were scored in 1979, the majority via the air route. Halfway through the 1980 season, *The New York Times* in its October 26, 1980 edition reported that there were twenty games in which quarterbacks passed for 300 yards or more, compared with fifteen the previous year in which there were three 400-yard performances, the first since 1976. Obviously pro football has moved in one direction to lessen violence, but more has to be done.

Why do anything about sports violence and its increasing prevalence and intensity? The authors would agree with Robert Yeager, author of *Seasons of Shame*, that "violence in sports is an important issue because sports

144   themselves are important—and in ways and to an extent they never were before" and "what is different is that our athletics have become a surrogate ethic in a secular time. There may be no other faith that binds us quite so universally." Whatever atavistic qualities that civilized man has sublimated, the predator instincts of human beings still have lurked close beneath the surface veneer of what passed for civilized behavior, and identification with the violence of pro football and other sports has allowed the passive, middle-class, average American a chance to safely rid himself of bottled-up violence and hostility without getting arrested—most of the time. Thus for the average fan, the pro players have become the "new gladiators" who wage war on the Sabbath and "ask nor give no quarter."

If sports won't clean up its act, then, the "Law Just Might." So says Arthur R. Miller, faculty member of the Harvard Law School in a column in the *Detroit News* of October 21, 1980. Such weighty legal periodicals as *The American Criminal Law Review* and *Wisconsin Law Review* have featured articles on sports violence and the criminal law. The January 1977 issue of *Trial* magazine is devoted to the matter of sports litigation. And as 1981 dawns, at least one congressman has attempted to make "excessive" violence on the playing fields a federal crime, punishable by a fine of not more than $5,000 or imprisonment not more than one year, or both. The Mottl Bill (introduced by Representative Ronald M. Mottl of Ohio) hearings were largely ignored by the sports establishment and the commissioners of the professional leagues. While it is unlikely that such a bill will pass in its originally proposed form, the very threat of federal legislation may bring about internal reforms. A court settlement of a lawsuit involving physical violence, with the infliction of criminal punishments against the offender in addition to punitive damages, would force the issue and bring a sense of urgency to controls and reforms.

One hopes that the impetus for needed restraints will come from within the sports establishment, even if this may mean banning certain players for life or for a season in order to protect the future of the sport. Long-range studies of the effects of injuries and disabilities on health and longevity may help players to understand the future consequences of the violence they accept and endure for the sake of earnings, glory, and press exposure. Fans need to understand the complex psychology of their involvement in sports and their role in being influenced by and influencing the violent excesses of a sport. They need to appreciate the skills of noncontact, evasion, and restraint as much as the head-on violence and confrontation. Violence in sports, however, is only symptomatic of larger problems of violence and aggression in society as a whole, and American society has many social problems to resolve before the cult and ugly realities of violence are confronted and seen for what they are.

Sources and Suggested Readings

Furlong, William Barry. "Football Violence." *The New York Times Magazine* (November 30, 1980), 38-41, 122, 124, 126, 128, 132, 134.

Morgan, Thomas B. "The American War Game." *Esquire* (October, 1965).

Roberts, Michael. *Fans! How We Go Crazy Over Sports* (Washington, D.C., 1976).

Runfola, Ross T. "Violence in Sports: Mirror of American Society?" *Vital Issues*, Volume 24.

Surface, Bill. "Pro Football: Is It Getting Too Dirty?" *The Reader's Digest* (November, 1974), 151-154.

Telander, Rick. "The Knee." *Esquire* (October, 1980).

Underwood, John. *The Death of An American Game: The Crisis in Football* (Boston-Toronto, 1970).

Yeager, Robert C. *Seasons of Shame: The New Violence in Sports* (New York, 1979).

Sadaharu Oh of the Toyko Giants smashing the home run which broke Henry Aaron's record. Oh is one reason why baseball is the number-one game in Japan. *(Asahi Shimbun)*

12

The American Sports Empire

William J. Miller

When Dr. Forrest C. "Phog" Allen, long-time University of Kansas basketball coach, asked the U.S. Olympic Committee to include his sport in the Amsterdam Games of 1928, it refused with the amazing observation that ". . . nowhere, except in the United States, is basketball played." Apparently, the elite group had not been informed that already forty-nine nations were enjoying the game. Today, that number has probably tripled. But basketball is not the only U.S.-originated game played internationally, since baseball and volleyball, as well, are true "world sports" to a degree astonishing to most Americans. The dissemination of baseball, basketball, and volleyball represent a kind of "American sports empire" to Western Europe, the U.S.S.R. (including Eastern Europe), Latin America, and East Asia. Significantly, they have helped to shape the American image overseas.

Baseball abroad owes much to player tours, the enthusiasm of American-educated foreigners returning home with the game, and the financial support of business interests. In 1874, the Boston and Philadelphia teams played in England and Ireland. A world excursion in 1888-1889 took the Chicago White Stockings of A.G. Spalding to Australia, Egypt, and the British Isles. Spectators obviously enjoyed the game but did not rush to play it. Just before World War I, John J. McGraw's New York Giants and Charles A. Comiskey's Chicago White Sox visited nine countries in East Asia and Western Europe. British King George V liked the game and commented on baseball's resemblance to cricket. Generally the British viewed baseball with modest interest. Japan, however, responded enthusiastically to the game. After preliminary visitations in 1908 and 1931, baseball executives dispatched an American League All-Star team in 1934, which made Babe Ruth a legend in Japan and led to the formation of the first Japanese professional league two years later. More recently Japan has hosted a big-league team each year since 1953. In addition, players and umpires have conducted frequent "clinics" in the fundamentals of the game in Japan and many other countries.

Following these first tours, Western Europe adopted baseball to a degree not realized by many Americans. Played both on an amateur and on a "semi-pro" basis (by U.S. standards), its organization resembles soccer, because generally athletic clubs and business organizations act as sponsors rather than academic institutions. Games take place on weekends or holidays. The sport attracts considerable support from middle and working classes, cheering for their factory teams. Soccer, however, remains decidedly the predominant spectator sport. Holland and Italy operate the best-established baseball programs, with France, West Germany, Spain, and Britain also supporting the game.

The Netherlands discovered baseball when J.C.G. Grasé, a Dutch schoolmaster just returned from the U.S., founded the Nederlands Honkbal Bond (Netherlands Baseball Association) in 1912, with business support. The game developed an enthusiastic following. After World War II, factory teams predominated in an eighty-four club, eight-league organization, divided into four classifications. The Main League represented the top circuit, playing a twenty-eight game schedule. Jan Hartog, a prominent businessman, headed the NHB, controlling some 9,000 players. "Haarlem Baseball Week" climaxed the season, pitting the best Dutch team against three others from among the top U.S. "semi-pro" clubs, U.S. military bases, or other European teams. Dutch players often worked with American clubs in Florida spring training. Fan interest, although enthusiastic, is not extensive, limited to fellow workers largely, with crowds averaging about three thousand. Terms like "slag" (strike), "wyd" (ball), "scheidsrechter" (umpire), and "werper" (pitcher) sound strange to American ears.

Italy adopted baseball after World War II, when two American sergeants (a superintendent of the U.S. cemetery at Anzio and his assistant) taught the game to Italian boys from the nearby village of Nettuno, using equipment left by departing GI's. Horace McGarrity and Jimmy del Sole, from the New York City area, persuaded Prince Steno Borghese of the noble Roman family, to lend part of his estate for playing fields. The prince then solicited the assistance of Italian business houses to found the "Federazione Italiana Palla Base" in 1952. Most clubs were attached to factories. By the mid-1950s, eighty-two teams made up leagues in three classifications. Teams contracted for American players but were limited to two, and none could pitch. Drawn mostly from the proletariat, spectator interest is intense within restricted numbers. Bad officiating prevails. Games feature frequent fights, debris thrown on the field, open threats to players, and the din from noise-makers, but everyone enjoys himself.

The United States has assisted by regularly donating equipment from American military centers. Also, prominent Italian-Americans established "Baseball for Italy" in 1958 as a working organization. Lou Perini, president of the Milwaukee Braves, Joe DiMaggio, famed Yankee slugger, and Yogi Berra, former catcher-manager of the Yankees, aided with equipment and traveling clinics. Italian teams in turn have frequently sent players, coaches, and managers to U.S. spring training camps.

Terms like "pallo" (ball), "battuta" (bat), "finito" (out), and "batta-

tore" (batter) abound, and Italian-American former players such as Di
Maggio, Berra, Vic Raschi, Carl Furillo, and Joe Garagiola make excellent
copy in Italian sports journals. One such publication, *Tuttobaseball*, from
Milan, gives American stars much exposure.

Other Western European countries have set up similar baseball organizations. France first saw the game during World War I when American
doughboys such as major leaguers Hank Gowdy and Christy Mathewson
taught the game to French "poilus." French soldiers attributed the American
ability to throw hand grenades great distances to their baseball skills.
Georges Bruni, a French baseball enthusiast, organized a league after the war,
but the game has not been extremely popular among the French. British
interest stems from the U.S. military presence in both World War I and II,
but that country can lay some claim to having originated the game from
"Town Ball" and "One O'Cat" (traditional children's diversions) and
"Rounders" (an adult pastime still played). Fred Lewis, a Boy Scout leader,
looking for some suitable activity for his troop, introduced baseball as such in
1912. Several club and factory teams around London emerged after 1918, and
more followed after World War II. Cricket, however, remained dominant in
Britain, and its superficial resemblance to the American sport probably prevented baseball from taking root in that country. West Germany first saw the
game in U.S. Army camps after World War II. The German Amateur Baseball
Federation was founded by a prominent industrialist, Claus Helmig. American touring clinics regularly visited German teams. The group of players and
umpires, headed by Red Schoendienst (then manager of the St. Louis Cardinals), which met at Wiesbaden in 1971, proved especially successful.

Since Western European baseball is largely a weekend diversion, the quality of play, even in Holland and Italy, is barely professional by U.S. standards. Generally, Europeans lack the agility developed only after years of
competition. Probably until baseball can attach itself firmly to the educational system so that the children can grow with the game, it will not have great
impact in Western Europe. Nevertheless, the sport does assist the U.S. image
there in a modest way as a symbol of social and political freedom to workers
and mercantile interests, but its following among fans is not substantial.

Eastern Europe exhibits no significant interest in baseball, perhaps
because its politically authoritarian traditions find the game's individualism
uncongenial. The Communistic model of the U.S.S.R., where sport is a
government-dominated function to rivet popular loyalty to the totalitarian
state on a mass basis, is emulated by the smaller countries but with national
differences. The Soviets stress above all the Olympic sports of which baseball is not one.

As a non-Communist state, Finland, however, presents an interesting
exception. Lauri Pikhala, a Finn just returned from the U.S., introduced a
"hybrid" of baseball to his country in 1919. "Pesapallo" placed the bases
in the corners of a triangle and the pitcher (throwing underhanded) only five
feet from the batter. A cloth-covered, relatively "dead" ball and slender bat

150   kept play within a rather small, rectangular area. Thus, more players were brought directly into the action by eliminating the dominant pitcher-batter duel. Also, fewer injuries occurred. Schools, labor groups, and army camps contributed 100,000 participants to the game by World War II, while the government regularly subsidized the sport, impressed by its considerable popularity and comparatively low cost.

Latin American baseball presents the most extensive organization outside of the United States and has sent hundreds of players to the major leagues in this country. In turn, American professional baseball regularly pays expenses for their young players to compete in the various Caribbean "winter leagues." Veterans often gain managerial experience as well. Many of the first winter leagues date from the turn of the century, but formal regional competition did not see realization until 1949, when the first "Las Series del Caribe" matched championship teams from Cuba, Puerto Rico, Panama, and Venezuela. When Fidel Castro's revolution withdrew Cuba, competition was continued with the addition of Nicaragua, Mexico, and the Dominican Republic to this "Caribbean Series" by 1970.

The Dominican Republic learned baseball (1891) from a Puerto Rican teacher, who had played the game with Americans, and Mexico first saw the sport when the Chicago White Sox visited in 1906. Organization, however, was slow in coming, since it was not until 1925 that the Mexican League was born. Only when Jorge Pasquel, the business tycoon, enticed American players to jump their contracts in 1946, did U.S. professional baseball admit the Mexican League with AA classification nine years later. Pasquel's inducements also forced American owners to grant the first player fringe benefits—direct representation and pensions—leading eventually to today's huge bonus contracts.

Emilio Sabourin, "the A.G. Spalding of Cuban baseball," introduced the sport to that country in 1874, establishing its first league four years later. U.S. professional baseball moved directly into Cuba when Bobby Maduro's Havana Sugar Kings played in the International League (class AAA) from 1954-1960. A respected baseball man, Maduro moved his franchise to the U.S., becoming Commissioner Bowie Kuhn's chief adviser on Latin American baseball after Castro's take-over.

Baseball continues under Cuban Communism as part of a centrally directed sports program. Cuban sport serves the socialist state as a government institution for national physical fitness. INDER (Instituto Nacional de Deportes, Educacion y Recreation) acts as coordinator through the schools, workers' clubs, and special sports schools. Cuba's Havana stadium, renovated in 1971, serves as a monument to Cuba's sports in general and baseball in particular. The INDER program has organized leagues controlling 493,000 players with teams based in cities and rural villages. A thirty-nine game series leads to a fifty-four game elimination from which an all-star team is chosen for international competition, used primarily for propaganda purposes in the rest of Latin America.

Cuban baseball teams have won four titles in the Pan-American Games since their inception in 1951, gaining three (1963, 1971, 1975) since Cas-

New York Giants Ruben Gomez, Willie Mays, and Herman Franks participating in winter ball in Puerto Rico, 1954. *(Wide World)*

tro's revolution—a positive example to all Hispanic-America of Marxist achievement. Baseball provides all Latin Americans with a field for equal competition with the "Yanquis" to the north. Recalling what he regards as the "imperialist exploitation" of the Monroe Doctrine, the Latin American often is willing to wager that a team from his hemisphere could defeat the best the United States has to offer. His aspirations frequently identify with Cuba's, especially when Castro speaks of the ultimate contest: "One day, when the Yankees accept peaceful coexistence with our own country, we shall beat them at baseball too and then the advantages of revolutionary over capitalist sport will be shown!" Many peoples of Central and South America await the outcome.

Historian Jonathan Kolatch rightly affirms that baseball in China stands upon a rich sporting tradition. Chinese "martial arts" (*wushu*) date from fifteen hundred years before Christ. Of these arts *taichichuan* ("bare-hand exercise") has been the most popular. Sports went virtually into a two-millenium eclipse, however, because the Confucian tradition stressed social harmony and the intellectual life. Not until the nineteenth century, did westernized military academies reinstitute organized sports. Then the Young Men's Christian Association (YMCA) established the first popular sports program for the cities in 1896, and baseball made a modest entrance eleven years later. The Nationalist movement also used sport to militarize the country after its victory in 1928.

When the Communist triumph created the People's Republic in 1949, a full-scale sports program to achieve popular physical fitness for jobs and national defense regimented the people in support of the state. Mao

152 Zedong's personal interest in sport inspired the effort. He created the National Games (1958), and baseball entered this competition in 1974. All
sports were administered through academic institutions, communes, urban
worker complexes, and "spare-time sports schools." Table tennis, basketball,
track and field, and volleyball ranked ahead of baseball, however, but a new
facility for the last sport was built in the late 1970s. What role the United
States will play in advancing the game is still to be determined in this era of
renewed Chinese-American cooperation, but baseball may provide some
common meeting ground.

Across the Formosa Strait, Taiwan (now the Republic of China) learned
baseball from the Japanese, who ruled the island from 1895-1945. After
liberation, a group of native Taiwanese desired to preserve the game. Hsieh
Kuo-cheng, a graduate of Waseda University (the "Notre Dame" of Japanese
college baseball) organized a six-team men's league and a similar organization
for boys in 1948. Visiting Japanese suggested the boys join the Little League
(ages 9-12). A Taiwanese team eventually won the "World's Series" in Wil-
liamsport, Pennsylvania, in 1969. Four successive titles (1971-1974), however, prompted opponents to complain of overage players and professional
instructors. But cleared of all charges, a Taiwanese team won again in 1977.
The success of the Little League program, in addition to Taiwan's remarkable economic advances over the same period, has done much to offset the
increasing diplomatic isolation of the country since her expulsion from the
United Nations in October, 1971.

Outside of the United States, baseball is most popular in Japan. Horace
Wilson, an American teacher, introduced the sport in 1873. The Japanese
embraced the game, played by a student elite, as an expression of an aggressive national character in the competitive spirit of Social Darwinism, a
dominant philosophy of the "Age of Imperialism," as historian Donald
Roden explains. Baseball would enable the Japanese to prove their equality
in the family of nations and thus to be rid of the "unequal treaties" as Japan
moved towards modernization in her Meiji Era.

For a long time strictly amateur, the sport organized the Japanese Professional Baseball League in 1936, two years after Babe Ruth's visit to Japan.
Even the war did not kill baseball as it continued on a reduced schedule. "To
hell with Babe Ruth" was the taunt of the Japanese soldier against the American GI in the Southwest Pacific. Under the Occupation, baseball was re-
emphasized to offset the warlike "martial arts," and the Pacific League was
formed with six teams in 1950. The older circuit continued under a new
name, the Central League. Team designations derived from sponsoring business firms: Yomiuri Giants, Nippon Ham Fighters. Crowds reached 100,000
even for high school tournaments in Tokyo's Korakuen Stadium.

Sadaharu Oh is the "Babe Ruth of Japan." Over a twenty-one year career
(1959-1980), this Giant first baseman compiled a .301 average and 868
career home runs (a record), while earning $7-1/2 million. He enjoys the
popularity of a film celebrity, a concert artist, and a sports hero in combination. Another star is Shigeo Nagashima, third baseman-manager for the

Giants, who once hit a "sayonara home run" (game-ending homer) in the presence of the emperor.

To give their hitting more punch, the Japanese began to import American *gaijin* ("outsiders") in the late 1950s. Each team is restricted to two foreign players, but the experience has not been all that pleasant. Americans resent the regimentation of Japanese baseball, especially spring training in January cold, protracted workouts even in the rain, and stifling dormitory atmospheres. The samurai ideals of respect for authority, group loyalty, and regard for old age and "face" are often beyond foreign comprehension. On the other hand, Japanese resent American abrasiveness and individuality, which often disturb the harmony (or "Wa") of the team. The behavior of many American players has not endeared them to the Japanese. Although often a home-run hero to many Japanese fans, to his teammates the *gaijin* is frequently an "outsider." The collective experience has not helped the American image in Japan.

Although invented by a Canadian, basketball is an American game that the rest of the world has adopted. One hundred forty-five countries have national organizations, presided over by the "Federation Internationale de Basketball Amateur." Since James A. Naismith created the sport in the Springfield, Massachusetts, YMCA (1891), that organization carried basketball to many countries. Fifty nations had adopted the sport by 1930, making it eligible for the Olympics of 1936. Before World War II, basketball had between eighteen and twenty million participants.

Today, forty million play in Europe alone on all levels. The European Basketball League controls the organized game in France, Belgium, West Germany, Italy, Spain, Poland, Czechoslovakia, Yugoslavia, the U.S.S.R., and Israel. Russia has dominated play since World War II. Again, like soccer, Western European teams are sponsored by athletic clubs and some business organizations rather than by schools. Well over three hundred clubs exist in Western Europe. Italy has twenty-eight teams, divided into A-1 and A-2 classifications, directed by the "Federazione Italiana Pallacanestro." Programs in other countries are similarly organized.

To offset Russian superiority, many Western European teams began importing American players in the mid-1960s. Rhodes Scholar Bill Bradley, formerly of Princeton University, commuted from Oxford University to play with Simmenthal of Milan. The usual player, however, is not quite equal to NBA calibre in the States. Teams are permitted two Americans, and there are probably as many as 2,000-3,000 from the States participating at the present time. Tall centers and forwards who can score between twenty and thirty points a game are most in demand. Contracts usually called for $20-30,000 a year, with most living expenses, in the mid-1970s. Those willing to bring their families, learn the language, and generally adapt to their environment usually prove successful. Bob Morse of the University of Pennsylvania has played eight years for the Varese team of Italy. Aulcie Perry of the Tel Aviv Maccabis has played four years, while Spencer Haywood, star of the 1968 Olympic team but released by the NBA, has found a new home with the Venice Carreras. Admittedly not up to American professional standards,

154   Western European basketball is somewhat slower but commands considerable following among working and business classes. The American player, in the overall, is popular and has credited himself with Europeans, enhancing his country's image to an appreciable extent.

Eastern European basketball strives to serve the totalitarian state but with highly centralized programs again differing in the various countries. Yugoslavia's teams have been quite successful, finishing second only to the United States in the 1976 Olympics. Czechoslovakia builds on the historic national physical fitness tradition of the "Sokol" (Falcon) movement dating from 1866. East Germany, which captured forty Olympic gold medals in 1976, follows the Prussian tradition of sports as a part of military training. All programs strongly emphasize the Olympic sports of which basketball is a part.

For the past sixty years, the U.S.S.R. has used sport to help change a backward, agricultural country of vast size into a modern technological state. As James Riordan, the sports historian, tells us, basketball entered Russia in 1906 when Mayak, a St. Petersburg athletic club, adopted the game and competed with the Bogatyr' Society. Mayak defeated a touring U.S. team in 1909. The Russian Revolution of 1917 eventually placed the sport under the Soviet Basketball Federation. First international competition sent a Soviet women's team to France in 1935. Just after World War II, the Soviets joined the European Basketball League, winning its championship eleven times. In addition, they have gained the world title twice and the Olympic crown once (in 1972). About three million of both sexes play the game in the U.S.S.R.

Latin American basketball has been most competitive. Miguel Angrel Moenck, a faculty member at the University of Havana, brought the game to Cuba in 1907. Puerto Rico first saw basketball in 1913, Mexico, Brazil, and others soon afterwards. A first overseas tour took Cuba to the Eastern U.S. to play Temple and Long Island Universities and Canisius College in December, 1943.

Communist Cuba's basketball belongs to the people as an instrument of public health and education and for propaganda beamed to other Latin American countries. She also tries to use the sport to break the U.S. trade boycott. Cuba attempted some "Basketball Diplomacy" in April, 1977, when she invited the two South Dakota senators, George McGovern and James Abourezk, to Havana to discuss a proposed diplomatic agreement with the U.S. Combined squads from their two state universities lost to stronger Cuban teams in a pair of games. These Cuban efforts failed to produce an accord, however, because Washington protested the use of Cuban troops in the Zaire invasion, aborting reconciliation.

Latin American basketball is at its best at the biennial Central American and Caribbean competition (started in 1926) and in the aforementioned Pan-American Games, played every fourth year. Since the latter's establishment in 1951, the United States has clearly dominated, except for a loss to Brazil in 1971. As expected, the U.S. triumphed over the Puerto Rican team in 1979 in the finals at San Juan, but an embarrassing situation arose as a result of Coach Bobby Knight's altercation with a policeman. Court action led to Knight's highly publicized racial slurs against the host country. Much was lost in this "ugly American" episode.

The Tientsin YMCA first introduced basketball to China in 1896, but it was Robert A. Gailey, Naismith's student, who gave impetus to the sport when he was appointed secretary two years later. Dr. Max Exner, general director for the "Y" in China, then established a general sports program for the country from 1908-1911. Basketball helped fulfill a genuine need. Exner also arranged for international competition by planning the Far Eastern Games between China, Japan, and the Philippines, played from 1913-1934. When Japan entered a "Chinese" team from their puppet state of Manchukuo in 1932, China entered the Olympics for the first time. Although not especially successful in Olympic competition, China also participated under its own flag in 1936 and 1948 before the Communist take-over. The People's Republic then successfully utilized basketball, among other sports, to achieve physical fitness on a mass scale. The visitor to China today frequently sees basketball courts in schoolyards, on communes, and in urban complexes, the game's American origin notwithstanding.

After Richard M. Nixon's visit in February, 1972, the game also played a part in *détente*. An American men's collegiate all-star team and the AAU girl's champions from Wahoo College in Nebraska played three games apiece in the PRC (June-July, 1973). The girls dropped their contests against a more experienced Chinese women's aggregation, while Coach Gene Bartow's men's squad swept their encounters. The Chinese invoked "Friendship First, Competition Second" frequently, as they entertained their visitors. Jiang Qing, Mao's wife, extended her hospitality in basketball's contribution to U.S.-Chinese reconciliation.

As a result, the People's Republic turned to Olympic competition by means of a new agreement with the International Olympic Committee in October, 1979. Relations had been broken in 1958 because of Beijing's objection to Taiwan's participation. The Chinese, as a consequence, made their first appearance at the Winter Olympics at Lake Placid in February, 1980. In the meantime, their basketball team had earned the right to represent Asia in the Summer Games to be held at Moscow the following July. The PRC, however, agreed to join the U.S. Olympic boycott because of the Russian invasion of Afghanistan. Thus, China forfeited her chance to participate again in the main competition of history's greatest sporting event.

The Olympics have never accepted baseball as an official sport, although "demonstrations" were presented in 1912 and 1936. Basketball, however, making its first appearance in 1904 at St. Louis as an exhibition, eventually received its official acceptance for the 1936 Games. Phog Allen, Dr. Naismith's colleague at the University of Kansas, presented the National Basketball Coaches Association's check for $6,400 between halves of a Jayhawks game for Naismith's trip to Berlin. There nineteen alumni from the Springfield "Y", all from the coaching staffs of Olympic teams, greeted the founder of basketball at a welcoming dinner. The U.S. swept through five games including the finale against Canada, which was played outside (required by the rules) in a driving rain, near an empty gymnasium.

From 1936-1972, the United States piled up an outstanding record of sixty-three victories. Such stars as Bob Kurland, Alex Groza, Clyde Lovellette, Bill Russell, Oscar Robertson, and Spencer Haywood ensured clear margins of victory. But in that last year, an experienced Russian team stopped the U.S. in the last minute of the final game, marked by confusion and questionable officiating. Aleksandr Belov sank a basket at the buzzer to win 51-50. Coach Hank Iba, trying to protest, had his pocket picked in the maelstrom. Soviet coach Vladimir Kandrashin had stated beforehand: "We want to prove that we can play with the Americans." No doubt they had, but the Americans refused to accept their second-place silver medals because of the officiating. Since Olympic competition is played under international rules, which permit more body contact than Americans are accustomed to, the U.S. is finding foreign competition increasingly challenging. Regaining the Olympic title in 1976 over Yugoslavia did not erase the wrenching memory of that Soviet victory at Munich.

Some reference should be made to the Harlem Globe Trotters, the goodwill ambassadors of basketball. Established by Abe Saperstein, a master promoter, in 1927, they long played seriously and competitively, but they tried crowd-pleasing antics and found their destiny. Their mentor gave them the designation "Harlem" to indicate that they were black and the name "Globe Trotters," because they were a perpetual road team. They entertained a record crowd of 75,000 at the Berlin Olympic Stadium in 1951 and then left on an extended tour of Latin America and Western Europe. Over ninety countries have seen their show, preceded by their famous warmup to "Sweet Georgia Brown." A recent national television appearance in honor of Chinese First Vice-Premier Deng Xiaoping's visit to the U.S. (February, 1979), only emphasized how the Trotters personify basketball as an international sport. Certainly the team is a demonstration to the Third World of how the United States strives to give opportunity to its minorities in fulfillment of its liberal heritage.

Our final American-born sport, volleyball, originated in the Holyoke, Massachusetts, YMCA (1895), through the efforts of William G. Morgan, another of Naismith's graduates. Volleyball commands more spectator and participant support than any other team sport except soccer. Fully seventy countries play the game. Its simplicity makes it accessible especially to "have not" nations. Unlike baseball and basketball, played abroad almost exclusively by club and business teams, volleyball has been adopted by many schools also, because of its appeal to both sexes, inexpensive equipment, and adaptability to both indoor and outdoor facilities. The YMCA controlled the sport until 1928, when the newly formed United States Volleyball Association took command and arranged the first national competitions. The U.S.S.R. followed with its own federation in 1933, Canada in 1953, and Britain in 1955. Already the sport was directed by the International Volleyball Federation, established in 1947, with headquarters in Paris. Now well-established, volleyball received approval by the IOC for competition in the Tokyo Olympic Games of 1964.

So many play volleyball abroad that it is probably relatively unimportant

Japanese and South Korean women square off in a volleyball match at 1976 Montreal Olympics. *(Wide World)*

that the U.S. has done rather poorly in international competition. Nevertheless, the American image has not been especially enhanced by its volleyball record in overseas contention. Americans have won three of the six competitions for men and only one for women at the Pan-American Games from 1955-1975 and none at all at the Olympic Games after 1964. In the latter competition Russia has won four titles, Japan three, and Poland one.

By way of summary, the "American sports empire," represented by baseball, basketball, and volleyball, has produced both positive and negative results for the U.S. image abroad. Western Europe beholds our three representative sports as modest symbols of American democratic freedom and individualism—reminders that the U.S. and Western Europe historically hold these ideals in common. Eastern Europe (especially the U.S.S.R.), in contrast, utilizes basketball and volleyball to compete against the U.S., especially in the Olympics, for the favor of the Third World. Latin America,

158 already penetrated by U.S. support of the winter leagues, carefully watches Cuban baseball and basketball contend with the "imperialist power" to the north, most notably in the Pan-American Games, where the Bobby Knight affair (1979) decidedly lessened American standing. China, which utilizes all three sports in a national program for physical fitness, may find that these sports open new areas of cooperation with the United States as the PRC moves towards modernization. Japan's passion for baseball intensifies with each visit from a U.S. major-league team, but this lift for the American reputation is somewhat tempered by the behavior of some foreign players, who refuse to conform to Japanese social standards.

In the overview, however, American sports have, in a modest way, enhanced their country's image in the eyes of the Free World.

Sources and Suggested Readings

Hollander, Zander, ed. *The Modern Encyclopedia of Basketball* (Garden City, New York, 1979).

Kieran, John and Arthur Daley. *The Story of the Olympic Games, 776 B.C. to 1972* (Philadelphia and New York, 1973).

Kolatch, Jonathan. *Sports, Politics, and Ideology in China* (New York, 1972).

Menke, Frank G. ed. *The Encyclopedia of Sports* (Garden City, New York, 1977).

Obojski, Robert. *The Rise of Japanese Baseball Power* (Radnor, Pennsylvania, 1975).

Riordan, James. *Sport in Soviet Society: Development of Sport and Physical Education in Russia and the U.S.S.R.* (Cambridge, 1977).

———— ed. *Sport Under Communism: The U.S.S.R., Czechoslovakia, the G.D.R., China, Cuba* (Montreal, 1978).

Spink, C. C. Johnson, ed. *The Sporting News* (Files: January, 1950-December, 1980).

Turkin, Hy and S. C. Thompson, eds. *The Official Encyclopedia of Baseball* (Garden City, New York, 1979).

Whiting, Robert. *The Chrysanthemum and the Bat: Baseball Samurai Style* (New York, 1977).

The Politics of the Olympics

William J. Baker
John M. Carroll

"The aims of the Olympic Movement," wrote Pierre de Coubertin in 1894, "are to promote the development of those fine physical and moral qualities which are the basis of amateur sport and to bring together the athletes of the world in a great quadrennial festival of sports thereby creating international respect and goodwill and thus helping to construct a better and more peaceful world." Since Coubertin launched the modern Olympics with the opening of the Athens Games in 1896, the ideals of the movement have been shorn and tattered by nations and individuals who have used the games for purposes of nationalism, political philosophies, and international diplomatic warfare. The games have become so commercialized and professionalized that the original aims of the modern Olympic movement are barely recognizable today. It is true that during the eighty-four-year history of the modern games, individual athletes, fans, and sporting associations have reaffirmed the ideals of Olympic competition. But in the period since World War II, the Olympics have increasingly become a tool of international politics. Today the games are as much a diplomatic confrontation as a sporting event; they are, as George Orwell succinctly put it, "war minus the shooting."

It is not surprising that the modern Olympic games have been shrouded in politics, because the movement began amidst the rumblings of intense European nationalism. Coubertin, a Parisian aristocrat, initially became interested in athletics because he sought a way to train French youth for an inevitable war of revenge against Germany after the defeat of France in 1870. Although he later became committed to the idea of promoting peace and brotherhood through sporting competition, Coubertin consistently viewed athletics in quasi-military terms. As leader of the International Olympic Committee (IOC), Coubertin fought many battles with national governments and political interest groups to establish the games as a successful enterprise.

Compared with more recent Olympics, the pre-World War I games were decidedly amateurish and haphazardly organized. They became increasingly

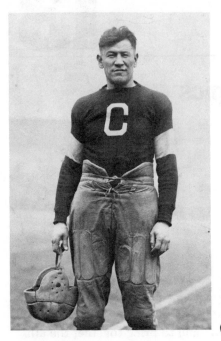

Jim Thorpe, Carlisle Indian School great, was
the decathlon winner of the 1912 Olympic
games and later starred in professional football.
(*St. Louis Post-Dispatch*)

popular, however, and reflected the intense political nationalism of the
period. In the 1908 London Games, for example, British Olympic officials,
apparently responding to anti-British sentiments in some American newspapers, seemed to delight in embarrassing the U.S. team and shortchanging
individual Yank athletes. On the whole, the 1908 Games were characterized
by bickering and strife rather than friendly competition and brotherhood.
Four years later in Stockholm, another nationalist incident erupted amidst
the splendor of the games. Athletes representing Finland, then a part of the
Russian Empire, were ordered by Tsarist officials to display a Russian flag
or no flag at all. In London in 1908, the Finns chose to march without a
flag. The 1912 Games provided the Finns with an opportunity to more
forcefully express their suppressed national sentiments. When a Finn, Hannes
Kohlehmainen, won the 5000-meter race, a Russian flag was raised. Kohlehmainen accepted the medal but, turning and pointing to the Russian flag,
declared in a loud voice, "I would almost rather not have won, than see that
flag up there." This incident was indicative of the fiery nationalistic passions
of suppressed peoples of Central Europe who would help to propel the world
to war in 1914.

These examples of political intrusions at the early games of the modern
Olympics, combined with paramilitary displays of flags and singing of
anthems and patriotic songs, were more expressions of chauvinistic nationalism than the kind of international political combat that would characterize
later games. As sport became more popular and highly organized in the Atlantic nations during the first decades of the new century, it became an

accepted tool of international diplomacy. By the end of World War I, this
trend was apparent both within and outside the Olympic Movement.

Interrupted by the war, the Olympic Games resumed in 1920 in Antwerp,
Belgium. The choice of Belgium as host country was indicative of the growing importance of sport and the Olympics in particular as a weapon in international diplomacy. The Belgians were awarded the games, originally slated
for Berlin, in part out of sympathy for their endurance of the German "rape"
of Belgium in 1914 and four years of occupation. In an action of great and
lasting consequence, the IOC decided to exclude certain countries from competition for political and humanitarian reasons. The former Central Powers,
Germany, Austria, Hungary, Bulgaria, and Turkey, were not invited to the
games of 1920 or 1924. The Western capitalist powers also made it clear that
Russia with its Bolshevik government was not welcome in the Olympic community. The Bolsheviks, who were not anxious to participate in capitalist-
run games at the time, were not invited to compete in the Olympics until
1948 and did not field a team until 1952. These decisions by the IOC and
the Western powers to punish countries because of their international conduct or political systems were particularly significant since they set
precedents which have increasingly infused politics into the Olympic Games.

The high-water mark of the Olympics as a political and nationalistic
spectacle in the pre-World War II era was the German Games of 1936. Adolf
Hitler, the German dictator who came to power in 1933, was determined to
make the Summer Games at Berlin and the Winter Games (begun in France
in 1924) at Garmisch-Partenkirken a showcase for Nazi superiority in military might, engineering skill, cultural achievement, and athletic prowess.
The modern Olympics had always been played amidst nationalistic symbols,
but the Nazis orchestrated an ultra-nationalistic display such as had never
been seen before. The games themselves seemed to pale before the political
spectacle that unfolded both within and outside the stadia. That the 1936
Olympic Games were a triumph for Nazism there can be no doubt. Some
historians maintain that the Games helped to legitimize Nazism in the eyes
of world opinion and encouraged Hitler to act more boldly in international
affairs thereafter. It is clear that other nations did not soon forget the "Nazi
Olympics" and the value of the games as a weapon in international politics.

What is most interesting of all is that the Summer Games of 1936 were
held in Berlin at all. Given the fact that nations had already been excluded
from Olympic competition for political reasons, clearly Germany should have
been expelled from the 1936 Games or the Berlin competition moved to another site. The Nazis violated humanitarian principles with regard to their
racial policies in general, and their specific discrimination against Jewish
athletes transgressed Olympic rules. Although this was well-known in the
international sporting community, Avery Brundage, the American president
of the IOC, gave Germany a clean bill of health in 1936 and helped to
squelch boycott efforts that were gaining momentum in several countries, including the U.S. In the end, only Spain boycotted the Berlin Games and organized the ill-fated Barcelona "People's Olympics." The Spanish boycott set a
precedent which was frequently used by nations in the post-World War II era.

Adolf Hitler signs autographs for admiring spectators during the opening ceremony at the Olympic Games in Berlin, August 1, 1936. *(Wide World)*

Although many Americans best remember the Berlin Games for Jesse Owens' exploits in garnering four gold medals and his alleged snub at the hands of Adolf Hitler, the German athletes actually won the competition. The Nazis' political and athletic triumphs as well as Owens' heroics were admirably captured on film by Leni Riefenstahl in her outstanding motion picture, *Olympiad* (1938). Germany's political successes and its allegedly superior society, however, did not last long. After a series of spectacular diplomatic triumphs, Hitler led his nation to war in 1939. Between 1939 and 1945, Germany and its "superior" Nazi system was ground to rubble by a coalition of Allied nations led by the United States, Russia, and Britain. The Olympic Games of 1940 and 1944 were cancelled, but many people looked forward to the Games of 1948 in the hope that they would reaffirm the Olympic ideals of peace, brotherhood, and cooperation. With Hitler dead and Nazism eradicated, the world awaited a new era of peace and tranquility.

It was not to come. The Grand Alliance of World War II broke apart by 1946, and two hostile superpowers, the U.S. and Russia, confronted one another in a world ravaged by war. An "Iron Curtain" decended upon Europe which divided capitalism from communism—two systems that were ostensibly incompatible and headed on a collision course. From Europe, the so-called Cold War, a war of strategy, propaganda, and limited conflict, spread to Asia, Africa, and Latin America. The frightening experiences of the 1930s seemed tame in comparison to a world-wide confrontation in which first one superpower, the U.S. (1945), and then the other, the Soviet Union (1949), acquired the means to annihilate civilization. In the Cold War confrontation, the imminent possibility of mutual destruction put a premium on winning battles through political maneuver and propaganda. It was in this atmosphere that the Olympic Games were renewed in 1948. Not surprisingly, the Olympics, as well as international sport in general, became a vehicle through which the Cold War was and is waged. The onset of the Cold War marks the beginning of a period of intense political activity in the Olympic Movement which makes it difficult today to separate sport from politics in the Olympics.

Amidst escalating Cold War tensions that engulfed Europe and spread to the Middle East, the 1948 Games were to be held in war-torn London. For the first time since 1912 Russia was invited to send a team but declined. The Soviets did not, however, pass up the opportunity to enter the Olympic propaganda battle. In late 1947, the Soviet press intepreted an American offer to feed Olympic athletes in London as a "Pork Trick" designed to enrich U.S. capitalists and provide an excuse in case the American team was defeated. The communist reasoning was that if European athletes emerged victorious, then the U.S. could claim that it was because of the American food. Another political issue arose at the Winter Games in Switzerland when two American ice hockey teams sought official status. The Russians accused the U.S. and Avery Brundage of dictating to Swiss officials as to which team would be accredited. Finally Rumania, a Soviet satellite country, walked out of the Summer Games after the IOC refused to appoint a Russian and Eastern European member to its committee.

The London Games were a distinct success. About 4,500 athletes participated despite the hardship of postwar conditions. The Soviets sent coaches and trainers to study Western athletic methods and to prepare for participation in the next Olympic Games. It was the Americans, however, who dominated the games. Led by seventeen-year-old decathlon champion Bob Mathias, the U.S. team reclaimed its Olympic supremacy which had been interrupted by the Germans in 1936. For Americans, the team's athletic triumph confirmed their nation's status as the number-one power in the postwar world. For the Soviets, the U.S. sweep posed a challenge to be met in the next Olympic Games. Both countries looked forward to the Helsinki Games of 1952 to test their athletic prowess and to enhance their political prestige in an increasingly bipolarized world.

Athletes assembled for the 1952 Games in an atmosphere of great world tension and strife. The Cold War had spread to Asia with the communist takeover of China in 1949 and the intensification of a struggle in Southeast Asia between French colonial and nationalist communist forces. American troops, under a United Nation's mandate, were openly battling communist armies in the stalemated Korean conflict. Beyond this, the Soviet Union had successfully tested an Atomic Bomb in 1949, and both the U.S. and Russia were busily developing hydrogen weapons. The international dangers and tensions were reflected in preparations for the Olympic Games. Columnist Arthur Daly expressed the attitudes of many Americans when he wrote in *The New York Times* on the eve of the Helsinki Games that "the Communist propaganda machine must be silenced so that there can't be even one distorted bleat out of it in regard to the Olympics. In sports the Red brothers have reached the put-up-or-shut-up stage. Let's shut them up." Daly's exhortation did not work.

American athletes did well at Helsinki, but the Russians stole the show and scored a propaganda victory. After a forty-year absence from Olympic competition, the Soviets entered contestants for every event except field hockey and won seventy-one medals, compared to seventy-six for the U.S. In the unofficial scoring system recommended by the *Olympic Bulletin*, Russia and the U.S. ended in a deadlock. The result stunned many Westerners who expected that Soviet athletes would falter in first-class world competition. Students of Soviet society knew, however, that communist leaders had built on the Tsarist sports programs and had made athletics an integral and highly organized part of Russian communist society. Soviet athletes were richly rewarded for outstanding performances in a sports system which had many of the manifestations of professionalism. But given the fact that few Russian athletes had previously competed against world-class competition outside the U.S.S.R., their achievements at Helsinki were indeed remarkable.

Within a year of the Helsinki Olympics, the tense Cold War struggle between the U.S. and U.S.S.R. began to moderate slightly. The Korean War, with the potential to escalate into a general conflict, ended in 1953. In the same year, Joseph Stalin, the brutal and paranoiac leader of Russia since 1924, died, and his successors promised "peaceful coexistence" with the West. Dwight D. Eisenhower became U.S. President and followed a policy toward the Soviet Union which oscillated between conciliation and hostility. His election coincided with the beginning of the decline of McCarthyism, which had poisoned the political climate in the U.S. and given impetus to Cold War tensions. In 1955 Soviet, American, British, and French leaders met in Geneva to discuss outstanding East-West issues. Little was accomplished at the meeting, but it did mark a thaw in Cold War relations. Despite the hopeful signs, the Cold War was not over. Both superpowers possessed the hydrogen bomb and made threatening gestures in regard to world trouble spots such as Germany, China, and the Middle East throughout the decade. International sports was still a field in which the two powers could engage in an all-out confrontation to test the mettle of their political and social systems without compromising their guarded commitments to "peaceful coexistence."

In 1956 the Soviets made a dazzling debut at the Winter Olympic Games in Cortina, Italy, after having refused an invitation to the Oslo Games four years earlier. A well-balanced Russian team won the overall unofficial point competition with the Austrians finishing a distant second. The Soviet victory in ice hockey over a favored Canadian team came as a shock to Western observers who had witnessed long-time Canadian dominance of the native North American sport. The feat was remarkable since the first Russian ice

hockey team had only been formed in 1946. Peace and tranquility reigned at
the Cortina Games, leading many sports enthusiasts to hope that the era of
high political drama at the Olympics was ending as the apparent easing of
East-West tensions continued.

Within the month prior to the opening of the 1956 Summer Olympics in
Melbourne, however, two political events threw the Olympic community
into turmoil. In late October, British, French, and Israeli forces invaded
Egypt as a result of the latter's attempt to internationalize the Suez Canal.
Surprisingly, the United States joined the Soviet Union in supporting a
United Nations cease-fire order. Egypt demanded that the IOC banish the
"aggressor" nations from the forthcoming Olympics. When the IOC refused,
Egypt joined with Lebanon and Iraq to boycott the Melbourne Games. This
marked the first use of the boycott in the postwar era and established it as
an important political weapon in the Cold War struggle.

The second political crisis began about a week before the joint invasion
of Egypt, and its impact was far more disruptive in terms of the games themselves. Beginning on October 23, Hungarian students and workers staged a
rebellion against the Moscow-controlled communist government in their
country. After some initial success, the revolt was ruthlessly crushed by a
Russian invasion spearheaded by tank columns. The Eisehhower administration, which advocated a "Roll Back" of communism in Eastern Europe,
denounced the invasion but did not intervene militarily. In protest against
the harsh but efficient methods used by Soviet soldiers against Hungarian
"Freedom Fighters," Switzerland, Spain, and the Netherlands withdrew
from the Melbourne Games. The Olympics went on, however, as Avery
Brundage of the IOC explained that "We are dead against any country using
the Games for political purposes, whether right or wrong." Despite Brundage's disclaimer, the 1956 Olympics marked an upswing in the number of
political incidents in the games and the use of the Olympics for political
purposes—a trend which accelerated in the 1960s and 70s.

In Melbourne, Hungarian spectators and competitors vented their anger
against the Soviet team. The Hungarians ripped the communist insignia off
their flag in the Olympic Village and replaced it with a flag of free Hungary.
In a dramatic incident, Hungarian runner Jozsef Kovaks, after finishing second to Soviet standout Vladimer Kuts in the 10,000 meters, made a point of
refusing to shake hands with the gold-medal winner. Mere snubs and jeers
turned to violence in a semi-final water polo contest between the two Olympic teams. The Hungarians utilized flailing elbows and roughhouse play to
build up a 4-0 lead going into the final minutes of the game. At that point,
a Russian swimmer retaliated against a shove by a Hungarian opponent by
butting him in the face, drawing a massive stream of blood in the water.
The Cold War had turned to hot conflict, at least in the water polo pool in
Melbourne. Despite the Russian-Hungarian animosities, the Soviet team
maintained its composure and posted ninety-eight overall medals to only
seventy-two for the United States, thereby winning the unofficial point
count competition. If the Olympic Games were an indication of sporting

superiority, the Soviet Union had emerged as the number-one athletic nation in the world.

After the Soviets successfully launched the Sputnik space satellite in 1957 and the American counterpart exploded on the launching pad the following year bringing forth refrains of "Flopnik" from critics, many Americans began seriously to assess the relative strengths of Russian and American societies. Amidst charges and allegations of a missile gap, a technological lag, and an educational crisis, American leaders began to place more emphasis on winning in any competition with the Soviet Union—including the Olympic Games. The 1960 Games seemed to offer some hope for a resurgence by the United States as the underdog American ice hockey team scored a stunning victory in that glamour sport of the Winter Games. Despite an overall Soviet victory at Squaw Valley, California, in 1960, Americans were encouraged by their team's strong showing and looked forward optimistically to the Summer Games to be held in Rome.

The American team failed miserably in its head-on competition with Soviet athletes in Rome. Although individual athletes such as Rafer Johnson in the decathlon, Wilma Rudolph in the women's dash events, Ralph Boston in the broad jump, and Cassius Clay in boxing turned in stellar performances, the American team was swamped in a sea of gold for the Soviet Union's "Big Red Machine." What was particularly disappointing was America's poor showing in track and field events. In the previous Summer Olympics, some Americans had accepted Russia's overall victory in unofficial total score philosophically, noting that the American athletes triumphed in the major or glamour events in track and field. In Rome, the highly touted American track team failed to win even in events that had traditionally been dominated by Americans.

The debacle in Rome stirred controversy in American political circles. John F. Kennedy, who had criticized Republican leaders during the 1960 presidential campaign for allowing America to fall behind the Soviet Union in a number of important fields, set the tone for the new decade in his 1961 inaugural address when he exhorted Americans to "pay any price, bear any burden" to preserve freedom, presumably by defeating communism. Apparent Soviet political victories in Third World countries, combined with its bold intrusion into the Western Hemisphere resulting in the Cuban Missile Crisis of 1962 convinced many Americans that a counter-offensive had to be mounted against the U.S.S.R. on all fronts. Sports and physical fitness were cited as two areas where the United States lagged behind Russia, and political leaders particularly focused on the training and quality of America's Olympic teams. Senator Hubert Humphrey spoke for many of his colleagues when he warned in a *Parade Magazine* article in 1963 that another Soviet sweep of the Olympics would allow "the Red propaganda drums" to "thunder out a world-wide tattoo, heralding the 'new Soviet men and women' as 'virile, unbeatable conquerors' in sports—or anything else." President Kennedy responded by creating the President's Council on Physical Fitness, which directed attention to the need to improve athletic programs in general and Olympic funding and training in particular.

The 1964 Olympic year started on a sour note for American athletes, who fared poorly at the Winter Games in Innsbruck, Austria. U.S. participants captured only one gold medal and came away empty-handed in the highly publicized ice hockey competition. It was another story at the Summer Games held in Tokyo. Apparently stirred by patriotic appeals to demonstrate American ability and resolve, American athletes made a strong showing in Tokyo. Led by a resurgent track and field contingent, the U.S. claimed ninety medals compared with ninety-six for the U.S.S.R. and narrowly missed overcoming the Soviets in the unofficial point totals. For some observers, the results showed that America could hold its own in the Cold War conflict and would not be swept away by the supposed red tide.

Shaken by the "eyeball to eyeball" confrontation of the Cuban Missile Crisis, which nearly resulted in nuclear war, Soviet and American leaders sought ways to avoid another direct clash between the superpowers. These efforts were highlighted by the installation of a direct "hotline" between Moscow and Washington (1963), the Nuclear Test-Ban Treaty of 1963, and the summit meeting between President Johnson and Soviet Premier Aleksei Kosygin at Glassboro, New Jersey, in 1967. The Cold War was far from over, but the direct confrontation of the superpowers had been muted. The scene of Cold War conflict shifted to Third World countries or to nations within the ranks of the U.S. and U.S.S.R. alliance systems. This trend in world politics was reflected in the politics of the Olympics in the early 1960s.

Earlier in the Cold War, the IOC faced several disputes concerning the recognition of communist bloc nations who sought to participate in the Olympic Games under their own flags. The most pressing of these political battles focused on Taiwan and the Peoples' Republic of China (PRC), East and West Germany, and North and South Korea. In each case, the IOC became hopelessly entwined in the web of Cold War politics by attempting to placate both East and West blocs in its policies relating to divided countries. After many years of heated debate and seemingly pointless quibbling, the IOC finally sanctioned the admission of East Germany (1968), PRC (1976), and North Korea (1976) as official participants in the Games. The dual recognition of East and West Germany and North and South Korea has worked well in recent years, but the solution with regard to China continues to spur international controversy. The whole problem concerning the recognition of teams purporting to represent sovereign states stems from the nationalistic orientation of the Olympic Movement. Because the IOC recognizes national committees and national teams rather than simply athletes from those nations, it has allowed itself to become a pawn in the game of Cold War politics.

Since the mid-1960s, the IOC has had to contend with another pressing international phenomenon, namely the emergence of Third World countries as a force in Olympic politics. The Bandung Conference of 1955, at which twenty-nine nations representing one-quarter of the world's population met to declare their "neutralism," signaled the beginning of the end of the bipolar Cold War world. These emerging nations, located mainly in the former colonial regions of Asia, Africa, the Near East, and Latin America, were highly nationalistic and sought recognition and respect in the world community. International sports and the Olympic Games in particular provided an ideal forum for Third World nations to attain those goals as well as for venting anger and frustration against a world political system which had long held them in the bondage of colonialism.

In 1962, President Achmed Sukarno of Indonesia hosted the first Asian Games in Jakarta. For refusing to grant visas to athletes from Israel and Taiwan to participate in the games, Sukarno was censured by the IOC. The Committee suspended Indonesia, pending guarantees that no further political discrimination would be practiced. Viewing this action as just another manifestation of Western imperialism, Sukarno organized a new format for sports in the Third World: Games of the New Emerging Forces of the Third World (GANEFO), which would be limited to Asian, African, Latin American, and socialist countries. After the First GANEFO were held in Jakarta in 1963 with sixty-eight nations invited to participate, the IOC threatened to ban all GANEFO participants from the forthcoming Tokyo Olympics. Since two of the forty-eight nations participating in the First GANEFO were the Soviet Union, which was the largest Olympic nation, and Japan, which was to host the 1964 Olympic Games, the IOC was forced to back down. In the wake of the GANEFO controversy, Asian and African athletes made their first significant showing at the Tokyo Games. This was perhaps fitting, since the 1964 Games were the first to be held outside the Atlantic community area. The emergence of the Third World nations at the 1964 Olympics also signified a drift of the Cold War conflict away from direct confrontation between the U.S. and U.S.S.R. and toward a struggle by the superpowers to win the "hearts and minds" of nonaligned peoples. In the area of international sports, the Russians appeared to be winning the contest.

The events in Mexico City, the site of the 1968 Summer Games, tended to confirm this judgment. Beginning in 1962, the Soviets, hoping to win the allegiance of black Africans, began a campaign to ban South Africa with its ruling white minority government and segregated system of apartheid from the Olympic Movement. The South African team was excluded from the Tokyo Games, but in early 1968 the IOC ruled that the apartheid system had been sufficiently revised to permit South Africa to participate in Mexico City. Thirty-two black African nations reacted furiously, threatening to boycott the Games en masse if South Africa competed. The IOC suddenly reversed itself in a decision which political observers at the time interpreted as a propaganda victory for the Soviet Union.

The Games at Mexico City seemed to confirm the contemporary view that the U.S. was losing the Cold War struggle in the Third World area. While South Africans, who enjoyed economic and political ties with the U.S. but not with the Soviet Union, stayed at home, black Africans performed brilliantly in Mexico City. At a time when a U.S. Government Commission headed by Otto Kerner reported that the main cause of race riots in American cities was white racism, black runners such as Mamo Wolde of Ethiopia and Kipchoge Keino of Kenya captured gold medals and the admiration of sports fans. Black American athletes, representing Harry Edwards' Olympic

Russia's Alshan Sharmakham-Edov scores in the Soviet Union's dramatic upset of the
U.S. team at the 1972 Munich Olympics. *(Wide World)*

Committee for Human Rights, who had earlier voted to call off a boycott of the Mexico Games after South Africa was banned, were determined to register a protest against racism and in support of black unity. In a dramatic incident, two American sprinters, Tommie Smith and John Carlos, gave "Black Power" salutes during a victory ceremony at which the U.S. national anthem was being played. The athletes were quickly sent home, but their defiant gestures became a symbol of the 1968 Olympics and an embarrassment for American leaders who sought to improve relations with Third World countries. The dramatic black protest and the violent and bloody rioting in Mexico City that preceded the Games seemed to overshadow the fact that the American team defeated the Soviets in the unofficial point totals for the first and only time in the postwar era. After 1968, it was becoming increasingly clear that the Olympic Games were an ideal forum for registering political protests and propagating political views.

The 1972 Summer Games at Munich tragically demonstrated how politically and commercially oriented the Olympics had become. In the early hours of September 5, the day American swimmer Mark Spitz won his record seventh gold medal, Palestinian (Arab) terrorists murdered two Israelis in the Olympic Village and took nine hostages. Finally, after fifteen hours of negotiations, which kept hundreds of millions of television viewers around the world glued to their sets, the authorities agreed to give the Palestinians and their hostages safe passage out of Germany. At a nearby airport, German sharpshooters opened fire on the terrorists, who retaliated in kind. Within minutes all nine hostages, five of the Palestinians, and three Germans lay dead or dying.

Incredibly, IOC officials ordered that the games proceed. "I am sure the public will agree," declared Avery Brundage, "that we cannot allow a handful of terrorists to destroy this nucleus of international cooperation and goodwill we have in the Olympic movement." Brundage and the IOC received a torrent of criticism for one of the most controversial sporting decisions since Commissioner Pete Rozell ordered National Football League teams to take the field the Sunday after President Kennedy was assassinated. Many critics suspected that commercialism as much as Olympic idealism prompted the IOC to decree that "the Games must go on." The Munich Games convinced many that the Olympics had become a monster—too big, too commercial, and too susceptible to political manipulation.

The Montreal Games of 1976 seemed to substantiate those charges. Canadian officials estimated that it cost $1.5 billion to stage the Games, more than six times the original estimate. Some observers wondered if any cities or government could afford to underwrite such expenditure in the future. In addition, a controversy over the participation of Taiwan caused political tension among the major powers. Canada, which did not diplomatically recognize Taiwan, refused to allow Taiwanese athletes to compete under the flag or name of the Republic of China. This resulted in a protest from the U.S., which included a threatened boycott. Even when Taiwan voluntarily withdrew from the Games, temporarily settling the controversy, American Secretary of State Henry Kissinger cancelled plans to attend the

Games in protest. Not to be out-done by the major powers, twenty-nine
Third World nations withdrew from the Games in protest against New Zealand's sporting ties with the white supremacist nation of South Africa. The
political and financial controversies surrounding the 1976 Games tended to
obscure the remarkable performance of the East German team and the
brilliant individual efforts of top-flight athletes such as Bruce Jenner of the
U.S. The diplomatic spectacle at Montreal, however, was only a foretaste
of the political whirlwind which enveloped the 1980 Games.

In early 1980 President Jimmy Carter announced that the U.S. would
boycott the Summer Olympics in Moscow unless the Soviets withdrew from
Afghanistan, a country they had invaded late in 1979. Calling the Soviet
provocation the greatest threat to peace in a generation, Carter put excru-
ciating pressure on American friends and dependents to join the boycott.
When the Russians refused to budge, the U.S. intensified its boycott efforts
and at the same time unsuccessfully appealed to the IOC to cancel or at
least move the Games out of Moscow. By the opening of the Moscow Olympics, Canada, Japan, and West Germany headed a list of sixty-two nations
who followed the American boycott policy.

The Moscow Games themselves turned out to be a political spectacle of
epic if not sometimes ludicrous proportions. Soviet authorities spared no
expense in attempting to utilize the occasion of the Games to promote their
socialist system. Not since 1936 had any country used the Olympics so
blatantly for propaganda purposes. Beyond that, some of the eighty-one
participating teams carried out makeshift protests against the Russian presence in Afghanistan or highlighting some other political issue. Sixteen teams
refused to carry their national flags in the opening ceremonial march. The
British team refrained from marching except for one individual who carried
the Olympic flag in place of the Union Jack. For New Zealand, five athletes
followed a raised black flag on which were superimposed a white olive
branch of peace and the five interlocking rings of the Olympic emblem.
From beginning to end, the Moscow Games were bathed in politics.

Alarmed by recent trends, critics of the present structure of the Olympic
Games have suggested reforms. One proposal is that the Winter and Summer
Games be held regularly at a neutral site—possibly Switzerland and Greece
respectively—to hold down expenses and to avoid the excessive use of the
Games for political purposes by the host countries. Some would-be reformers want to abolish chauvinistic symbols such as national anthems and flags.
Still other critics concerned with the different standards of amateurism in
the East and West blocs would simply throw the Games "open" to the best
athletes, whether they be amateur or professional by any standard. Few have
suggested that the Olympics be abolished altogether.

Despite the increasing political orientation of the Olympics, individual
athletes have often exemplified the ideals of the movement through their
performances, courage, and acts of international friendship. The courage of
German broad-jumper Lutz Long, who walked arm-in-arm with Jesse Owens
at the 1936 Games before a disapproving multitude fed on Hitler's propaganda of Aryan supremacy, the warm friendship of high jumpers John

Thomas of the U.S. and Valerii Brumel of the U.S.S.R. during the height of the Cold War, and the incredible performance of the 1980 U.S. Olympic ice hockey team which defeated a vastly superior Soviet team on the ice at Lake Placid, N.Y., are but a few examples of Olympic ideals in action.

Outstanding feats and acts of courage and brotherhood, however, do not change the fact that the Olympics have been overwhelmed by political forces. This is unlikely to change so long as the Cold War continues and nationalism remains as a driving force in the world. The Olympics simply have become more politics than sport.

Sources and Suggested Readings

Brokhin, Yuri. *The Big Red Machine: The Rise and Fall of Soviet Olympic Champions* (N.Y., 1977)

Edwards, Harry. *The Revolt of the Black Athlete* (N.Y., 1969).

Espy, Richard. *The Politics of the Olympic Games* (Berkeley, Calif., 1979).

Gilbert, Doug. *The Miracle Machine* (N.Y., 1980).

Lapchick, Richard Edward. *The Politics of Race and International Sport: The Case of South Africa* (Westport, Conn., 1975).

Lucas, John A. *The Modern Olympic Games* (San Diego, 1980).

Mandell, Richard D. *The Nazi Olympics* (N.Y., 1971).